Another Hand on Mine

Another Hand on Mine

The Story of Dr. Carl K. Becker
of the Africa Inland Mission

by William J. Petersen

McGRAW-HILL BOOK COMPANY
New York / Toronto / London / Sydney

ANOTHER HAND ON MINE

Library of Congress Catalog Card Number: 67-13515

First Edition   49593

To ARDYTHE
for enriching my life

Acknowledgments

Once I thought that authors filled their Acknowledgments page with trivial things. After two years of interviewing, researching, writing and editing, I now know differently.

Scores of people merit my deepest gratitude for their gracious assistance—people like ex-Sunday-school teacher Anna Kraedy, druggist George Heiges, physician Robert Hunter, dentist Gordon Bornemann and minister W. A. Masteller . . . relatives like sister Helen Shollenberger, son Carl Jr., and daughter Mary . . . missionaries like John Kuhn, Vera Thiessen, Carolyn Saltenberger, Harry Wilcke, Herb Atkinson, Edna Amstutz, Mary Heyward, Jewell Olson, Margaret Clapper, Agnes Bell, Stan Kline and many more . . . missionary executives like Sid Langford and Harold Amstutz . . . Reader's Digest editor Clarence Hall who graciously shared a goldmine of research already done on Dr. Becker . . . Jean Phillips of the American Leprosy Missions for files of information and excellent photos . . . Robert Wilson of The United Evangelical for valuable counsel.

Nor can I forget the kindnesses of world-famed leprologist Robert Cochrane, who took time from a busy schedule in his London office to open his notebook to me. . . . Nor the hospitality of Paul Stough at the A.I.M. rest home in Nairobi, dentist Dale Walker in Nairobi, and Norman Weiss in Bunia. . . . Nor of the skill of M.A.F.'s Gordon Marshall, who flew me from airstrip to airstrip in between cracks in the clouds. . . . Nor of charming Alice Wentworth Douglin and her husband Deighton as well as the entire CBFMS crew at Goma, Congo. . . . Nor of Yonama, Melona, Benjamina and other African assistants who spent an afternoon with me at Nyabirongo.

And, of course, I am grateful to the Beckers, who have never wanted publicity and who have secretly dreaded the publication of a biography, but who graciously opened up heart and home to me in the foothills of the Mountains of the Moon.

Others too deserve mention . . . the board of directors of the Evangelical Foundation for a leave of absence to visit Africa . . . *Eternity's* editor-author Russell T. Hitt for innumerable reasons . . . editorial assistant Miriam Cox Moran, who did double-duty in my absence . . . typist Lyn Mease . . . translator Millie Horner . . . and people who prayed for me, for I of all plodding authors was standing in need of it.

An endless list of names? Perhaps to you, but to me wonderful, wonderful people, without whose help this book would not be possible.

Contents

1
The Eye of a Tornado

"Nothing almost sees miracles but misery. Miracles and martydoms tend to bunch about the same areas of history—areas we have no wish to frequent." c. s. LEWIS

Along a slender reddish-brown thread that winds insistently through a green tweed jungle, flecked with tan mud-and-wattle huts, is a startling patch called Oicha. Only the most detailed of maps dignify it with a name, usually badly misspelled, for Oicha itself (pronounced Oh-each-ah) seems more a mistake than anything else, a bold divot out of a monotonous broccoli-green fabric.

Here in Congo's vast Ituri forest giant mahogany and ironwood trees shoot 150 to 200 feet into the sky; magnificent ferns, including great fields of the maidenhair variety, burst out from the moist shade; vivid orchids and poinsettias slash majestically across vine-colored gray tree trunks.

And through the interlacing green foliage romp black and white Colibi monkeys, chit-chattering endlessly at each other or at tiny, flitting birds, brazenly scarlet or luridly yellow; underneath, black and green deadly mamba snakes slither stealthily over exposed roots or dangle flauntingly from low-hanging branches. Only occasionally is the serenity startled by a leopard's cough, a jackal's wail or an owl's screech.

This is the Ituri forest, primeval and irrepressible, unsullied and unmanageable, except for the patch called Oicha.

From the air, Oicha looks roughly like the imprint of a divine hand pressed down hard, with rigid fingers stretching stiffly out into the jungle. In the palm of that hand, a hospital sprawls its building across a clearing. A stream, grandly called the Oicha River, cuts uncertainly across the palm like a lifeline and helter-skelter roads form the indistinct creases.

Along the insistent reddish-brown dirt road that is the closest thing

3

to a highway that eastern Congo knows are plodding motley Africans
—tiny Pygmies wearing nothing but a bark cloth; mothers clad in
gaudy swaths, toting infants on their backs and balancing bottles on
their heads; leprosy sufferers hobbling painfully, resting momentarily,
then hobbling a few more steps toward Oicha. In unison they step to
the side, merging into the jungle to let a rickety truck go by, loaded
with more motley Africans for the clearing in the jungle.

At Oicha, 2,000 Africans, some who have come hundreds of
miles, stand in various lines, waiting to talk to a soft-speaking white
man or one of his African assistants. To all of these, Oicha is not a
hole in the jungle, nor a gargantuan hand; it is "a place of miracles."

At least that is the way it appeared in July, 1960. That month was
historic for Congo and decisive for Christian missions. For some it
was the beginning of the end, and for others it was the end of the
beginning. But for Dr. Carl K. Becker, who sat calmly behind a
rough-hewn desk in his Oicha dispensary, it was business as usual.
This veteran missionary, whose thinning white hair, rimless glasses
and easy smile projected a fatherly image, leaned far over the desk to
catch the woes of an African tribeswoman detailing her medical
history. His eyes were fixed intently upon her. Though the nation was
erupting around him, nothing was so important right then as this
woman's health. With his stubby fingers, he picked up a pen and
scribbled a note for the pharmacy; then after speaking a quiet Swahili
word of comfort, he sent her on her way.

He awaited the next patient. Instead, a fellow missionary poked
his head in the door. "Excuse me, Doctor."

Dr. Becker motioned him in.

Sweat rolled down the missionary's forehead. "We've got to get
out of here, Doctor. I've just come from Beni, and that whole town is
going crazy. All the Belgian officials have deserted the place, and
even the Greek merchants are packing up. They say we'd better get
out of here while we can."

Dr. Becker wished he didn't have to think about it. He wanted to
call in the next patient and get on with his work. He stared at the
desk. A decision had to be made soon, and he knew what the decision would have to be—especially because of the women.

You would think that Oicha in the middle of a jungle wouldn't be
bothered with political unrest, he thought to himself. People around
here didn't even know what independence meant. Yonama, his African medical director, had admitted to him only a month ago that

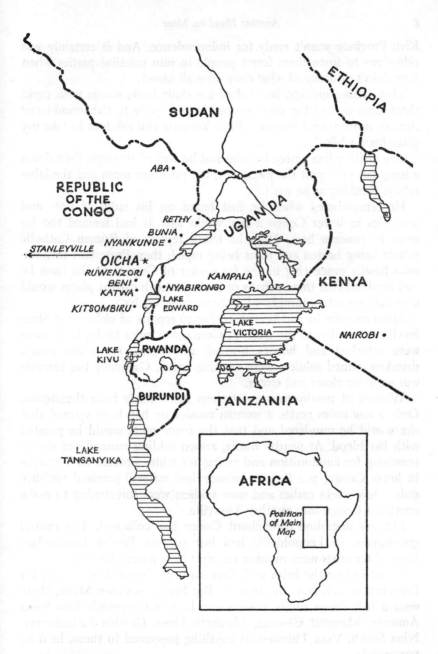

SUDAN

ETHIOPIA

REPUBLIC
OF THE
CONGO

ABA •

STANLEYVILLE

RETHY •
BUNIA •
NYANKUNDE •
OICHA ★
RUWENZORI •
BENI •
KATWA •
KITSOMBIRU •

UGANDA

LAKE
EDWARD

KAMPALA •
• NYABIRONGO

KENYA

LAKE
VICTORIA

NAIROBI •

LAKE
KIVU

RWANDA

BURUNDI

TANZANIA

LAKE
TANGANYIKA

AFRICA

Position
of Main
Map

Kivu Province wasn't ready for independence. And it certainly was ridiculous to force these forest people to join political parties when they didn't understand what they were all about.

Then, rising quickly, he pushed his chair back, strode with rapid short steps toward the door, opened it and spoke to the round-faced African nurse seated outside. "Find Yonama and ask him to take my place for a while."

The waiting line parted for him and he walked through, then down a long dirt path past the pharmacy, the injection room and the laboratory, thinking as he went.

He remembered when he first heard on his radio of riots and atrocities in lower Congo a few weeks ago. It had seemed too far away to concern him. Then he heard reports of Roman Catholic priests being beaten and nuns being raped; then Protestant missionaries hastily evacuating in the far corner of Congo. At the time he had doubted that those squalls of unrest in such distant places would ever develop into a tornado of destruction at Oicha.

More recently he had been listening to reports of violence at Stanleyville, 400 miles to the west; in Goma, 200 miles south, Europeans were attacked and houses burned; at Watsa, 175 miles north, drunken, armed soldiers were running amok. Gradually the tornado was whirling closer and closer.

Women at nearby mission stations had already been threatened. Only a few miles north, a woman missionary had been warned that she would be murdered and that the fence posts would be painted with her blood. At nearby Bunia, armed soldiers roamed the streets searching for ammunition and asking for white women. In Thysville in lower Congo, 300 Belgian women had suffered personal violence only a few weeks earlier and now soldiers were threatening to make northeast Congo into another Thysville.

Military discipline throughout Congo had collapsed. The central government of Leopoldville had lost control. Patrice Lumumba's band of terrorists were running rampant in northeast Congo.

He walked up the brick walk that led to his house. If it weren't for the women, he'd stay, he thought. But besides his own Marie, there were a half dozen single missionaries he was responsible for—Edna Amstutz, Margaret Clapper, Elizabeth Frost, Carolyn Saltenberger, Nina Smith, Vera Thiessen. If anything happened to them, he'd be responsible.

Now for the past few days he had been hearing rumors that the government post of Beni had been getting jittery. And Beni was only twenty miles to the south. Plenty of soldiers there too. What if they suddenly decided to defect to Lumumba's party?

He wasn't surprised that the Europeans were fleeing from Beni. Just yesterday, Beni's only doctor had brought him two patients for surgery that would have been easy to handle. Made some lame excuse about being too busy. Obviously, he was planning to evacuate.

Suddenly he spotted Vera Thiessen, walking briskly on the road, coming from her chores at the leprosy camp. "Vera," he called.

She stopped and waited for him where the brick walk met the station road.

"Vera. Bad news!" He watched to discern her reaction. He guessed that she wouldn't be any more anxious to leave Oicha than he.

He told her the report about trouble in Beni. "Spread the word quickly, but quietly. We'll have to get out of the country until the storm blows over. Tell everyone to be ready in one hour." He glanced at his watch and then at her. She seemed stunned. "It's no joke, Vera. Tell everyone to pack one suitcase; that's all." He was making his decision as he spoke. Usually he liked to ponder his moves more carefully.

Vera started to leave.

"Oh Vera, one other thing. Better not tell the Africans yet. Might get them too excited."

In his five-room brick house, he broke the news to Marie; her jaw dropped as he spoke. However often they had discussed it as a possibility, he had never thought it would happen; apparently Marie hadn't either. It would be just as hard for her to leave as it would be for him. Oicha was home, and had been for most of their thirty-one years on the mission field.

They selected clothing quickly and shoved what they could into their suitcases—one apiece.

"We have to leave everything else here?" she asked.

"We'll be back." He noticed she was looking at pots and pans, the same ones she had brought to the field a generation ago. "Nobody's going to steal those anyway, Marie."

A quick rap at the front door and a sing-song "Hodi" (May I come in?).

It was the voice of Benjamina, his top African assistant in surgery.

"*Karibu*," the doctor sang back. In a clean white coat, the medical assistant appeared.

"*Habari gani?*" (What's the news?) The doctor wondered if Benjamina would notice the suitcases. Apparently not; he seemed too excited.

A woman had just been brought in to the hospital to deliver her baby, Benjamina explained. Nurse Carolyn Saltenberger was there and had told him to call the doctor. The patient needed a Caesarean section. "Come quickly."

The doctor nodded. It may delay our leaving a bit, he thought, but he had no choice. The Lord certainly wouldn't want him to let that woman die in childbirth just because of some arbitrary timetable he had set up. It must be God's will. He had been looking for some indication of God's leading, some straws in the wind, some fleece on the ground. This was it.

Benjamina left and the doctor walked back into the kitchen with Marie.

"You heard?"

"Yes."

"Tell Vera and she can pass the word to the others that we will have to postpone our leaving for a couple hours. They'll understand."

Marie went out the back door to Vera's house; Carl Becker left by the front door for the operating room. By the time the Caesarean was completed, a second emergency, a strangulated hernia patient, had arrived. When that was done, he spoke quietly to his nurse, "I think it's too late in the day to leave now, Carolyn."

She nodded.

"I'd rather not be on these roads at night. In the present state of affairs you never know what you'll run into."

That evening the missionaries all gathered at the Becker home, listening to the radio, hearing the latest news, none of which was good. The doctor was still seeking straws in the wind, directional signals from God, to change his mind, to reverse his decision. He sent Harold Olsen, a young, first-term missionary from Indiana, to check on the situation in Beni, to see if law and order had been restored yet.

He knew that only one or two of the fourteen missionaries at Oicha desired to leave; some of the others were openly dissatisfied with his decision to evacuate. He confessed to them that he was not happy with the decision either, but under the circumstances it was the only one that could be made.

They talked about the principle of missionary evacuation. "Aren't missionaries supposed to be martyrs?" asked one, half in jest.

Dr. Becker explained that the problem on Congo in 1960 was not cannibalism versus Christianity; it was now black skin versus white skin or simply a matter of getting in the way of rioting, rampaging Congolese soldiers. "If evacuating Congo meant betraying Christ, no one here would be voting for it," he reassured them.

Soon he led them in a simple prayer meeting, on their knees in the living room.

Finally late in the night Hal Olsen returned. Dr. Becker recalled that his wife had been quiet all evening. Now she brightened up.

"How did it look, Harold?"

"Not good, Doctor." He was still breathless. "I couldn't tell if the government was still in business there or not."

"See any soldiers?"

"About fifty or sixty, I guess. But you sure wouldn't want them as bodyguards."

All was quiet for a minute. Dr. Becker knew that they were waiting on him. He had been hoping, praying for a sign to stay, but all the signs seemed to be marked "Run, don't walk, to the nearest exit."

"How do you women feel about it? Do you feel safe staying here one more night?"

Heads were nodding, though no one was doing much talking. It was his decision to make; he knew it and they knew it. He continued. "That settles it. After morning rounds tomorrow—"

"Tomorrow's Sunday, Doctor," Margaret Clapper, veteran missionary to the Pygmies, interjected.

He wasn't sure what she meant by that remark. He looked momentarily in her direction to see if she was going to explain it. She didn't, so he continued, "After morning rounds tomorrow, we will evacuate."

The next morning Dr. Becker woke up at five o'clock as usual, read his Bible, prayed and sought God's direction. A Bible verse jumped into his mind, a verse he had adopted as his own for 1960. And, strangely enough, it seemed to contradict his plans. He leafed through the Bible to Exodus 14 where Moses was encouraging the Israelites who were being hotly pursued by the Egyptian hordes:

"Fear ye not, stand still, and see the salvation of the Lord, which he will show to you today."

Quite clearly, that verse seemed to advise him to "stand still." He shook his head, not understanding what God was trying to tell him. He tried to evaluate his own prejudice: frankly, he did not want to leave Oicha, for there was so much work to be done. If the Belgian doctors were all evacuating, there would be no one left for hundreds of miles to minister to the diseased and suffering. It didn't make sense to go when there would be more work than ever. Yet since he was responsible for the entire missionary group, common sense dictated that all missionaries evacuate Oicha as soon as possible.

He tried to analyze their course of action. Had they made mistakes in reaching their decision? He could think of only one—they had not told the African medical staff of their plan. Perhaps this was wrong. If the missionaries walked out suddenly, how would this be interpreted by the African Christians? For that matter, how would it be interpreted by the entire non-Christian African population of the area?

While making his hospital rounds, Dr. Becker was rethinking his course of action. Afterward, he shared his revised thinking with the other missionaries. "I think we should stay for the morning church service; it will give us a chance to explain to the people why we have to leave. Then we can grab a quick bite to eat and leave early this afternoon."

He searched their faces for negative reactions. Everyone seemed to agree.

The main Oicha church was already well filled when the Beckers arrived that morning—750 or 800, he estimated. He walked up the rows of long, low wooden benches to sit near the front, for he had a special announcement to make. In the middle of the service, Pastor Zefania called on Munganga Becker. It wasn't often he spoke at church, and when he did he knew that the people regarded it as a special occasion. But it seemed more than that today; there was an air of expectancy among the congregation.

In simple Swahili, he explained the situation. "It is not that we want to leave, but we feel that there is nothing else we can do." He noticed the deathly silence of his audience; even the bawling babies seemed momentarily stilled. "We won't be gone long; as soon as things quiet down, we will come back." He explained how the hospital would carry on under his trained African staff with Yonama

Angondia as medical director. All the books, the accounts and the keys would be turned over to the African board of trustees.

After the service, Yonama, Zefania, two church elders and another medical assistant converged on the doctor. They listened as he explained the problem to them in more detail, especially the rebellion at Beni. It wasn't safe for the women to stay at Oicha any longer.

"We will go to Beni and ask them to guarantee your safety," Yonama said emphatically, his arms flying out in forceful gestures.

"I'm afraid it won't do much good. I doubt if you'll find anyone sober at Beni," the doctor responded.

Yonama glanced at his new wrist watch. "Can you wait until two before you leave? That will give us enough time."

In his mind the doctor refigured the time they would need to get from Oicha to the border by nightfall. "All right, we will wait until two."

As the Africans dashed off, the missionaries gathered for a light lunch before departing. It was a solemn meal. Carolyn Saltenberger tried a quip. "Reminds me of a passover."

No one said a word.

"Oh, you know, the passover meal—the way we're eating in a hurry so we can escape the Egyptians."

The Old Testament allusion brought Dr. Becker's focus back once again to that verse, "Fear ye not, stand still, and see the salvation of the Lord." Despite all the adverse circumstances, he felt he was defying God's will by planning to evacuate. Was the Lord reminding him of this verse again for a purpose? Yet, except for these slim threads of subjective guidance, everything else was urging him to lead the band of missionaries out of the Congo as soon as he could.

He knew it wasn't like him to be so indecisive. He had a reputation for making strong decisions, carefully reasoned. Yet by the end of their "passover meal" he was trying to hedge his decision. He wondered, he told the others, "if the situation at Oicha had really worsened sufficiently to warrant our leaving." But the plans remained; the group would leave when Yonama returned or at two o'clock, which ever came first.

Two o'clock came first. By this time the missionaries had dispersed again to their own houses and the Beckers were looking impatiently out their front windows. Carl Becker noticed a crowd forming on the station road in front of his house, no doubt a band of church members waiting to wave goodbye. But ten minutes later when he looked out again, the area was black with hundreds of faces. There were Pygmies, sufferers from leprosy, men in business suits two sizes too small, other men wearing only an undershirt and a pair of khaki trousers, women encircled with bright flowery prints, men with tribal markings scarred into their faces, women whose heads had been shaped in infancy.

Carl Becker tried to be patient, but today patience didn't come easily.

"It's getting close to three," Marie reminded him.

With a glance at his left wrist he acknowledged it.

"Don't you think we'd better leave soon, so we can get out of the country before dark?" Marie prodded.

"I think we'd better wait for Yonama anyway."

"What could change the situation now?"

He didn't know. Suppose they did bring back some drunken administrators who pledged safety to the missionaries. What good would that do? Maybe it was just that he wanted to be assured that he wasn't going against God's will.

He rose to look out the window again. "How many hundreds of people are out there, Marie?"

"Looks like thousands to me."

They waited longer. Three o'clock bent into three-fifteen and then into three-thirty, and finally they heard automobile horns blaring above the din of the crowd outside. The crowd parted like the Red Sea to let Yonama's committee re-enter the mission compound. But it wasn't only Yonama's car; behind it was a sleek black Cadillac and then, like a little toy being pulled behind, came a jeep crammed ridiculously with Congolese soldiers.

Dr. Becker opened the front door to see the visitors brought by Yonama. Yonama leaped out of the front car, propelled his way through the crowd, and rushed to the doctor. Dr. Becker had often seen his effervescent assistant excited before, but never so elated as this. Yonama spoke between quick gasps for breath. "We couldn't —find the—local officials anywhere. —We were just about—to return to Oicha."

"But who are these men that you have brought with you?" asked the doctor impatiently.

"Important people, *Munganga*, very important people. —We saw them inspecting the government post. —One is a government minister—all the way from Leopoldville;—the others are officials of

Kivu Province—up from Bukavu;—the captain of the army came
along too. —They arrived in Beni today to steady it—to make sure it
doesn't fall—into the hands of Lumumba's forces."

The delegation of officials emerged from the Cadillac and marched
stiffly to the Becker home. The crowd was cheering madly now. As
Dr. Becker received them into his house and introduced them to his
wife, he wondered if it were only a coincidence that responsible
officials from the central government had come to stabilize the shaky
government post at Beni just at the time that Yonama had arrived.

Inside, one after another of the Congolese officials gave a flowery
oration in French, detailing how much all of Congo had appreciated
the doctor's work and asserting that they would do anything for him
if only he would stay. They assured the doctor that Lumumba's political party would not gain control of Kivu Province and that the
missionaries would be safe at Oicha. After listening out the florid
orations, Becker pondered a French response. He always felt unsure
of his self-taught French and now especially so. Finally, he replied,
"We don't want to leave either. It is only because we have felt that it
is unsafe for our women that we have considered leaving. If you can
guarantee safety for the women, all of us will be happy to stay."

The army captain threw back his shoulders as he replied that he
not only would guarantee their safety but would also send a permanent detachment of soldiers to guard the houses of the single women,
if Dr. Becker requested it.

The doctor mused over the idea for a moment. He wondered how
his unmarried nurses would react to having a permanent native
bodyguard, and then replied blandly, "No, I don't think that will be
necessary."

"But will you and your nurses be willing to stay at Oicha?" The
official from Leopoldville anxiously sought a definite answer.

The doctor smiled. "With your guarantees of safety, we will all be
willing to stay."

The Congolese delegation broke out in hearty applause. Then
abruptly they about-faced and marched outside to address the crowd.
Dr. Becker walked out with them. Jubilant cheers seemed to rend the
jungle. The doctor heard his name called out repeatedly, "Beck-air,
Beck-air," and "Munganga, Munganga" (Doctor, Doctor).

The officials raised their hands for silence and the noise was
quickly muffled. They spoke sternly, warning the people not to
damage the hospital property nor to molest the missionaries. Then

they said, "The government of Congo stands behind this hospital. And anything done to this hospital or to these missionaries will be considered a crime against the Congolese government."

The crowd stood in awe as the officials edged their way toward their Cadillac. Then one of the Congolese leaders realized he had forgotten to say something. Halting, he raised his hand for continued silence and then shouted out, "The Beckers have promised to stay at Oicha."

Wild shrieks erupted from the mob, and a jubilant demonstration began which lasted nearly a half hour.

That evening as Dr. Becker stepped out of his house, he found an elderly woman crippled by leprosy waiting for him. Her face lit up, even as tears rolled down her cheeks. She wiped her eyes with a dirty cloth, and looked up at the doctor. All she could say was "*Ahsante, ahsante, ahsante*" (Thank you, thank you, thank you) and then she broke down and wept some more.

The doctor doubted no longer that he had made the right decision.

For the next two weeks, Dr. Becker heard reports of more and more missionaries evacuating their stations. Assemblies of God missionary Jay Tucker in Paulis (martyred five years later) radioed for a plane to come to his station; other missionaries from the Assemblies of God mission, from Heart of Africa mission and from Unevangelized Fields mission stopped at Oicha on their way out of Congo into Uganda. Then Plymouth Brethren missionaries and other Africa Inland Mission workers evacuated. From the south, Conservative Baptist missionaries packed up and left. Almost every day missionaries stopped at Oicha, sampled some of Marie's cooking and then hurried off to safety in Uganda.

At three thirty, Wednesday afternoon, July 20, 1960, an African ran up the road with a message, an SOS from three missionaries. Mr. and Mrs. Hans Schuezger and Annie Cowell, A.I.M. missionaries at Bogoro, 100 miles north, were trying to escape to Oicha, but were trapped by Walesi tribesmen. Dr. Becker knew what that meant. Only two days before, the Walesi had stopped 125 cars with fleeing Belgians from Bunia and had stripped the passengers of everything— suitcases, watches, rings, shoes.

Immediately and almost automatically, Dr. Becker set off in his car with an African medical assistant to rescue the endangered missionaries. He was hoping he could reach them by dark.

Not too far up the road, the two men encountered a Walesi roadblock. Faces painted and wild-looking, a mob of Africans brandishing spears and bows and arrows rushed toward the car. Boldly the doctor rolled down his window, stuck his head out and waved at them. Then he thought he recognized a couple of them and called them by name. Immediately their attitude changed.

"We don't want to hurt you, *Bwana*, but we are afraid. The whites are coming to kill us."

The doctor stepped out of the car and walked to the Walesi in short quick steps. "You know that we will not hurt you," said Dr. Becker. "Some of you have come to the hospital at Oicha, and you know how we love you."

"But where are you going, *Bwana*?" asked one.

"You are not leaving us, are you?" asked another, digging his spear deeply into the brown soil.

"No, I am on my way to Mount Hoyo to find three missionaries who need help. Will you let us go?"

"You promise that you are not leaving us?"

"Yes, I promise. I am only going to Mount Hoyo, and then I'll be coming back as soon as I can."

With this promise, the savage-looking Walesi lifted their roadblock and the Becker car was allowed to pass. Dr. Becker and the medical assistant sped along the jungle road. It was after five now and dark comes with surprising suddenness at six in Congo.

Soon he saw dust billowing on the road ahead; it was a whole convoy of vehicles coming toward him down the road.

It must be more Belgians from Bunia, he figured. He pulled off to the side to let the cars and trucks pass. But the first one stopped as it pulled alongside him.

"Where are you going?" A voice hollered in French.

"To Mount Hoyo, to rescue some Protestant missionaries," Becker shouted back.

"It's no use. Go on back. The two of you will never make it."

"What's the difficulty?"

"Impossible. Those Walesi leaped down on the roads and beat our men up. They took money and jewelry. Some soldiers rescued us; otherwise we'd all be lying there yet. You can't reason with them. You had better go back."

"Thank you for the advice," the doctor acknowledged.

The convoy moved on. Finally the African medical assistant looked at Dr. Becker. "Are you going to turn around, *Munganga?*" The doctor glanced at the African. "Are you afraid?"

The African didn't answer the question. Instead he said, "God has helped us save many lives on the operating table, *Munganga*. Maybe He will help us save three more on Mount Hoyo."

Dr. Becker's foot was already on the gas pedal.

Soon they were out of the dense forest and into the rolling hills. It was close to six now. The sun was ready to drop into the Ituri Forest behind them, and the dusk made visibility poor. Suddenly the African cried, "Watch out!" The doctor slammed down on his brakes. He had spotted it too—a ditch slashed deeply across the road. The car screeched, skidded, swerved and finally nosed gently into the muddy ditch.

Instantaneously the Walesi swooped down from a hill to surround the car.

Dr. Becker stepped briskly from the car to meet them. "*Yambo*" (How are you?), he greeted, as if they were his long-lost relatives.

"*Yambo*," they returned the familiar Swahili greeting.

"*Habari gani*" (What is the news?), Dr. Becker continued the Swahili banter, taking the offensive from the Walesi.

Some of them now recognized Dr. Becker, and soon they were gathering behind the doctor's car pushing him out of the ditch, singing in rhythm to aid in the forward thrust. Once again the missionary's car was on its way. "*Ahsante*," called the doctor out his window; and mud splattered by the whirring wheels for their kindness, the savage Walesi sang back "*Ahsante sana.*"

A few miles farther on Dr. Becker turned off the main road onto a side track climbing to Mount Hoyo. Here was territory which Dr. Becker did not know so well. And it was also territory that did not know him so well. He needed his headlights now. He was sorry he hadn't made it sooner, for the night brought fear and encouraged savagery. His headlights pierced into a mysterious darkness, until they focused on a crowd of Africans gathered around three trees which had been felled across the track to form a roadblock. Far in the background he discerned three white faces.

"This is it," Dr. Becker told his companion. As he stepped from his car, he was more elated than afraid; in fact, his calmness surprised him. He called from within for wisdom, and he was reminded again of that verse from Exodus: "Fear ye not, stand still and see the salvation of the Lord."

Clearly these Africans would not be so easy to talk with. They were wild-eyed, drunk with liquor, hemp or marihuana. These were the ones that the Belgians had said couldn't be reasoned with. The stench of stale liquor was strong.

"We have come to help our friends," Dr. Becker told them. He kept his hands at his side. Some sudden gesture might anger them. "Will you let them come with us?"

They refused. Never, never, never! But they seemed more stupefied than stubborn.

Dr. Becker tried to reason, but the Belgians were right, it was impossible. He turned his back and trudged slowly back to his car to figure out a new approach. Finally one who seemed more in control of himself than the others came up to him, touched his elbow and said, "All right, you take them, but we will take the car and all they have with them."

The doctor shook his head. He climbed over the tree trunks and walked over to the missionaries who were held captive. Hans Schuezger, a Swiss-born missionary, was obviously shaken.

In broken English, he told Dr. Becker, "I am glad you have come, but it is no good. We have tried to talk to them, but they are out of their heads. I do not know what we can do."

Dr. Becker smiled and put his hand on Schuezger's shoulder. "God will work it out, Hans—somehow."

He walked back to another group of Walesi standing on the other side of the roadblock.

"How long are you going to keep my friends here?" he asked.

The Africans shrugged.

"What will we have to give you before you let them go?"

They pretended they weren't listening.

Becker, feigning disinterest, turned his back on them and began to walk toward still another group of drunken Africans. Then he heard one Walesi running up behind him.

"Bwana, give us 3,000 francs and we will let them go."

Now Dr. Becker had the advantage. He laughed and shook his head. "Too much." He did not have 3,000 francs (about $60) with him. So he turned away again.

This time the African caught him on the shoulder. "How much do you have, Bwana?"

The doctor pulled out his wallet and showed him 600 francs. "That's all," he said, and started to fold it up and put it back in his pocket.

"No, *Bwana*, that's enough; that's enough."

And for the ransom price of $12 Hans Schuezger, his wife and Annie Cowell were released. The roadblock was moved to let Hans Schuezger drive his car past, and then Dr. Becker escorted them along the winding trail back to Oicha.

It was ten-thirty that evening when the two cars finally arrived back in the relative safety of the Oicha station. Alternating between worry and prayer, Marie Becker and the others had finally sent two Africans in a truck to try to locate the doctor. They met him on the road.

Dr. Becker was tired, plenty tired, when his car stopped in front of his house that night, and he would have liked to go right to bed. But no sooner did he have the Schuezgers and Miss Cowell billeted for the night than nurse Carolyn Saltenberger came up to him and said, "I hate to tell you this, but there's a woman in the maternity ward and . . ."

"I might have known, Carolyn; get her into the operating room and I'll be right over."

During the next few weeks more missionaries came past Oicha on their way out of Congo. By mid-August, 1960, only a handful of missionaries remained in all of northeast Congo, except for those at Oicha, who were living in the eye of a tornado.

2
Exodus and Ambush

After that, things never returned to normal. As Dr. Becker recalls it, "Congo sort of blew up in our faces."

When a friend wrote to him of his tremendous faith, he responded quickly that it wasn't a matter of his faith, but rather of God's faithfulness. "We aren't thinking as much about faith as we are about the reality of the One in Whom we have confidence."

And when someone wrote saying how wonderful it was to know that in spite of all the problems "no harm would ever come to them," he responded that he never had that assurance. That is what made it even more amazing. "With mass evacuation of the Belgians and the literal breakdown of the government, with drunken soldiers fully armed—pretty much on a rampage—barriers on the road all around us, no harm actually did come to us," but Carl Becker staunchly denied that this was because of his faith. No, it was because of God's faithfulness. Another hand was on his.

The brightest spot of all in 1960 was the coming of Dr. Herbert Atkinson to join the staff at Oicha. Barely out of med school and seminary, the square-jawed, bespectacled thirty-year-old general practitioner left his wife and three children behind in East Africa and waded into the turmoil of Congo while all the traffic was going the other way. He arrived July 22, much to the astonishment of fleeing Europeans and to the jubilation of Dr. Becker. Even more elated were the Congolese medical assistants who took heart on seeing an eager white face join the staff.

"The Little Doctor" the Africans called him, but not because of his height. He was about as tall as Dr. Becker's five feet eleven inches, and his build was stockier, less wiry. But Dr. Becker had long held the title of "Big Doctor," more from veneration than anything else.

Through his wife, Frieda Paul Atkinson, a second-generation Congo missionary, he had known of the almost legendary doctor at

Oicha. And he had hoped for the privilege of working with him, though he knew that not all physicians had found it easy to work with the hard-driving, disciplined Carl Becker. But intrigued by the challenge, he was delighted when he heard that he had been assigned to the jungle station of Oicha. Knowing the mountainous overload of medical work that sixty-five-year-old Carl Becker was carrying, he ventured into Congo, when all the other missionaries were fleeing.

Becker's favorite teaching technique was learn-by-doing, and consequently Atkinson was thrown into the most complicated of medical procedures immediately. Once Atkinson told a nurse, "I wish he'd let me stand behind him and let me watch him as he worked." But there was more than enough to keep two doctors busy at Oicha treating 2,000 patients a day and performing 3,000 surgeries a year.

Shortly after Atkinson arrived, Dr. Becker had to leave Oicha for a few days to meet with the missionary field council to discuss future plans. As field director of the Africa Inland Mission for Congo, Becker bore much of the responsibility for charting A.I.M.'s course during those turbulent days.

As soon as Becker had departed, Atkinson was confronted with a major tragedy. A family—father, mother and two small children, all savagely beaten by thieves—was brought to him. He examined them quickly and shook his head, appalled by the brutality. The father had his head slashed through to his skull, a big gash across his back and another across his chest; his knee cap was cut in two, fingers on both hands were torn wide open. His two little children had deep arm wounds, but the mother was the worst of all. Her right hand had been hacked off at the wrist, and it was hanging by just the skin. The third finger of the same hand was smashed and she had large wounds in her upper arm and knee, and the index finger was cut off the other hand.

Nurses Carolyn Saltenberger, Jewell Olson, Vera Thiessen and the chief African assistants worked smoothly with Dr. Atkinson. With Gray's *Anatomy* and Bunnel's *Surgery of the Hand* propped open before him, Atkinson worked steadily throughout the day, delicately repairing the shredded bodies.

When the "Big Doctor" returned a few days later, the patients were all recuperating and the "Little Doctor" had received his baptism in missionary medicine.

As the Congo situation seemed to stabilize, Atkinson's wife, Frieda, brought their children to Oicha and joined her husband. Most of the other missionaries who had evacuated in July and August also returned during the months of September and October. They had thought that conditions had returned to normal, but they had all been fooled.

By the end of the year soldiers seemed to be everywhere—both Congolese and United Nations—and roadblocks were appearing unexpectedly in the strangest places. Any time a car was halted at a roadblock, the outcome was unpredictable. The hospital was jammed with accident patients and with people wounded in attempts on their lives or beaten up at roadblocks.

Food became scarce, drug and medical supplies critically short. The solitary drugstore in that section of the Congo was closed down for two good reasons: no drugs and no pharmacist.

Previously, European patients had been a helpful source of income for the hospital at Oicha, but now all the Europeans in the area had evacuated. The number of African patients, however, continued to mount. More African patients, fewer supplies and less money than ever. That was the plight of Oicha late in 1960.

Ever since the July crisis Dr. Becker had kept in close radio contact with the major Africa Inland Mission stations in Congo. News was becoming gloomier every day. At Blukwa, missionaries were warned that they would have to join Patrice Lumumba's MNC party or be put in jail. Plymouth Brethren missionaries in nearby Nyankunde were threatened with beatings. To the south, a United Nations medical unit sent to help the Congolese had been jailed.

Then early in January, 1961, a coup d'état by Lumumbists overthrew the Kivu provincial government. Throughout the month, tension mounted. At one mission station, missionaries were placed under house arrest. In another place, missionaries were herded into prison. In several others, missionaries were pushed and slapped around. Anti-white feeling was running high. Congo was ready to explode.

Late that month the American Consul in Kampala, Uganda, radioed all missionaries in Kivu and Orientale Provinces of the Congo to evacuate immediately. The consulate had apparently intercepted a message from Moscow to Stanleyville, inciting Lumumba's supporters to begin massacring all whites, regardless of nationality or occupation, until rebel leader Patrice Lumumba was released from prison. Supposedly, Congolese soldiers were already fanning out from Stanleyville on this mission. Consequently, missionaries were urged to

evacuate Congo as soon as possible by any means they could and at
any place they could.

As Congo Field Director, Dr. Becker alerted the 130 A.I.M.
workers scattered throughout northeast Congo. Some fled immediately on a northern route around Lake Albert into Uganda. Others in
the southern sector of A.I.M. territory headed south to Oicha to join
the missionaries there. Because Dr. Becker had carefully laid out
detailed plans for evacuation in previous field council meetings, there
was little confusion now.

Veteran missionary Paul Stough, attempting to lead one contingent of missionaries out of Congo, was halted by drunken soldiers at
the legal border exit of Kasindi. Discouraged, the group headed back
to Oicha to convey the news to Dr. Becker.

At the Becker house the following evening, all the missionaries—
Stough's contingent from the north, the Oicha missionaries and
others joining them from outlying mission stations—met to make
their plans. It was a sombre occasion. For missionaries who had
spent their lives in Congo, it meant abandoning all they had. For first-
term missionaries like the Atkinsons it raised questions of why God
had brought them to Congo if they would be forced to return immediately to the States.

Six months earlier those who evacuated felt they would return
before long, but now the missionaries felt that evacuation would be
permanent.

The discussion lasted for hours. Becker tried to organize it. In his
mind, there were two questions to be decided.

Should they all leave? Certainly, single women and mothers with
young children should leave; he had no question about that. But
should he himself leave? Should he leave seriously ill patients in the
hospital? Should he leave an area of several thousand square miles
that had no doctors whatever? He was nearly sixty-six years old now
and had lived a full life. Why shouldn't he stay?

On the other hand, as field director of the Congo missionaries for
the African Inland Mission, he would set an example which others
would follow. If he stayed, others might foolishly imitate his action.

The second question to be settled was whether they should leave
by an official route. Paul Stough's group had been turned back at
Kasindi. Chances were, that a new convoy would be turned back
from any legal border crossing.

Then Herb Atkinson and Hal Olsen spoke up. They had just returned from a trip to the Uganda border to pick up medical supplies. There they had met a European count who owned a large plantation straddling the Uganda-Congo border.

"He said he was here a few years ago." Dr. Atkinson continued, "and he was most appreciative of the medical help he received. Well, to make a long story short, he offered to be of assistance to us."

"He said there is a little side road that leads to the plantation." Hal Olsen picked up the conversation. "I know where it is, and we could escape through his plantation into Uganda."

Andrew Uhlinger protested against the idea of using an illegal exit. "If the Lord wants us to get out, He will open up a legal border post," he argued, but the majority felt that the escape exit through the European count's plantation had been provided by the Lord, and since the American Consul had urged them to evacuate anywhere they could, this was sufficient authority. Uhlinger was outvoted.

Before the evening ended, Dr. Becker realized that the group felt strongly that all the missionaries should leave together. Both Becker and Uhlinger were inclined to stay, but they were willing to go along with the others.

After the long session, Becker and Atkinson rounded up the leaders of the African staff, carefully explained the situation, handed over the keys and prayed earnestly with them.

Then a few hours of restless sleep.

The night air was chilling. Dr. Becker felt it in his bones. Not that it was any colder than any of the hundreds of other Congolese nights when he had been roused at 3:00 A.M. by a rap on the window. But this night was different. The moon was big and brassy, almost defying anyone to sneak out of Congo tonight. The grass was damp, the air was damp; Marie's arthritis would start acting up if it hadn't already.

The convoy of nine cars was ready to leave now. The wives, children and single women were already seated in the cars; only the men were still outside, whispering in stage whispers their final arrangements.

It was all settled now; Hal Olsen would lead the way in the pickup truck. He knew where the turn-off was, and he was carrying the planks which would be converted into a crude bridge when they reached the final river. Next would come Paul Stough, and then Herb

Atkinson, who had just discovered that his headlights weren't working. Dr. Becker was happy to be at the tail end, the last to leave
Congo, driving right behind the Uhlingers.

With plans finalized, the men quickly walked to their cars, and the
procession began, moving slowly off the station property. Then leaving Oicha's sanctuary in the forest, they turned south onto the main
road that leads to Beni.

"Marie, you're quiet tonight."

"Uh-huh."

"I feel the same way you do." He saw her turn for a last look at
moon-lit Oicha before it was lost behind the giant trees of the Ituri.

Strange what had happened in the past six months, since that
delegation of Congolese officials had guaranteed their safety and
since the Schuezgers had been rescued from Mount Hoyo.

Driving by the Beni airstrip, Dr. Becker glanced to see if there
were any soldiers on duty. It seemed deserted. Only the moon spar-
kled down the 800-yard airstrip carved out of the jungle. It looked
more like a golfer's fairway, with not an airplane standing anywhere.

The convoy moved slowly, but steadily toward the border. It could
not be a hurried trip because of the condition of the roads and
because of the probability of unexpected barricades around any corner. About an hour out of Oicha the convoy stopped. Dr. Becker
stepped out and looked up the line of cars. The headlights showed
Harold Olsen and Paul Stough clearing away some branches in the
road.

"Just some fallen branches," Dr. Becker reported to Marie as he
climbed back into his car. "So far, so good, and we're almost halfway
to the border."

The convoy began moving again. Marie was becoming more talka-
tive now. "I can tell; you're still not convinced about leaving."

"Would you expect me to be?" The remark came out a bit shorter
than he had intended.

"No." Then she paused before adding, "Don't you think it's God's
will?"

She had read him perfectly. He felt that evacuation with the rest of
the missionaries was what he had to do, and yet he certainly wasn't
content in that decision. It was more than a sorrow about leaving
Oicha, it was an internal unrest. Yet as Congo field director for the
Africa Inland Mission, he had no choice.

He riveted his eyes on the taillights of Uhlinger's car and followed dutifully. Soon the convoy slowed to ten miles an hour.

"What do you think is the trouble?" asked Marie.

"The turn-off must be around here someplace. Hal probably wants to make sure he doesn't miss it. It's little more than a trail, you know."

Thirty seconds later, the convoy edged off the main dirt road onto a small track that led to the plantation of the European count. The track became narrower and narrower, and as it shrank in size, the holes increased.

How far they progressed the Beckers could not judge, but the time consumed was longer than they had anticipated. At one brief halt, Dr. Becker glanced at his watch anxiously. Softly, he expressed his concern: "I was hoping we'd make it before dawn."

Finally the convoy stopped in complete silence.

"I think this is it." Becker half spoke to Marie and stepped from the car.

All the men walked up to join Harold Olsen at the front of the convoy. There ahead of them was the stream dividing Congo from Uganda.

Suddenly Olsen put his hands to his forehead. "Oh, no." He dropped his head in disgust and then confessed. "I forgot to bring along those planks to make a bridge."

The men were silent momentarily. Then, "We ought to make you go back to Oicha to get them," someone kidded.

Now the doctor spoke. "The streams don't look too deep. Maybe we won't need a bridge. Why don't you try your truck on it, Hal?"

Despite the rocks in the stream bed, Olsen's truck made the crossing easily. Stough's car followed, then Atkinson's. One by one they crossed the dividing line. A long, low station wagon was momentarily snagged, but made it across with the help of manpower.

Finally, as the sun's rays started to lighten the sky over Uganda, all the cars had crossed the stream except those belonging to the Uhlingers and the Beckers. Then as Andrew Uhlinger climbed into his car and was starting to make his descent into the stream bed, Dr. Becker heard a raucous war cry behind him. He glanced back to see a dozen Watalingi tribesmen leaping down over the hillside, shouting their way through the elephant grass. Each seemed armed with either a bow and arrow, club or spear.

Dr. Becker stood motionless; the other missionaries clustered around him. With their big eyes almost popping out of their sockets, the Watalingi seemed half-crazed. Running down the hill behind the savages was a well-dressed African, evidently the leader of the group. He was attempting to keep the Watalingi under control.

There was something familiar about that leader, Becker thought, as he watched him, shouting at the savages. And then he recognized him. He was a Congolese official whom he had treated at the hospital.

"You cannot leave," shouted the arriving official. "None of you can leave. We will take your cars away from you." He stepped forward and nodded to his men. "Hand over your car keys to me." The Watalingi moved in and began shoving the younger missionaries.

Dr. Becker walked quickly to the official. "A good leader controls his men. If you have a problem, let's talk about it. We are your friends, not your enemies."

The official barked an order and his henchmen drew back. Dr. Becker breathed a bit more easily.

The European plantation owner joined the missionaries and moved alongside Dr. Becker. "Let me handle this, Doctor," he whispered. Then he turned on the African official and berated him for stopping the missionaries. After a few minutes of emotional outbursts back and forth, the European called Dr. Becker aside and said, "Listen, Doctor, these Watalingi can't be reasoned with; there's only one thing that they understand, and that's brute force."

The doctor shook his head.

"Listen to me, Doctor," the European continued. "I've got a pistol in my pocket; just give me the word and I'll use it. It's your only chance."

"No, I don't want anything of that kind happening. We'll work something out." He raised his hand and waved the emotional European away.

The Congolese official then drew close to Dr. Becker. "Where are the keys to your cars? Give them to me before my men get out of hand."

Dr. Becker glanced at the tribesmen surrounding the official. He was not anxious to tussle with them. But on the other hand, he did not want to see the women and children forced to return to Congo.

"Tell me," he finally asked, "why don't you want us to leave?"

"This is an illegal border exit."

"But some of our people tried to leave at Kasindi, and were not permitted to leave. So we were told by our government to leave any way and any place we could."

"But my government tells me I must not let you go."

There must be more to his hostile reaction, Dr. Becker thought. So he decided to probe further. "Listen, other white people have fled from Congo and you have not stopped them."

"Maybe, Dr. Becker," the official finally confided, "maybe we would not have stopped this group either if you had not been along."

Becker smiled. He felt he was finally getting somewhere. "Do you want to arrest me? Am I a prisoner?"

"Oh, I would not say that you are a prisoner. But you must not leave. I cannot and will not allow it."

"Well, then," Dr. Becker finally saw the way out. "To tell you the truth, I don't really want to leave anyway. So suppose I stay in Congo and you let all the rest leave."

"I cannot do that," said the official.

"Why not?" asked Dr. Becker. "You said that if I weren't in the group you might have let them escape. You see, my car is still on the Congo side of the stream."

"Yes." The African official smiled at the wise decision. "But what about the other car?" He motioned to Uhlinger's vehicle.

"I think that he might like to stay, too," said the doctor, winking at Uhlinger.

"You will turn your cars around and go back to Oicha?"

"Yes, you can depend on it."

The missionaries whose cars had crossed the stream seemed perturbed at the decision. Herb Atkinson seemed especially bothered. Finally he went to Dr. Becker and said, "I can't let you and the Uhlingers go back to Congo alone. I'm going with you."

"No, Herb, we can take care of ourselves," the doctor insisted. "God's hand is upon us."

But Atkinson would not give in. And for the second time in six months, he kissed his wife and children good-bye and turned to enter the no-man's land which was called Congo.

And the five—the veteran Uhlingers and the Beckers, and the rookie Dr. Herbert Atkinson—headed back to Oicha, not knowing what they would face in the days ahead.

"You know, Doctor," said Herb Atkinson as they began the long drive in the early daylight back to Oicha, "many people when they get to be your age are content to live in the past. But you always seem eager to look ahead to the future."

3

A Time to Be Born, a Time to Die

"Every human soul has a complete and perfect plan cherished for it in the heart of God, a divine biography which it enters into life to live." HORACE BUSHNELL

The clouds hung low over the Becker household that day in 1895 when John F. Becker was buried. Left behind were a grieving widow and three growing children: Helen fourteen, Carl eleven, and Frank seven. And all of Manheim, Pennsylvania, mourned with them.

John Becker was only forty when he died. He had not distinguished himself in the four decades of his life, as some of his brothers had. Two of them were doctors, and two were prospering farmers in the lush Pennsylvania Dutch farm country around Lancaster County.

Some folks thought that when he married into the Kline family, descendants of early settlers in Lancaster County, it would be a turning point for John Becker. And when he left the coal business to join a cousin as a co-proprietor of a general store in Manheim, they thought he might become a successful merchant in town. A thin, frail man, he yielded to his wife Ella's persuasion to move into the fashionable three-story brick "mansion" on South Charlotte Street in Manheim. It wasn't really a mansion, but the residents of Manheim didn't have many others to compare it with. Built by the town eccentric, it was a clumsy double-gabled house with a large porch and an iron spiked fence all around it. Inside, it was adorned by mahogany woodwork throughout.

Manheim itself is a pleasant town separated from the nearest sizable city of Lancaster by ten miles of rolling fields and bountiful farmland. It was founded in 1762 by German Baron William Stiegel, who started manufacturing flint glassware and made a fortune. But his generosity got him in trouble and only fourteen years later, by the time of the American Revolution, he was in debtors' prison because he had given away more money than he had.

Manheim was built around the town mall, with churches sprinkled liberally throughout the area. South of the city, toward Lancaster, were its biggest industries which included two large foundries. Most of the homes in the city were modest but clean and neat. Most—the Becker's was an exception—were built fronting on the main avenues of the town.

Life in the Becker home had been easy and quiet, with family games of croquet in the front yard. Though raised in a relaxed atmosphere, the children obeyed well and were taught to be helpful around the house.

John Becker had been a member of the Brethren Church, but in Manheim he joined his wife's Reformed Church, and soon was chosen a deacon.

Shortly after Carl was born, John Becker started a Sunday school in an area two miles southwest of Manheim, called Sporting Hill. He had received permission to use the local school, but in a short time the school board evicted them. Helped financially by Ben Hershey, owner of one of the town's foundries, he built a small chapel for the Sporting Hill community and gradually, the little Sunday school of Sporting Hill developed into a sizable church congregation.

In order to give his wife Ella a rest, John often took the three children with him on Sunday afternoons and strolled the two miles to the Sporting Hill Sunday school. It was a long walk for little feet, especially that long, winding hill at the end; and it was a long Sunday-school hour, especially after having attended Sunday school at the Reformed Church in the morning. But young Carl looked forward to it.

Life wasn't always so pleasant for John Becker. A failure in the coal business, he was rapidly discovering that the general store would not support the families of both his cousin and himself. And so he sold out—seemingly a failure again.

The fashionable house on Charlotte Street had to be sold too, which hurt Ella deeply; and finally John took his family to Lancaster while he tried his hand at the hotel business. Once again he felt he could not succeed.

Shortly before tuberculosis conquered him, he returned his family to Manheim, moving into a small frame house on Main Street. And then TB devastated him, as it had two of his brothers, and John F. Becker lay in a casket, as the family mourned.

What had he done in life except raise a family and start a Sunday school? Was there anything for which he would be known?

Carl Becker was finishing ninth grade at the time. His teacher, A. K. Kauffman, recalls, "He was one of the youngest in the group—some were several years older—but Carl earned the highest grades in the class. He was quiet, almost bashful among the older pupils, but he enjoyed fun, had a good sense of humor and took part in many extracurricular activities."

Understandably, young Carl became more serious about the meaning of life and death in those days. Though he had been brought up in a Christian home, Christianity had never become personal to him. Then the pastor of the big brick German Reformed Church announced a catechism class, which Carl attended faithfully. "It was the first time that I ever came in contact with the real meaning of the Christian faith," he recalls. Toward the end of the instruction, the minister confronted Carl with the question: "Are you going to accept this or not? It's up to you? It's not automatic. You have to make a decision." He could not rest in his father's faith or his mother's goodness. The decision had to be his.

Carl was ready to make his decision. After that, he recalls, "there were real changes in my life. I lost the desire to do some of the things that the rest of the gang were doing."

The gang was a fun-loving, outdoor-appreciating group, several from his Sunday-school class, which spent summer nights camping on nearby Mount Gretna. But some activities, washing dishes or gathering firewood, weren't so pleasant, and when the air was heated with hot and loud arguments, young Carl Becker, one of the smallest of the group, stepped in to settle the dispute. He became the gang's chaplain, praying before each meal.

Coupled with his deep interest in camping was his interest in athletics, especially swimming and tennis, and a mechanical curiosity. To win a steam engine, he and pal George Heiges one fall went house to house throughout Manheim selling magazine subscriptions. George didn't get anything, but Carl got his steam engine. In his mind he laid plans for new and faster airships, toy engines and steamships.

Though reserved and somewhat bashful, Carl possessed a determination that was awesome. What he went after, he got.

But the most important influences in his life came through his church. Accommodating 350 parishioners in its sanctuary, it was a very influential church in town. Within the congregation was a small core of mission enthusiasts, led by Ben H. Hershey, founder and owner of the Hershey Machine and Foundry Company, and his nephew Jack Nissley, who served as general manager. This group met weekly for Bible study, usually in the Hershey home.

One of the members was Anna Kraedy, Carl Becker's Sunday-school teacher. Actually, she taught all the boys in the church who had grown out of short pants. The class fluctuated in size almost as much as it did in age, but usually diminutive Anna Kraedy had about a dozen youngsters to contend with.

And sometimes it was definitely a contention. Outside the church, a swarm of bees and the mischievous boys often got together. Sometimes the Sunday-schoolers raided the hives and brought the wax into class with them. During the lesson, they kneaded bee's wax while Anna Kraedy was trying to teach. Some of the boys used a sharp pin to good effect in provoking a fellow pupil.

Like any normal boys, they delighted in asking questions designed to stump the teacher; for example, "Will the head of John the Baptist be in heaven?"

Yet through her love and concern Anna Kraedy deeply influenced the boys in her class. Carl Becker was only one of many. Sometimes she told missionary stories which she had heard only a few days before at the Hershey's Bible study class. When she told how Hudson Taylor had left the shores of England and went to China by faith with no guarantee of support at all, Carl Becker was deeply stirred.

He knew what it meant to need money. His mother, who loved the finer things of life, was forced to work every day in a factory to feed and clothe her children.

Because of Anna Kraedy's love for the Bible, Carl began to spend more time in reading Scripture for himself, and it wasn't just a few verses of Scripture hastily scanned before jumping into bed. That's what concerned his mother. Afraid he was wearing himself out reading the Bible, Mrs. Becker went to Anna Kraedy. "I'm worried, Anna. I know this sounds like a strange request, but I wonder if you could do something about it. You see, he's reading five or six chapters of the Bible every night before going to bed. It's too much for a boy his age. Anna, could you calm his religious enthusiasm down a bit?"

Anna Kraedy never even tried.

One Sunday morning Mrs. Kraedy reported to her class that the Africa Inland Mission was thinking about going to the heart of darkest Africa to a dangerous section of Belgian Congo where the gospel had never been preached before. The pioneering missionaries would have to camp out night after night with wild animals threatening and savage tribes surrounding them. Young Carl Becker was all ears.

A precocious child, he graduated from high school at the age of fifteen, the valedictorian of his class of eight members. His valedictory address was entitled "Qualification for American Manhood." Though he could hardly see over the podium and his voice had not yet changed, it was obvious that he understood what manhood was all about.

"The kind of men needed to better this nation are those who are unselfish and fearless, not passengers to be borne along by the labor of others. Success comes only to those who lead the life of endeavor."

Ella Becker, his mother, was very proud. She had worked hard to see that Carl had finished high school. She realized his capabilities, realized that her son Carl could make his mark in life. She had outfitted him well, especially considering her modest income, and his classmates had noticed his handsomeness, neatness and good grooming.

Once when older sister Helen was squabbling with Carl, Mrs. Becker admonished her. "Treat him well, Helen; you're going to live to be proud of him some day."

After high school, Carl received a scholarship to Mercersburg Academy, a highly recommended Reformed Church prep school not far from Gettysburg. A few years later, Calvin Coolidge sent his son to the same school. Sixteen-year-old Carl Becker distinguished himself both in the classroom and in athletics, setting a quarter-mile record for the school at the time. The following year, until money ran out, he went to Ursinus College, another Reformed Church institution, located about twenty-five miles northwest of Philadelphia. Returning to Lancaster County, he accepted a position as a teacher at a rural school for a year, and then returned to Manheim to work at the Bond Foundry and Machine Company as a clerk.

He wasn't through with his education yet, but he knew it would have to wait awhile. While his older sister Helen was at a teachers' college, he would stay home to support his mother and younger brother. After Helen graduated and became established in teaching, he could resume his schooling again.

At times he grew impatient with waiting as the months dragged into years; and at times his impatience turned into discouragement, as he wondered if he would spend his life as a clerk for a foundry. His mother wanted more for him, and he did too.

One good thing about being back in Manheim, however, was the privilege of attending the Bible study group that Anna Kraedy had told him so much about.

Some church members at the Manheim Reformed Church resented this little group; they thought that it would soon split their congregation and begin its own church. And some of the group members were in favor of the idea. They thought it would be a good idea to pull out of the Reformed Church because there were so many lukewarm members there. But Ben Hershey said, "No, I think we ought to stay in the church and bear our influence there." And that's what they did.

Carl Becker did too. He took on a boys' Sunday-school class, part of the class that Anna Kraedy had taught. Besides Sunday-morning lessons taught unspectacularly, Carl planned special hikes for the boys and he marched them militarily down the main highway to their camping grounds. The boys loved it. One of the boys, John B. Kuhn, influenced both by Anna Kraedy and Carl Becker, later became an outstanding missionary with the China Inland Mission.

Among the missionaries that Ben Hershey brought to Manheim to speak to their Bible study group were Charles E. Hurlbut and Lee Downing, two early leaders of the Africa Inland Mission. When Downing stayed at Manheim for three weeks, Carl Becker became acquainted with a missionary for the first time.

Still undecided about his future plans, Carl approached the missionary for guidance. Lee Downing drew the teen-ager apart and sat beside him on the Hersheys' sofa. He mentioned the desperate need which the Africa Inland Mission had at that time for medical missionaries.

When Carl asked if healing bodies was as important as preaching or teaching the gospel, Downing stressed how doctors could open doors for Christianity by overcoming prejudice and breaking down superstition. "We think of the medical missionary as the advance agent of the gospel," he said. He also pointed out that many mission-

aries had been dying of malaria and blackwater fever because no
doctors were there to help them.

The boy was impressed, deeply impressed.

Medicine had always fascinated him, and gradually it became
more clearly his goal. Would he become a medical missionary? He
certainly thought about the possibility, and when he was at the Bible
study group, he felt urged in that direction. But at home he wavered.

Jacob Nissley, Hershey's son-in-law and the foundry manager, was
desirous of seeing Carl Becker go to the mission field. The profits
from the Hershey foundry as well as individual donations from em-
ployees supported twelve missionaries in China and Africa. But Nissley seemed particularly eager to have a missionary go out right from
Manheim. And he had his eyes fixed on young Carl Becker. One day
he told Carl, "I know that you've thought about the idea of becoming
a missionary. Well, you know that the Hershey Foundation supports
a lot of them. What I'm meaning to say is this: If we can ever
be of help to a future missionary, let us know."

But young Carl wasn't sure he was going to be a missionary. Long
years at a medical college came first, and then he felt he would be
better able to chart his future.

So when sister Helen had completed teachers' college and had
become established in the teaching profession, Carl Becker began
writing for catalogs from various medical schools. He pored over
them trying to decide which one he should select. At a complete loss,
he threw up his hands in despair and visited a local physician to ask
his advice.

"I don't know, Carl; there are a lot of fine medical schools in
Philadelphia. But, say, I just received a catalog from one of them this
morning." And the Manheim doctor reached deep into his waste-
basket and pulled out a catalog labeled Hahnemann Medical College,
Philadelphia.

"I've never heard of it." Carl spoke uncertainly.

"Good school," the doctor said with authority and plunked the
catalog into the boy's hand.

And on the basis of that recommendation, Carl applied the next
day.

A few weeks later, he waved his acceptance papers in front of his
mother and brother. But the closer it came to September, 1916, when
he was slated to enter Hahnemann, the more uncertain he became.

The uncertainty was largely financial. He had only $100 saved for his education, and some had already laughed at him for thinking he could get through a six-year med course on that amount. Everything seemed against him. He had been forced to drop out of college after one year, because of finances. His financial needs would be even greater in med school. And he had been out of school for five years. Would it be possible for him to stand the strain of working a heavy schedule on top of studying long hours at medical school? He had always done well at school, but he knew med school would be more intensive than anything he had ever faced before. He looked again at the Hahnemann catalog and shook his head. There were names of courses which he couldn't even pronounce, let alone define.

Finally, he dropped to his knees beside his bed. "Lord," he prayed, "I haven't done much for You yet that has counted for anything, and maybe I never will—" He thought about his words in prayer. He wished he could pray like Lee Downing or Ben Hershey or even like Anna Kraedy. But his words came out cold and clumsy-like, without the soft reverence of Thee's and Thou's. Yet it was the only way he knew how to pray.

"But, Lord, if You help me get my medical education and help me to become a doctor, I will give You everything."

He stopped praying for a minute and considered what he had just uttered: Did he really mean it, he wondered. And then his head sank deeper into the bed as his words were almost smothered by the blankets, "Yes, Lord, everything."

4

The Making of a Medic

In 1916, after a five-year hiatus from books, twenty-two-year-old Carl Becker walked up the stone steps of Hahnemann Medical College. In the pocket of his neatly pressed suit was $125, and with this sum he was to obtain a medical education.

He looked at the massive building with awe. When he finished—if he finished—six years from now, he would have an M.D. after his name, a degree that would enable him to heal the sick and suffering. One year of pre-med schooling, four years of medical training, and one year of internship—would he make it?

He didn't know much about medical schools, didn't know if Hahnemann was better or worse than others in the Philadelphia area, but the catalog was certainly impressive.

Established in 1848, Hahnemann had grown until it had thirty-eight instructors and professorships in everything from ophthalmology to gynecology. It housed an outstanding anatomical museum, and a library of 18,000 volumes. Adjoining it was a 250-bed hospital, the first hospital in the United States devoted to homeopathy.

Homeopathy, he found out after he arrived, is a philosophy of medical treatment founded by a nineteenth-century German physician named Samuel Hahnemann. Hahnemann's curiosity was aroused by his experiments with Peruvian bark. He discovered that symptoms produced by a drug on a healthy body are similar to the disease the drug cures. It confirmed an old medical proverb, "Like cures like," and upon this theory he founded his system of medicine.

The hospital, founded five years after Hahnemann's death, offered an education comparable to that of other medical schools, and perhaps superior to many, because it was trying to prove itself to the traditional schools of medicine. There was very little difference in its classroom work, since homeopathy differed not in the diagnosis but in its philosophy of treatment. And since many of the early homeo-

36

pathic zealots had passed from the scene by the time Becker began his training, Hahnemann was already offering a more standard approach to medicine than it had in its pioneer days.

When Hahnemann's registrar introduced Carl Becker to a fellow student who needed a roommate, the student looked Carl over skeptically and remarked, "I guess he'll be OK, if he studies."

That was one thing Carl Becker did. He studied when he was eating his lunch, he studied when he was riding a streetcar to school, he studied between classes. He had to scrape the hours to the bone and make good use of all of them.

They told him it was an impossible load to carry, working six hours every night from 6:00 P.M. until midnight behind a soda fountain in the Reading Terminal basement, before returning to his third-floor room on Girard Avenue with three easygoing roommates to study for the next day's assignments.

During the summer of 1917, he saddled himself with an even more strenuous load, adding to his nightly stint behind the soda fountain, a daytime job in the Reading Terminal delicatessen. It meant fifteen hours of work a day. His Manheim friend George Heiges kidded him that his work slicing meat in the delicatessen would be good training for his future in surgery.

Amazingly, his health held out, though he feared that his family history of TB would catch up with him. Knowing that his thin frame seemed to be the type to be prey to tuberculosis, he was reluctant to be tested for the disease. But finally he surrendered to the tuberculin test. Much to his amazement, he showed no signs of a TB infection. He couldn't believe it; there must have been some mistake, he thought. But he was taking no chances. He wouldn't be tested again.

Carl Becker's closest friend at Hahnemann was burly Bob Hunter. They had much in common—but not their physiques. Hunter resembled a rugged football lineman; Becker, who spread 130 pounds skimpily over his 71 inches, looked more like a scared jackrabbit.

Both top-notch students, Carl and Bob competed vigorously in the classroom. Their competition was just as keen on the athletic field. Two or three times a week they boxed together. "I could beat him with one hand tied behind my back," said the broad-shouldered Hunter. It wasn't a boast; it was merely a fact stated in admiration of Carl's spunkiness.

Another link between the two was Hunter's father, a warmhearted Christian believer with whom Carl Becker talked for many hours on

Sunday afternoons. Though Bob Hunter shared neither Becker's nor his father's enthusiasm for spiritual things, he soon recognized that Becker's faith was the genuine article. He respected it, because it wasn't something worn on the sleeve. Hunter says, "It was something deep—and very real."

"The only way I can describe him is—different. He was different —that's all. He would sit down with a sandwich and a book and eat and study totally oblivious to the noisy game of pinochle being played alongside of him."

"Yes, he was different. He was friendly with everyone and very well liked, but not very many people got to know him below the surface. He had no real social life, but whenever we went someplace together he always insisted on paying his own way—even though money wasn't nearly the problem for me that it was with him. I guess he didn't want to sponge off anyone."

During his first year at Hahnemann, war was closing in on America. For two years the United States had managed to stay out of the European conflagration, but the fire was spreading, and it seemed inevitable that Yankee doughboys would be sent overseas.

President Woodrow Wilson, re-elected for a second term, had pledged to do all that was in his power to keep America out of war. But after repeated sinkings of American ships, and after repeated warnings to Germany with no effect, Wilson made the big decision. On April 3, 1917, Carl saw the headlines of the *Philadelphia Bulletin* on a Broad Street newsstand: WAR! SAYS WILSON: BIG ARMY NEEDED.

Writing to his Manheim pal George Heiges who was already in France, Carl confided that he didn't know how long it would be before he too would be called into the Armed Forces.

Carl was also worried about finances. By dogged work, he had been able to pay for board, room and tuition at Hahnemann, but the sum of $125 which he had brought to Philadelphia was now depleted and his job at the Reading Terminal each evening was barely keeping him financially afloat. His one suit was nearly threadbare, and his one pair of shoes had been resoled for the last time, the cobbler said.

That fall, when a medical reserve corps was organized at Hahnemann, Carl decided to enlist in it. His enlistment meant no change at all in his daily routine—at least for a while. But then as the dogwoods of eastern Pennsylvania exploded in blossom in the spring of 1918, the German Army began exploding an offensive in France against the Allies and the situation did not look at all bright.

For weeks the reservists gossiped about rumors of their activation. Newspapers were devoured religiously to glean some advance clue. And then it came. The Enlisted Reserve Corps of the Army of the United States, Medical Section, was officially activated.

Carl didn't know how to react to the news. It might mean a further delay in his medical education; it might mean long years of waiting. "Actually," his friend Bob Hunter recalls, "all it meant to Carl was free board and room, $30 a month in wages, and best of all, for Carl, a spanking new Army uniform. It was a Godsend to him."

The activated Reserve unit moved the boys from their rooming houses to the local armory, but allowed them to continue their regular Hahnemann medical training, tuition free, under the auspices of the United States Medical Corps. Military discipline was imposed, but this was no hardship on Carl who had long imposed upon himself a more rigid discipline. While he had to stop his soda-jerking at the Reading Terminal, in its place he received $30 a month with practically no new expenses.

After his discharge following Armistice Day, 1918, and for the three remaining years at Hahnemann, Carl made good use of his army coat and shoes.

Carl Becker hadn't much time for girls. So determined was he to get his medical degree that his social life had been terribly neglected. That's what his younger brother Frank said one Christmas vacation when Carl was back in Manheim.

But reluctantly Carl double-dated with brother Frank to a young people's social at the Reading Evangelical Congregational Church. Frank's girl brought along for Carl a young Reading schoolteacher named Marie Bodey. Carl usually felt out of place at such events, but Marie Bodey, an attractive large-boned brunette with a full face and sad eyes, intrigued him.

Like Carl, she had come from an old German family in Pennsylvania Dutch country, was raised in a German Reformed Church and was one of three children. After an education at West Chester State Normal School, she began teaching at Langhorne, a few miles north of Philadelphia. Out of curiosity, she visited a Billy Sunday evangelistic campaign in Philadelphia and was spellbound by the evangelist's flamboyant approach.

In her home town of Reading a short time later, Evangelist Henry

W. Stough, following the Billy Sunday pattern, was holding revival services in a huge specially constructed wooden tabernacle. Marie Bodey walked in one evening, still remembering the message of Billy Sunday, and when Evangelist Stough urged sinners to come forward for salvation, she walked down the sawdust trail.

Serious and sensitive by nature, she pursued her new-found faith passionately, joining Reading's First Evangelical Congregational Church, where she found a Bible-centered emphasis, and then seeking to share her faith with her immediate family. Her younger brother, Allen, was the fruit of her soul-winning efforts.

Carl and Marie's courtship bore no resemblance to a whirlwind. At times Marie became discouraged with Carl's lack of intensity, for although he wrote frequently, he saw her only occasionally. One night he confided, "Marie, I want you to understand one thing. Before I went to med school, I made a promise to God, a promise that if He would give me an education, I would give my life to Him. I don't know what this will mean, Marie; I don't know if it means I'll go to China or Africa as a missionary or what. But He has first claim to my life. And I thought I had better warn you about it."

Marie was thrilled with the warning. That was the kind of man she wanted to marry, a man upon whom God had first claim.

In his senior year at Hahnemann, Carl's friend Bob Hunter battled with diphtheria for six weeks, forcing him to miss an entire course in nose-and-throat. After Hunter had recuperated, Carl decided to tutor him, and using nurses as guinea pigs, he went painstakingly over the material Hunter had missed.

At the end of the year, the Hahnemann registrar revealed that there was a tie for top honors in the class, two students with "not one-tenth of a point separating them." The two were Carl Becker and Bob Hunter. Hunter received special praise, because he had missed so much instruction and yet tied Becker at the top.

(A year later when both medics took the Pennsylvania Board of Medicine examination, competing with doctors from all the medical schools of the state, Becker ranked first, and Hunter was a close second. Both were granted licenses to practice medicine in the Commonwealth of Pennsylvania.)

As graduation day approached, while most students were showing signs of excitement and release from tension, Carl Becker was becoming depressed. When Hunter questioned him about it, he responded, "It's my clothes, Bob. I wish I could get something decent to wear for graduation." He was still wearing his army shoes and the remainder of his clothing was almost as old. Carl explained that he didn't care much about it himself. "But my mother and sister will be coming to graduation and I don't want them to feel ashamed of me."

A week later, Carl burst into Hunter's room with rare exuberance. He was sporting a new suit, new shirt, new tie, new shoes.

"What did you do, Carl, rob a bank?" Hunter exclaimed.

"No, I just sat down and asked the Lord about it," Carl answered simply. And then he went on to explain how five checks suddenly came in the mail—"one from a fellow I had loaned some money to about three years ago. I thought he had forgotten all about it. Another came from Jacob Nissley in Manheim—he wanted to give me a graduation gift and didn't know what I needed most—so he sent a check for $50. And then there were three smaller checks. Before I knew it, the Lord had sent in more than $100."

He left Hunter shaking his head in amazement, not only at the miraculous arrival of the checks, but also at Carl Becker's childlike faith.

While Carl Becker was in his year of internship, Jacob Nissley asked him to come to the *Sunday School Times* building to meet Charles Hurlburt of the Africa Inland Mission. While Becker had heard him speak previously in Manheim, he had never met him.

Hurlburt was a tall, impressive, almost overwhelming man. His deep tan and leathery skin reflected the many years he had spent in the heart of Africa, and his voice evidenced his urgency for Christian missions. He told Carl Becker of a new area in Congo which had just been opened in the past two years, a place with the strange name of Nyankunde, a tribe called the Babira which numbered 150,000 to 200,000 people, who had no missionaries at all. He told of the need for medical missionaries to prepare the way for the evangelists and Bible teachers in this area. He told of witch doctors who killed more people than the slave traders and who took advantage of the tribespeople by fear and superstition.

"We've been praying for new missionaries, Carl, especially doctors." Hurlburt laid his hand heavily on Carl's shoulder. It was a firm, strong hand, a fatherly hand. The man's intensity bothered Carl. "I hope the Lord leads you out to Africa when your training is finished."

Jacob Nissley had been standing in the background. But finally he moved forward to say, "He'd make a great missionary, Dr. Hurlburt; and we too are praying that the Lord will lead him out there."

Carl Becker didn't know what to say. He remembered the night when he had dropped along the side of his bed and had prayed fervently, "Lord, if you give me a medical education, I'll give you everything I am, everything I have." Now, his medical education was nearly completed, and he was wondering if it perhaps had been a rash promise. Perhaps God didn't want him on the mission field. And he knew one other thing: Someone was going to have to provide for his mother. Now that he had been trained in medicine, it was natural for the burden of the provision to fall on his shoulders rather than on his sister who was struggling with a schoolteacher's salary.

No, he told himself, he just couldn't go to the mission field immediately. He had other obligations. And he recalled a verse in the Bible he had recently seen. "If any provide not for his own, and specially for those of his own house, he hath denied the faith, and is worse than an infidel."

But he would not forget the plea of Charles Hurlburt, nor the prayers of Jacob Nissley. Indeed, he could not, for the Lord would not let him.

5

The Pride of Boyertown

"Our lives are our own to spend, but we spend them only once."
J. OSWALD SANDERS

Two eligible young bachelors began their medical practices in Boyertown, Pennsylvania, in June, 1922. Their names were Carl Becker, M.D., and Gordon Bornemann, D.D.S., and they lived at 29 and 31 E. Philadelphia Ave., respectively. Both had offices underneath their second-floor apartment, and both found favor with Boyertown residents immediately.

Boyertown was centered between the larger communities of Reading, Allentown and Pottstown and was overshadowed by all three. Old-time residents there had to fight for the town's identity, and merchants kept trying to entice residents to shop locally rather than traveling ten, twenty or thirty miles away to one of the bigger sister cities.

Because of its precarious economic position, a strong community feeling was built in Boyertown. Whenever a merchant closed up shop, a lawyer joined a Philadelphia law firm, or a physician died, it was a blow struck at the heart of little Boyertown. Like the littlest schoolboy who has to fight the class bullies waiting on every corner, so Boyertown felt that it had to battle for its own existence against Allentown, Reading and Pottstown.

Thus, when in quick succession Doctors Ludwig, Oberholzer and Merkel had been removed from the Boyertown scene due to death and other causes, the Chamber of Commerce swung into action to recruit the best young medical student they could find. If they didn't, Boyertown residents would soon come to depend on one of the larger rival cities for medical assistance.

Twenty-eight-year-old Carl Becker, M.D., walked into Boyertown in 1922, after six years of medical training; a thriving practice was already waiting for him.

When he had first received the Boyertown plea, Becker was thrilled with the opportunity, but a bit puzzled with what to do about it. He had no money with which to buy needed medical equipment, so how could he establish his practice? But he remembered what Jacob Nissley had mentioned to him six years before: "If there's anything I can do for you, let me know." Carl never liked the idea of asking for charity, but the Boyertown proposition was not charity; this was a sound business proposition. So Carl Becker asked Jake Nissley for a $2,000 loan.

Nissley was agreeable. "But, you know, Carl, that all the profits that are earned through the Hershey Company are dedicated to the Lord for the support of missionaries. We're glad to loan you the money, but don't forget the terms of the loan."

The practice grew like a magic beanstalk. Becker's manner inspired confidence and his dedication to the work enabled him to handle twice the load of the average country doctor. Despite his youth, he had the bearing of an experienced country doctor with his gentle, assuring bedside technique and his understanding eyes.

After hours, Physician Becker and Dentist Bornemann sprawled together on his living room floor and tried to build some simple crystal sets. Both were born tinkerers, and for them it was a relaxation to use a soldering iron to put together a radio set at the end of a day. When completed, the radios were taken out on house calls and left at needy homes.

Throughout his early months at Boyertown, Becker's trips to the Bodey home in Reading became more and more frequent. And then in September, the schoolteacher and the country doctor were married in a simple parsonage wedding at the First Evangelical Congregational Church in Reading.

After the marriage, Marie set up housekeeping in the second-floor flat at 29 E. Philadelphia Avenue. Marie, a practical-minded realist, quickly adjusted to life with Carl Becker. She learned that he might absentmindedly put on different colored socks if he was preoccupied in thought. And she learned too that he was often unpredictable.

Shortly after their first child, Mary, was born in 1923, Carl bought her a toy train. Since Mary was too young to play with it herself, he set it up himself, winding the seemingly endless track throughout the house, into Marie's spotless kitchen, into the dining room underneath the table and around the chairs and into the living room under the big leather sofa. Mary enjoyed it all right, but not so much as Carl Becker and neighbor Gordon Bornemann.

The Pride of Boyertown 45

The next year, Carl presented Marie with a huge Graflex press camera, so big and clumsy she could hardly lift it. He couldn't understand why she didn't seem to appreciate it. Nor could he understand why she didn't seem to appreciate the ugly little Boston terrier named Bud which he gave her the following year.

In spare moments, when Gordon Bornemann and Carl Becker weren't tinkering with crystal sets to give away, they tried to keep physically fit with assorted athletics. Behind their offices on Philadelphia Avenue, they constructed a tennis court, and when it was completed they spent time chasing tennis balls across neighbors' yards and shaking them out of the neighbors' trees.

When Boyertown opened its new indoor pool, Carl Becker and Gordon Bornemann were given a special dispensation to splash around after hours in pitch darkness between ten and midnight.

As a general practitioner, Becker touched all branches of medicine, but Boyertown residents regarded him as a specialist in maternity cases.

Early one Sunday morning in the middle of a bitter winter storm, Carl Becker was roused out of sleep by two farmers. One of them explained that his wife was in labor and that the doctor must come quickly. Becker dashed out the door right behind the farmers and jumped into their sleigh, which took him far out into the country, to see the expectant mother. It was a false alarm.

In the middle of the afternoon, he was called out again, and after making the long trip, he discovered that it was another false alarm.

Finally in the middle of the night, the men came a third time. They told him, "We're sure about it this time."

As Becker was about to join them, they said, "By the way, Doc, you may have some trouble tonight; there's no electricity out our way."

Becker went back and roused Bornemann to assist him. Rather than go by sleigh this time, Becker used his car. It was no false alarm. The woman was having difficulty and Becker determined that it would have to be an instrument delivery. With Bornemann administering the ether, and one of the farmers holding a dim flashlight, the little baby was safely delivered.

But false alarms like that didn't seem to rile Carl Becker; in fact, very few things ever got under his skin.

One time, however, he received a phone call from a farmer who said his children were sick in bed with diarrhea, and he requested that the doctor come out immediately. Jumping into his car, he raced

—which was the only way he knew how to drive—several miles to the farmhouse.

When he arrived, he discovered the children were outside playing, seemingly in the best of health. As he walked somewhat puzzled to the house, the farmer met him at the door.

"I thought you said the children were sick," the doctor questioned.

"Well, it wasn't exactly that." The farmer hemmed and hawed. "It's, well, it's something else." The farmer seemed embarrassed and ashamed to say any more. Dr. Becker followed him through the kitchen piled with dishes and up the stairs into a bedroom, where the man's wife was groaning in bed.

She was in labor. After examining her, Dr. Becker knew that he would need his instruments from his office in Boyertown in order to bring her through. For once Becker was irritated. "But why didn't you tell me on the phone that she was in labor?"

The farmer hesitated. Then he said with reddening face, "Doctor, there are just some things that a Christian man doesn't talk about."

The doctor sped back to Boyertown at breakneck speed and returned with the instruments in time to save the life of both the mother and the newborn baby.

As Becker's practice continued to grow, he hired two nurses and a secretary and bought more medical equipment. He even wrote to Hahnemann to send another alumnus to work with him. A young M.D. came and worked with Becker for a few months but left in consternation. "Nobody can keep up a pace like that without going crazy," he said.

The loan which Becker had received from Jake Nissley was being rapidly repaid—in fact, much more quickly than Nissley had anticipated. But each time a payment was made on the loan, Nissley reminded Becker, "Don't forget the terms of the loan, Carl; don't forget the terms of the loan."

Carl Becker had almost forgotten.

It wasn't that he had forgotten God. No, not at all. It was just that life had become complicated with cares, pressures and responsibilities. Everything had seemed so simple and clear-cut when he had made that promise to God ten years ago. But it wasn't that simple any more.

He had a responsibility to his mother, to see that she was properly provided for. After all, she had sacrificed for him; it was only right that he honor her and provide for her in these later years of her life. And so she had come to live with Carl and Marie at Boyertown.

But he had to admit that he was glad when he made his final payment to Jacob Nissley. Nissley kept reminding him of that earlier promise. How could Nissley know what the Lord wanted from his life? He resented the implication that he was a heathen for remaining in Boyertown.

He couldn't deny that life in Boyertown had been good to them. He had become prosperous, and had achieved status in the little community. No longer did he have to wonder where the money would come from. No longer did he have to pray for cash to buy a new suit of clothes.

One day a government official from Washington, D.C., was traveling through Pennsylvania and became ill near Boyertown. Dr. Carl Becker came to his rescue and restored him to health. The official was deeply impressed with the Boyertown physician. "Dr. Becker, you shouldn't have buried yourself in Boyertown; your future is limited here, you know. A man with your gifts and capabilities could make a name for himself in a big city. Why don't you come down to Washington?"

After the official had left, Dr. Becker was thoughtful. Had he buried himself in Boyertown? Was there more of a future elsewhere? If God had given him medical ability, was it right for him to stay in a small isolated town? He pondered these questions seriously.

There was still another possibility. A businessman in Boyertown had once suggested to him that he think of founding a hospital there. The idea intrigued him. When he mentioned the thought casually to members of the Chamber of Commerce, he found them excited about it. His mind was already making plans about how it could be started. Since he had his own X-ray equipment and private laboratory, it wouldn't be hard at all to launch a small hospital. And once started, it could grow and grow and grow.

But then came a third possibility.

A letter came from Dr. Charles Hurlburt of the Africa Inland Mission. It told the tragic circumstances of the death of Dr. Elizabeth Morse Hurlburt, who died at Aba station in northeast Belgian Congo. Dr. Hurlburt's son Paul had cabled home with the sad news and the explanation was in two words: "Blackwater fever."

Now the need for missionary doctors in Congo was greater than ever. An urgent request had gone out to all the friends and family of the Africa Inland Mission "for the raising up of a doctor to take the place of Dr. Elizabeth Morse Hurlburt."

The letter lay on Dr. Becker's desk for several days. A letter like that was difficult to answer. To refuse Dr. Hurlburt made you feel like a horrible sinner, yet Dr. Becker carefully penned his reply. He appreciated Dr. Hurlburt's remembering him from their one short meeting at the *Sunday School Times* office in Philadelphia. And he certainly hadn't forgotten the mission field or the particular needs of the Africa Inland Mission. However, at this time, he had a responsibility to his mother, he explained, and it would be impossible for him to leave her until she was properly provided for.

After he sealed the letter, he felt a bit dissatisfied with it. He was sure that Dr. Hurlburt wouldn't think that the excuse was adequate. But each man has to make his own decisions before God, he told himself, and this seemed to be the course he had to take.

Whether the decision was right or wrong, the thought of going to the mission field was pushed farther and farther back in Becker's mind.

Life in Boyertown was good and pleasant. He was a man held in esteem by the entire community and was netting a salary of well over $10,000 in those pre-depression years. Yes, life in Boyertown was full of rewards of all sorts.

It was about this time that an uneducated country preacher came to Boyertown. W.A. Masteller, a thirty-seven-year-old former miner from northern Pennsylvania, had been in the ministry for only two years, handling a circuit of four churches in the coal-mining regions north of Scranton. He felt unsure of himself as he took the pastorate of the Boyertown Evangelical Congregational Church. It was a small, insignificant church, with only a few more than 100 members. The two big congregations in town were the Reformed and Lutheran churches, each claiming more than 1,000 parishioners.

Most of the people in the Evangelical Congregational Church were simple Christian folk, people with not much more education than Masteller himself. That was why he was surprised that Carl and Marie Becker came so regularly to church.

Masteller knew well the Becker reputation. He also knew that the rival ministers were both vying to get the Beckers to join their congregations. And frankly, Masteller didn't know why they didn't. What could these educated people get out of simple messages from an uneducated preacher?

Yet the noted doctor would come in the small church, sit in the last pew, next to the aisle. With his hand on his chin, he sat fixedly throughout the sermon, staring with his small intent eyes directly on the minister. Masteller, though five years Becker's senior, held the doctor in awe.

One night after the evening service at the church, Marie Becker asked Masteller to come over to their home. Dr. Becker wanted to talk to him about something. Masteller prayed much about that interview for he felt inadequate to handle it.

The meeting was casual. Over coffee and doughnuts, they discussed Biblical matters together. Then, almost as Masteller was about to leave, Marie tugged on Carl's sleeve. "Why don't you tell Reverend Masteller why we asked him over here tonight?"

Dr. Becker glanced down at the floor, almost bashfully, back at his wife, then at the minister. "I've been wondering, Pastor, if you would feel that I was worthy to become a member of your church?"

Masteller was dumbfounded. Finally he replied, "Dr. Becker, the only requirement we have for church membership is that a man be truly born again."

Dr. Becker nodded. "Yes, I know, but I see all those wonderful Christian folk in your church and I don't know if I measure up."

Masteller smiled. "Dr. Becker, you measure up just fine!"

Later Masteller asked the doctor why he chose his church when so many other larger churches and well-trained ministers had obviously been angling for him. Becker responded, "The other ministers give me textbook preaching; I can read that in books if I want to. You preach from personal experience. That's what I need."

Charles Hurlburt had not given up on Carl Becker. Though he was an old man now and no longer could return to Africa, he still had Africa in his heart. Retired to California, he promoted missions in whatever way he could. When a New Jersey physician wrote to him, volunteering for missionary service, Hurlburt wrote back immediately. "By the way," Hurlburt added at the conclusion of his letter, "there is a doctor in Boyertown, Pennsylvania, named Carl K. Becker who should be going to the mission field one of these days. Please contact him for me and see what his plans are."

In the summer of 1928, the New Jersey physician made his first contact with the Boyertown doctor. He reported back to Hurlburt, "As yet he has no plans—no immediate plans—for the mission field."

It was on a cold, blustery night that winter, as the windows of the Boyertown apartment were rattling from the wind. Marie was check-

ing on the two children, Mary, five and Carl Jr., two, to see if there
were any drafts blowing upon them. Carl Becker was in his study.

Marie returned from the bedrooms, just as her husband emerged
from his study.

"Sit down, Marie," he said. "I have something important I want to
talk to you about."

Marie seated herself quietly on the leather sofa.

"Marie, I've been praying." He spoke quietly, calmly, but he
didn't know exactly what he would say to her. "And as I speaking to the Lord He spoke to me." It sounded strangely mystical, but
he didn't mean it that way. Carl Becker had always believed in
prayer, and had always set apart time to seek the Lord's help in his
work. Sometimes his contacts with the Lord weren't as personal as
they should have been. Lately, he hadn't been experiencing the answers to prayer which he had experienced in earlier years. But still he
prayed. And sometimes as he talked to God, he felt the still, small
voice of the Holy Spirit within him communicate with him.

Marie was looking at him intently, but she said nothing.

"Marie, when I first started courting you, I told you of my promise
to God."

Marie nodded.

"I don't know if I've kept that promise very well. Tonight the
Lord spoke to me about it."

"What do you mean, Carl?"

"I think that God wants us to be missionaries, but I don't know
exactly what to do about it." Then there was quiet. Carl was half-waiting for Marie to say something, and half-thinking he should say
more.

"What was the name of that mission leader you talked to once?"
she finally asked.

"Oh, you mean Charles Hurlburt with the Africa Inland Mission."

The next day he wrote to the Brooklyn office of the A.I.M. for the
address of Hurlburt, and receiving in return a very short note containing Hurlburt's California address, he corresponded directly with
the aging missionary pioneer. In less than a week, Carl Becker received a night letter from California. Hurlburt was jubilant about
hearing from him. It was an answer to prayer, Hurlburt said. There
was a great need for doctors in Congo. How soon could he be ready
to go?

Becker was overwhelmed by the response. But hardly had he

digested the first night letter than he received a second, and then a third. All were urging him into action. There was no doubt now about their future course. The die had been cast.

Seven years earlier, Marie would have had few problems about going, but now it was different. She had two children, six and three, and they were going to be taking them to the heart of darkest Africa. When she mentioned the possibility to a neighbor, it didn't help her confidence to be told, "Your children will never come out alive."

In addition, Marie's mother was suffering from high blood pressure. How would she stand the shock of seeing her only daughter going to Africa? The Bodeys had already lost one son; now all they had left were Marie and her younger brother, Allen. Marie worried about how to break the news.

Carl Becker had problems of his own. His first step was to establish a trust fund for his mother. From accumulated earnings he could provide for his mother to live comfortably for the rest of her life. Next he would sell his home and dispose of his practice.

What Carl hadn't counted on, however, was the reaction of the town. When word seeped out that Boyertown's favorite physician would be deserting them for a hole in the jungle somewhere in Belgian Congo, the community was aroused. It was a blow to community pride.

The Chamber of Commerce appointed a committee to talk some sense into Dr. Becker's head. They had heard him speak of his dream for a hospital in Boyertown. Surely if they would raise the money for the establishment of that hospital, he would change his mind.

Dr. Becker listened patiently as the committee made their carefully outlined presentation. He was moved by their interest in him, but when they had finished, he said, "I've made a promise to God. My time in Boyertown has been sort of borrowed time. You wouldn't want me to go back on a promise to God, would you?"

The committee filed out of the Becker home and made plans for an indirect attack. "There's no sense in talking to him," said one.

But another committeeman said, "Let's see if we can make some headway with Reverend Masteller."

Masteller had never had a delegation from the Chamber of Commerce visit him before, but he graciously received them. Slowly they presented their case to Masteller. They made it sound as if the entire future of Boyertown was at stake. There certainly was a great deal of

good that a Christian doctor could do in Boyertown, they told
Masteller.

And Masteller agreed. "Don't think I won't be sorry to lose the
Beckers too. But his decision is between him and the Lord. It
wouldn't be right for me to intercede."

Then one merchant jumped to his feet and said, "Listen, Reverend, I'm going to lay it right on the line. My wife is getting hysterical
about this thing. She's going to have a baby soon and nobody can
deliver that baby but Dr. Becker."

The other committemen nodded in hearty agreement. "Please,
Reverend, see if you can talk some sense into his head," one of them
added.

"No, I can't do that, and he wouldn't listen to me if I tried,"
Masteller explained. "Besides, with the tremendous practice that he
has built up in Boyertown, we can get any number of M.D.'s who
would jump at the chance of taking over for him. But I sure don't
know of anyone who would be willing to substitute for him in Africa,
do you?"

The committee had lost round two of the fight to keep Carl Becker
in Boyertown. After a strategy huddle, it was time for round three.

A public meeting was called in the National Bank Building. Its
specific purpose was to keep Dr. Carl K. Becker in Boyertown.

Sponsored by the Chamber of Commerce and widely publicized,
the meeting attracted some 400 civic-minded Boyertown residents
who packed the hall in an attempt to dissuade the thirty-five-year-old
doctor. Becker himself would have avoided the gathering if he could.
He was deeply embarrassed, and only reluctantly did he finally appear at the rally in his honor. Then standing before an applauding
crowd, he lifted his hands and the crowd slowly hushed to hear his
reply. He expressed his appreciation for their coming; he admitted
that he was deeply moved by seeing such a large crowd of friends
and neighbors. "But years ago I made a promise to God, and I can't
go back on that promise."

News of Dr. Becker's decision so delighted Jacob Nissley and the
Bible study group in Manheim that they pledged to take over Dr.
Becker's personal support of $60 a month as well as pay his passage
to Africa. And a group of Boyertown citizens banded together to
help Dr. Becker purchase drugs and medical supplies for his ministry
in Congo.

Then came the first jolt of his missionary experience. It happened after his practice had been disposed of, after his home had been sold and after the day of departure had been set. It was then he discovered that Charles Hurlburt was no longer with the Africa Inland Mission. Carl Becker had been accepted as a missionary with a mission that he had never heard of—the Unevangelized Africa Mission—and not with the Africa Inland Mission.

Dr. Becker pieced together what had happened. When he had written to the Africa Inland Mission, their Brooklyn headquarters had given him the address of Dr. Hurlburt as he had requested, without mentioning that he was no longer with the A.I.M. And Hurlburt had apparently assumed that Becker had known that he had recently formed a new mission, the Unevangelized Africa Mission.

But by this time, Carl Becker had made so many arrangements and had made such a determined stand before all the residents of Boyertown that he couldn't do an about-face now. He didn't understand why the Lord had added this new complication, but he was convinced as ever that the Lord was in control of the situation. There would be no backing down now.

In August, 1929, just before the big stock-market crash, the Beckers prepared to leave, taking more than ten tons of equipment, including their big, black Buick.

A farewell service was planned at the tiny Evangelical Congregational Church during the week before their departure. Late in July the Reformed and the Lutheran ministers had come to Masteller's parsonage offering their more spacious auditoriums to accommodate the crowds who would attend the farewell. Masteller agreed that it would be a good idea to switch the service to another church, but decided to check with Carl Becker first.

Becker listened thoughtfully to the offer and then said, "No, you're my pastor, and this is my church, and this is where I want the farewell service. I'm not interested in big crowds of people. I'm interested in the Christian folk who have come to mean the most to me."

And so the roads around the tiny Evangelical Congregational Church of Boyertown were jammed with traffic on a sweltering evening in August, 1929. Many drivers, seeing the crowds milling on the outside of the church, didn't even bother to stop.

Little Boyertown was saying good-bye to its country doctor, a doctor who was going someplace in Africa, he wasn't sure exactly where, and under the auspices of an embryonic mission board, he wasn't sure exactly what.

6
Stranded at Katwa

Carl Becker had to admit that he felt a bit uneasy as he followed his family up the Leviathan's gangplank in mid-August, 1929. He was thirty-five now, too late in life to go on a wild-goose chase halfway around the world.

He knew what his Hahnemann friends would say about it, and he would have to agree. It was foolhardy, crazy, stupid. It was certainly ridiculous to leave a $10,000-plus income to earn $60 a month; to leave a town which would give him anything he had ever wanted and all he had ever dreamed of to go to a primitive outpost he knew nothing about; to go out with a mission board that no one he could find had ever heard of; to leave dependent parents, one of whom was in poor health; to take susceptible young children into one of the most disease-ridden areas of the world; to venture from peaceful Boyertown into an area peopled with tribes that the Belgian Army still hadn't subjugated.

Sometimes he wondered about it too. Maybe when he discovered that Hurlburt was no longer with the Africa Inland Mission he should have changed his mind. Maybe—but it was too late now. He was on shipboard. Hurlburt's night letters with cryptic, urgent pleas to hurry to the Congo as soon as possible had done the job. The Beckers boarded ship less than five months after they had made their decision.

After crossing the Atlantic, traversing Europe by train, hopping another ship across the Mediterranean to Egypt, and changing to still another vessel down the Red Sea into the Indian Ocean, they finally docked at the historic seaport of Mombasa, alongside the exotic island of Zanzibar.

"Are we there yet, Daddy?" asked Mary.

"Not yet, not yet," replied her father, more impatient with the length of the journey than with the question of his child.

The train they took to Nairobi was nicknamed "The Iron Snake," for it coiled around jungles and deserts and hissed over mountains and rivers. The children excitedly eyed the giraffes and ostriches, the gnus and zebras, while Carl pointed out the cocoanut palms and baobab trees, and Marie gasped at the precipitous drops at the side of the trestles.

Nairobi, Carl thought, ought to provide some answers to his questions, for only thirty-five miles northeast of Nairobi was the Africa Inland Mission headquarters at Kijabe, where his old counselor Lee Downing was stationed. Perhaps Downing would give him some straightforward answers.

So after touring the large Kijabe mission station, Becker started firing questions.

Downing explained the situation to the best of his knowledge. After Charles Hurlburt had resigned as general director of the Africa Inland Mission in 1924 because of poor health, he was appointed director emeritus, and the home council of the mission, which had been Hurlburt-directed for a quarter of a century, reorganized itself. But in less than two years, the indomitable Hurlburt had recuperated and wanted to get back into action again. Seeing great opportunity for missionary expansion south of the Africa Inland Mission territory in Congo, he suggested that the A.I.M. move in that direction. When the A.I.M. replied that because of lack of personnel they were unable to serve any more territory to the south, energetic Charles Hurlburt, though over sixty-five, said that he would get the job done himself. And appointing his son Paul as field director, he organized the Unevangelized Africa Mission and began recruiting. Others of his family joined his foundling mission, including his daughter and son-in-law, Agnes and James Bell, who wanted to start missionary work among the Pygmies of the Ituri forest. In 1928, the first contingent of some ten stalwarts went to their field in Kivu Province, Congo. Following now a year later, the Beckers were the first reinforcements.

"I really don't know what you'll find at Kitsombiro," said Downing. "You'll just have to find that out for yourself."

"How dangerous will it be for the family?"

"I don't know that either," answered Downing. "But I know this. The natives have been restless throughout this whole area lately. There's been a big uprising not far from here that has all of us at Kijabe quite concerned. And these things have a habit of spreading."

"And you think there might be trouble in Congo then?"

"It's hard to say. But Kivu Province has always been a trouble spot for the Belgians to handle. Those tribes around there take anything as an excuse to cause trouble."

Leaving Kijabe by train, the Beckers passed through more game country and then through cultivated plantations—sisal, coffee and cotton—farmed by British settlers. At the Victoria Nile, they transferred their possessions to a wood-burning steamer, propelled by a paddle wheel at the rear. After crossing Uganda's Lake Kioga, they bumped along on the back end of a truck to a hotel at Masindi. Early the next morning, they rode down to Lake Albert and were herded into a small boat. The ride alternated between discomfort from clouds of mosquitoes and drenching by violent thunderstorms. The cabins were so hot and dirty that the Beckers moved out on the deck to sleep, but there the malarial mosquitoes swarmed after them. Staying awake all night, Carl sprayed and shooed the mosquitoes mercilessly.

Landing on the Congo side of Lake Albert on October 5, they were driven the last 300 miles of their 10,000-mile journey in a travel agent's Buick, not too unlike their own, which, like most of their belongings, was still on its way. After stopping their first night at a small mission station called Nyankunde and obtaining permission to drive through the gold and platinum mining area, they continued on their way, driving through a section of the Ituri forest, spotting a few Pygmies along the road. Then, as they reached higher country, the road began to wind and reel. A few miles south of the town of Lubero, the journey finally ended, except for the final twenty-minute hike up a trail on a hillside to the station called Kitsombiro. They had traveled nearly 12,000 miles in about eight weeks.

"Welcome to Kitsombiro," Paul Hurlburt greeted them cheerily. He was a tall, erect, ramrod sort of man, the image of his pioneering father.

They introduced themselves awkwardly and then Hurlburt took the Beckers on a quick tour of the place.

Kitsombiro station consisted of two grass-roofed mud huts and one tent. The Paul Hurlburts with their five children—the sixth was coming momentarily—bulged out of one mud hut, while the Bigelows with their one child lived in a smaller one. Two women lived in a tent off to one side.

"You can share our hut," Paul Hurlburt offered generously, "until we can get a brand new home built for you."

Marie and Carl, with six-year-old Mary and three-year-old Carl Jr., along with suitcases and a small sampling of furniture, squeezed into one tiny room with four mud walls, a mud ceiling and a mud floor. A native bamboo mat adorned the floor. The wash stand was made of boxes, and clothes were hung in a wardrobe trunk. Marie promptly hung a picture on the wall to make the mud room feel more like home. But for some reason, it didn't help much.

"Can we live like this?" Marie whispered to Carl so that the Hurlburt clan in the next room would not hear.

"I think we'll have to," her husband replied with a grin.

"But where will I cook?" asked Marie, who prided herself on her Pennsylvania Dutch culinary artistry.

"The kitchen is out in back," he whispered.

"That's what Paul Hurlburt told me, but I looked and all I saw were three large stones."

"That's your kitchen, Marie."

So she learned to cook on three large stones. She was assisted by a lovable and overeager African who was the most genial and least sanitary person she had ever met. His hands were caked with filth; he had a perpetually runny nose, and the only way she could converse with him was by sign language.

Not content with sign language, Carl tackled the native language immediately. Since there were no textbooks and since the other missionaries were themselves just beginning to learn the tribal tongue, he devised his own system. On little cards he scribbled Kinandi words on one side and on the other the English equivalent. Carrying them in his pocket, he referred to them in every spare moment.

He also spent considerable time studying his books on tropical medicine. Strangely enough, despite the fact that he was practically on the equator, he was finding more cases of pneumonia, influenza, bronchitis and tonsilitis than he was of malaria, dysentery, yaws and leprosy.

After entering the native grass huts, Carl Becker understood better why so many of the people were sickly. Each hut had only one small opening for a door; there were no chimneys. He wrote Gordon Bornemann: "To enter one of these huts at night is almost stifling. The goats and sheep are allowed to remain with the people. No wonder fifty per cent of the babies die in infancy. No wonder colds and pneumonia are so common. If you can imagine living in this cold climate with little or no clothing, in overheated huts at night and such, it's not strange at all."

Though Kitsombiro was perched on a ridge a chilly 8,000 feet high and though the climate was damp, the Wanandis wore little else besides loincloths—more technically a bark cloth around the hips supporting a piece of bark cloth between the thighs. In addition, the women sometimes wore goatskins well treated with castor oil.

Yet Dr. Becker didn't have a rushing business. He was the only doctor for miles, and there was sickness, disease and death all around him; yet he couldn't do much to alleviate the suffering if the patients didn't seek his help.

For two months before Carl Becker had arrived in Kitsombiro, the Hurlburts had been clearing away the wood and underbrush to build a little hospital for him. They had tried to interest Africans in helping with the project, but they had little success.

"What's wrong?" Carl finally asked Paul Hurlburt.

"It's the hold the witch doctors have on these people," replied Hurlburt. "You're a competitor, you know."

"You don't think it's anything more serious than that?" asked Becker. He still remembered Downing's warning of a possible native uprising.

"That's bad enough. These Wanandi feel that if they're disloyal to their witch doctor, he will curse them with evil spirits and these evil spirits will kill them. Might as well die a slow death of pneumonia as a quick death by the curse of evil spirits."

"Do you think the witch doctors might stir up trouble for us?"

"I don't know, doctor; but this area's a tinderbox. One spark could ignite the whole thing."

Two days later as Becker stepped outside his hut, he eyed a strange-looking piece of bamboo in front of his door. Examining it, he found that inside the bamboo were castor oil, egg yolk and leopard hair all wrapped together. Not knowing what it was, he took it to Paul Hurlburt.

Hurlburt studied it for a moment. "There's no doubt about it, Doctor. You've been cursed—cursed by the witch doctor."

Becker laughed. "What am I supposed to do now—take the next boat home?"

"Don't take it too lightly," replied Hurlburt.

The doctor was surprised at Hurlburt's reaction. "You don't take it seriously, do you?" the doctor asked.

"No, of course not, but all the Africans know now that the witch doctor has put his curse on you. So they'll be watching you closely from now on. If you stumble as you come up a hill, it will be because of evil spirits; if a patient of yours should get suddenly sick and die, it will be because the evil spirits are cursing you; and if anything more serious happens, they will credit it to the evil spirits."

Dr. Becker didn't bother asking him to explain what he meant by "more serious."

Hurlburt looked off over the hillsides, over 100 native villages which could be spotted from the ridge on which Kitsombiro rested. Then he spoke again. "There are thousands of people in those villages, Doctor, thousands of people who have never heard of Jesus Christ. What happens to you and to your medical practice in the next few weeks may either open the door to them or slam it tightly shut. It's something to pray about, isn't it?"

That weekend Carl bumped along on the back of Hurlburt's motorcycle to a mountain path, and then trekked up a mountainside to a little village. Together they walked quickly to the headman's hut and asked permission to hold a meeting in the village. Even before the permission was granted a crowd was gathering. Africans circled the two white men, and drove their spears deeply into the ground, making an iron ring around them. In fractured Kinandi, Hurlburt and Becker tried to tell about God and His Son Jesus Christ. Carl drew a simple picture in the ground showing how Jesus had died on a cross for them. As one spoke, the other watched the audiences for suspicious actions, hoping that none of them would suddenly leap up and grab his spear.

There seemed no response to the gospel message, just a few nods and murmurs. But Carl Becker was exhilarated by the opportunity to share his faith with someone who had never heard before.

"There'll be another time," said Hurlburt, "and maybe another time one or two will understand enough to respond."

A few days later as Dr. Becker stepped out of his hut at Kitsombiro a thin Wanandi woman sat, hunched over, on his doorstep. She wanted to see the white witch doctor, she said.

In faltering Kinandi, the doctor spoke to her, finally determining that she had a serious hernia condition. She explained hesitantly, and in response to his prodding, that she had consulted several different witch doctors, but after trying an assortment of painful remedies they had said she couldn't be helped. In desperation, she had been willing to try the foreign witch doctor.

Upon examination, Dr. Becker assessed the damage that the competition had done. Her condition was certainly serious; she needed to be operated on very soon.

This might be the breakthrough they had all been praying for; but he knew very well, also, that it might just as easily be the "slammed door," or even the "spark" to ignite the tinderbox. After all, this woman was in bad condition. Any surgeon even under the best of conditions would consider her to be a risk, a fifty-fifty chance at best. And he knew very well that he was no surgeon. His training at Hahnemann had only given him a surface knowledge of surgery. At Boyertown he had continually referred most of his surgical cases to appropriate specialists.

Minor surgery was one thing, but major surgery for a general practitioner?

"I'm sure I'm going to have to tackle more and more of these cases in the days ahead," he told Marie. "I might as well start now."

"But you don't have all your medical equipment yet."

He knew that too. Most of his medical supplies had not arrived as yet. They were coming by freight.

There was no operating table. "What about our wooden kitchen table? That should be good enough," volunteered Paul Hurlburt. Becker accepted the suggestion.

There was no nurse either, but Marie could be drafted. There were things that she had learned by osmosis, so to speak; at least Dr. Becker hoped so.

Marie turned to scrubbing down the kitchen table with antiseptic while Carl went to scrub his hands and arms with soap and hot water. Just because he was now in Africa was no excuse for slipshod practices of sterilization.

He glanced out the door. At least a dozen file-toothed Wanandis had gathered out there stone-faced, expressionless. But he had an idea what was in their minds. Little children, pot-bellied with hideous umbilical hernias, pushed in closely to watch the excitement, too. There was no need for Paul Hurlburt to clear any more land if this operation failed. Everything seemed to hinge on one trivial hernia operation, and the odds seemed stacked against him.

A kitchen table as his operating table, a schoolteacher as his nurse, and a mud hut with manure-plastered walls as his sanitary hospital.

What if he should fail now as a missionary doctor after having the world at his feet in Boyertown? After all, he had seen no visions from God, he had heard no voices from the sky, saying, "Go to Kitsombiro." Maybe he had been all wrong about coming. Maybe it was stubbornness on his part rather than a divine dedication. It wasn't always easy to distinguish between the two.

He had responded to a promise he had almost forgotten, a still, small voice deep within him, and an opportunity to meet a great need. And on that basis he had given up everything in Boyertown for the nothing of Kitsombiro. Doubts seemed to be giant-sized in that damp little mud hut, and his missionary call shriveled to a shadow.

"I think the table is ready now, Carl," Marie said, breaking into his thoughts.

The Wanandi woman was brought in and strapped onto the table. Her eyes grew half-dollar size as she saw the gleaming instruments beside her.

Dr. Becker grasped his wife's hand. "Marie, let's pray first." He prayed briefly, pragmatically and fervently, committing the success of the operation to the Lord. Then, on opening his eyes, he said, "Marie, we'll do our best, and the rest will be up to Him."

He glanced a last time at the vulture-like African villagers peering in from outside, and then turned to the terrified woman on the table. In Kinandi he spoke softly to her, and was pleased to see her relax a bit. Then he nodded to Marie to begin giving the anesthetic.

Marie was performing well, better than he had hoped, and he was pleased that his own stubby non-surgical fingers were reacting well, too. Minutes later, after the patient was closed up, Dr. Becker noticed Marie glancing over at him for an indication of success or failure. He pulled down his mask. "Congratulations, Marie; so far so good."

"So far?"

"Yes, her convalescence is going to be extremely important. We'll fix up a tent for her in the back, and as my head nurse you'll have to keep an eye on your patient."

In the afternoon a torrential Congo rain burst out of the sky and splattered itself out on the patches of brown soil. The convalescent tent sagged in places and heaved with the gale-sized winds.

Suddenly Marie shouted, "Hey, she's running away."

Carl glanced out the windows in back and saw their prize patient, clad mainly in a white abdominal dressing, crawling out of the tent, struggling to her feet and scrambling toward the bush. "Get her back in there; she's your patient."

Grabbing an umbrella, Marie chased after her, slipping perilously in the mud, finally catching her by the arm. Holding an umbrella over her stubborn patient and at the same time yanking her back toward the tent with vigorous jerks, Marie scolded, "No, no, no; you mustn't run away." And the woman, not understanding a word of English, retorted in a fluently vivid torrent of Kinandi.

Marie won the argument, through superior strength rather than debating finesse, and returned the patient to the tent.

Much to Dr. Becker's amazement, the patient's escapade did not harm her. Speedily recovering, she was able to be released to her village in a few days. And she took back with her a firsthand report of the excellent care which she had received at Kitsombiro.

Soon the word of the new doctor spread across the ridges and people came even from distant villages for some of the doctor's special medicine. "You should have seen the natives here today," Carl wrote enthusiastically to Dr. Bornemann in Boyertown.

Though most of his medical equipment still had not been delivered, he worked over plans for a small hospital and several native wards. The only thing that hampered him was a lack of funds. "Funds for the construction of the buildings are not in hand. But since with cheap labor an efficient group of buildings can be constructed for a very moderate sum, it seems inconceivable that such a need will not be met by Christian friends in America."

It was unusual for Dr. Becker to say anything about lack of funds in a letter to the States. And as the months of his early experiences went by, he said less and less. But his financial problems mounted, and rather than leaning on man for help, he was forced to lean on the Lord, even as he had first learned at medical school.

While Carl was thinking about building a hospital, Marie was planning a home for their family. Obviously, they couldn't live in the one room of the Hurlburt's hut indefinitely. She found her site—a scenic plot on top of a high hill—and boys were hired to clear the ground and carry bamboo poles to the site. A path was cut down the hillside to a valley below where Marie had already started a vegetable garden.

Their new mud hut was to be a mud mansion, containing two

bedrooms, a dining room, storage room, pantry, office and a bathroom. The bathroom would be a plain room equipped with a large galvanized tub in it for bathing purposes. An outhouse would be erected about thirty feet away. Marie had to live with the fact that there would be no kitchen in her new mud hut either. "There's too much danger of the roof catching fire if you cook in the house," Hurlburt had warned her. So the cooking would have to be done in back.

Marie had chosen her site wisely. So now, when the hut was finished, they could look out from their front door across a hazy panorama of green hills and blue valleys. They could count scores of fires as evening came, each designating a native village, and from their home they would be able to hear the singing of the tribal dancers and the frantic beat of the drums.

Sometimes Becker would travel to these villages during the week to take care of a sick African or to check up on a patient who had come once to Kitsombiro for treatment, but who had not returned for a second appointment. Because the tribes of the area seemed intelligent, he had assumed that they could follow his instructions on how to take their medicine and when to come back, but such was not the case.

Once he had given a patient a bottle of medicine to take at regular intervals, with the promise that when it was finished he would return to Kitsombiro for more. Becker had expected him back in a week, but when one week stretched past two weeks Becker went to find him. The patient was lying in his hut, obviously not recovered from his malady.

"Where's the medicine I gave you?" Becker demanded.

The infirm man pointed up. Becker looked through the murky smog of the hut and saw the unopened bottle of medicine, suspended by a red cord from the grass roof of the hut. The man had thought that the bottle of medicine would ward off the evil spirits that supposedly had caused the disease.

An African whom Becker had given six pills to take, one every day, was discovered wearing the pills around his waist as a charm band.

A few incidents like that convinced Dr. Becker to change his medical procedure.

Shortly after much of their more than ten tons of equipment came, including the X-ray equipment and their Buick, the Beckers were transferred to another station of the Unevangelized Africa Mission, a station called Katwa, about fifty miles north of Kitsombiro. Like Kitsombiro it was set on top of a steep escarpment of the Kivu hills. But unlike Kitsombiro, it seemed to have possibilities for the growth of a large medical facility.

It was at Katwa that Dr. Becker erected his first hospital, and most of it he did himself. The structures themselves were primitive, mud-brick buildings. And over the mud brick was applied a plaster of cow manure and mud. Mold, all the colors of the rainbow, could be seen on its walls, so while the walls were still moist, they were whitewashed with wood ashes. The floors too were of mud, although later they were carpeted with stalks of elephant grass. These stalks, standing eight feet high and two inches thick when cut, roughly resembled cornstalks.

The beds also were constructed from the cornstalks. Into this primitive setting, he incongruously introduced his modern X-ray machine, powered with gasoline engines.

It was shortly after arriving in Katwa that Dr. Becker received his introduction to leprosy. Sufferers from leprosy had been sauntering around the mission station. Cast out of their own villages, they had nowhere else to turn.

"What do we do with them?" one of the missionaries asked the new doctor.

"I don't know much about leprosy myself," admitted Becker, "but I know it's a contagious disease, resembling tuberculosis in some ways; and leprosy patients like TB patients need to be isolated."

Since there was no extra land at Katwa's mission station for use as a leprosy colony, Becker went to the local chief to ask permission to use a hill near their present station. The old chief did not seem anxious for his land to be used as a retreat for leprosy patients and told Becker so, spitting some juice on the soil for emphasis.

"But the more patients we have in the camp," argued the doctor, "the fewer there will be outside, and the fewer of your tribe there will be who will get the disease."

With that point Becker won the argument, and the chief granted permission for the use of his land. Four native huts were constructed on the next hill and leprosy victims came by the dozens.

Yet the doctor was dissatisfied. Leprosy (now called Hansen's disease) was one prevalent tropical disease for which there then was no cure and little effective treatment. Certainly the care they could give to the patients at Katwa was better than the witch doctors who only applied a herb preparation over the spots that raised blisters on top of the sores. But Katwa's treatment didn't seem much better. The chaulmoogra oil he used helped prevent the spread of the disease but only rarely did it heal it. As a Belgian prospector who managed a gang of 100 Africans told him one day, "My men tell me you have medicine for everything but leprosy."

Some day, Becker told himself, he would have a medicine for leprosy too.

Meanwhile the doctoring business boomed. Using the front porch of the Katwa home as a dispensary, he had 75 to 125 Africans coming each day for a variety of ills. And within a year's time the leprosy colony grew to more than 80.

But all was not peaceful in Carl Becker's mind.

He was bothered by the existence of two neighboring missions, the Unevangelized Africa Mission and the Africa Inland Mission, working so closely to each other, yet having little to do with each other. "Why do we need two?" he asked Paul Hurlburt one day. He also saw problems between missionaries, petty disagreements and bickering, that disturbed him deeply. He could understand such problems if they arose among non-Christians, but not among Christian missionaries.

But these were not the only problems which Dr. Becker faced. Not long after he and Marie had moved to Katwa, they received a jolting letter from Jacob Nissley of Manheim.

It was a long, involved letter, explaining financial matters. In brief, the Hershey Machine and Foundry Company of Manheim, which had faithfully supported up to a dozen missionaries for years from its business profits, had been hit hard by the depression. "We regret this very much, but because there were no profits at all this year, there is nothing in the fund to distribute to our missionaries."

Nissley went on to say that he would try to pick up Carl Becker's support personally, but even though it was only $60 a month, he was not sure how long he could do it as an individual.

"What are we going to do?" Marie asked.

Carl had no answers. He felt separated from everything. The Unevangelized Africa Mission was shaky enough. It had no funds at all. Obviously, it took money to run even a small dispensary, dispensing medicine to 100 patients a day. His family had to be fed and clothed. This was his God-given responsibility, too.

Carl Becker had real doubts now. He was a doctor, a medical man, trained in science, trained to examine, to question, even to doubt. Had he been trained as a minister or as a teacher he could close the hospital work completely. He had no training in theology, either at a Bible school or seminary. He was only a layman.

"What am I doing on the mission field, anyway? Am I sure that I am called of God to be here?" he asked himself once again.

Perhaps it would be best for him to return to Boyertown, or to start a practice in Washington, D.C. Perhaps God would have him return home and from his earnings send out other missionaries who would be better equipped to teach or preach than he had been.

It was something that he could share with no other person except Marie. But he could also pray; he could ask the Lord to guide him through his Word. After all, what could he do about it anyway? He didn't even have the money to return home. He was stranded at Katwa.

Strange how fast your fortune could be reversed. Two years earlier he had enjoyed an easy living; now he had nothing.

Stranded. Alone.

On a floor slatted with stalks of elephant grass he dropped to his knees and prayed. "Lord, you know both our needs and our doubts. Supply our needs and banish our doubts. They are all in your hands. Amen."

7

SOS from the Pygmy Forest

"Faith accepts quiet guidance; only unbelief demands a miracle."

K. D. MOYNAGH

In 1931, Carl and Marie Becker were not the only ones who had deep thoughts about what they should do in the future. Agnes and Jim Bell, Charles Hurlburt's daughter and son-in-law, did too. Stationed only sixty miles north of Katwa at a hole in the Ituri forest called Oicha, Jim Bell heard about the biennial conference for Congo missionaries of the Africa Inland Mission and asked Carl Becker if he would like to accompany him to it. Becker agreed eagerly.

Under the theme, "Christian Fellowship," 120 missionaries—all except Carl Becker and Jim Bell associated with the Africa Inland Mission—gathered at Aba in Congo's northeast tip, making reports, talking about new plans, and praying earnestly.

Faced with financial strain due to the world-wide depression, many of the missionaries were struggling with the same problems that Carl and Marie Becker were confronting.

The high point of the conference came on the last afternoon, an afternoon of prayer that Jim Bell was to conduct. "We were practically all melted to tears," stated the official report, "and were made very conscious of the working of the Spirit of God in our midst. Difficulties vanished, mountains became plains, unwilling hearts were made willing. Before closing, Mr. Bell felt moved to ask who would devote one hour or more each day to prayer and communion; practically everyone rose to his feet in response. By God's grace, if each one is faithful to this purpose, it should mean more to the work in this field than anything we have yet realized. Without a doubt, God was leading that afternoon." One of those who stood to his feet was a visitor from Katwa. He felt, without a doubt, that God was leading him too.

Shortly after the conference both the Bells and the Beckers applied

67

to the Africa Inland Mission to be accepted as missionaries. Carl Becker's two visits to A.I.M. stations—Kijabe to see Lee Downing, and Aba at this conference—had been high points in his two-year missionary experience. Besides, Carl Becker had never understood the reason for the existence of the U.A.M., which in his mind was a needless breakoff from the Africa Inland Mission. And since a new doctor had recently been added to the Katwa staff, he felt that this would be an ideal time to resign.

After being accepted as A.I.M. missionaries, the Beckers were assigned to work at the hospital at Aba, which was lodged between mountain ranges adjoining the Sudan border and was the Congo headquarters for the mission.

Filling in for a furloughing missionary doctor, Carl Becker spent much of his time visiting the mission stations of the area. Though he preferred his own aging Buick, the time-honored vehicle among A.I.M. medical men was a Harley-Davidson motorcycle. Eight years before Dr. Becker joined the mission, Dr. C. L. Trout first introduced motorcycles to missionary service, and while some of the earlier medics nearly lost their sanctification over the failure of some mechanical part, followed by an inevitable three-months wait for a replacement, yet a Harley-Davidson did chop a ten-day safari into a bite-sized two-day trip.

By the time Dr. Becker arrived on the scene, motorcycles were standard equipment. But his brief experience with motorcycles did not endear them to him. Once, sliding on wet grass, his cycle struck a rock, catapulted him into a ditch, and then aimed unerringly at him as if to finish him off.

Bruised but not injured severely, he decided to renew his friendship with his Buick.

But even the Buick had difficulties in Congo. Nighttime driving was especially hazardous. Once, when turning a sharp corner, he almost crashed into an elephant; he decided to ignore the animal in the hope that it would go away. After ten minutes in pitch darkness, he turned on his lights again only to discover the huge pachyderm standing just outside the car door, caressing the Buick with his trunk. Now becoming impatient and not believing that God would want a stupid animal to delay His work, he slapped his horn forcefully, and the frightened elephant gamboled off like a jilted suitor into the surrounding bush.

As Becker station-hopped through northeast Congo, his medical reputation spread. Many Africans walked more than 100 miles to reach the Aba Hospital. One of the most memorable was Kasulu, an Azande tribesman who lived 175 miles away and who suffered from a hernia so large it hung down to his knees. With what must have been great pain, he walked all the way to Aba for an operation. Afterwards, Dr. Becker told him that he had a need bigger than his physical need; he was carrying a load of sin on his back, bigger than his hernia had been. In his hospital room, Kasula became a Christian.

Missionaries too turned to Dr. Becker for help. Some, like Plymouth Brethren missionary Bill Deans, were apparently headed back to America for health reasons. Two missionary doctors had already given up on Deans; one had suggested that he be a missionary in a desert land because of his severe rheumatism. Under Becker's simple treatment, Deans' condition cleared up and he stayed on the field to become one of the outstanding Congo missionaries of the century.

While the medical ministry was gratifying, the financial problem of the Beckers was still acute. It was the policy of the Africa Inland Mission never to ask for money, and Carl Becker agreed with this principle. But it wasn't always easy to live that way.

Jacob Nissley did what he could, but his contributions never came up to the $60 a month that had originally been pledged. And gradually Nissley's support dwindled as the depression continued to drain his resources. More and more Carl Becker was forced to depend on God; there was simply no one else to whom he could turn. And whenever the financial picture appeared darkest, a check would come in the mail from some unexpected source.

After living in this way for some months, Carl and Marie learned that it was senseless to worry. God's provision never came too late; why should they doubt the Lord? So carefree was their family life that their children were totally unaware that financial problems existed at all. Daughter Mary recalls, "We never heard anything about money worries that I can remember. I don't believe anybody worried, actually. It was the Lord's work and He would see to it that we had what was necessary, and through one instrumentality or another, He did."

In spite of the fact that the Africa Inland Mission had more than its share of outstanding medical missionaries, Dr. Carl Becker quickly gained notice. It was more how he did things than what he did. The intensity with which he threw himself into his calling was almost overwhelming. A slight, unassuming man, he spoke clearly and slowly to his patients as if there was all the time in the world and they were the only people in the world. He never wasted words; for that matter he never wasted anything, and least of all time.

His attitude toward the African was unique. It was not uncommon then for Belgian mining officials to bring Africans to him who had been injured in mining accidents, not because they wanted to save a patient, but because they didn't want Africans to die on their hands. One mining official brought a casket along with an injured African so that Becker could bury him quickly.

But Dr. Becker's attitude was different. Said one European who couldn't figure out this strange American, "Occasionally, I've seen him become irritated with Europeans who try to crowd in and demand preferential treatment, but I've never seen him lose patience with an African."

And when a missionary would complain vehemently about these irresponsible, unpredictable, unethical Africans, especially in certain tribes, saying, "Well, I suppose that's the African for you." Becker would quickly correct his fellow missionary: "No, that's human nature for you." He had seen the same characteristics in men in Boyertown.

"Another thing about Dr. Becker," another missionary noticed early in the doctor's missionary career, "he never gives up when he knows he is right. He is a never-give-up-man."

Carl Becker never could be told that something was impossible. The feeling grew among his associates that if they told him something was impossible, likely as not he'd consider it a challenge to do it himself.

This was what happened once when his X-ray machine broke down. Another doctor suggested that he get professional help to have it repaired. "It's impossible for you to fix that broken-down thing, Dr. Becker."

He shouldn't have said the word "impossible." Although Dr. Becker spent twice as much time, money and effort doing the job himself as it would have cost to have it repaired professionally, he wouldn't give up, and eventually he fixed it.

Still shy and retiring, despite his competence, he was certainly not the life-of-the-party type. In social groups he would most likely be off in a corner with a guest that no one else was bothering to talk to.

But wherever he went as a missionary he was noticed. Sometimes he resembled Elijah's whirlwind, sometimes a crackling fire and sometimes a still, small voice, but he always left his mark on missionaries and Africans alike.

Early in 1934, Jim Bell, who was trying to reach Pygmies from his little hole in the Ituri forest, sent a plea to Field Director George Van Dusen for a doctor. To others in the Africa Inland Mission, there wasn't much sense in stationing a doctor at Bell's tiny mission station of Oicha, but he wasn't a man who could be easily denied.

Dr. Ralph Kleinschmidt, having returned from his furlough, resumed his role as head of Aba's Greenlawn Hospital, making Carl Becker, the junior member of A.I.M.'s three Congo doctors, expendable for the call.

"Why do they need a doctor down in the jungle?" asked Dr. Becker.

"Well," replied Van Dusen, "every few years the Africa tribes around that area sponsor circumcision rites for the Pygmies. They call it the nkumbi. And at these rites the boy is initiated into the life of the village, making him fit to join his ancestors when he dies. All boys between eight and twelve are required to be circumcised at this time."

"Sounds like a pretty gruesome ritual."

"Yes, that's what Bell says. For six months prior to the circumcision ceremony the Pygmies subject themselves to one form of torture after another in order to get themselves ready. Then comes the final act when a crazed and often drunken witch doctor performs the delicate cutting of circumcision."

"But what could I do about it?"

"Nothing, really. But Jim Bell is bothered because boys who have professed Christianity are also compelled to go through this vicious ritual. If there were a doctor there, he could perform the operation on the Christian boys."

Van Dusen went on to explain that it would be only a temporary assignment for Dr. Becker, although Bell would try to talk him into staying permanently. Perhaps it would be well to have a mission hospital somewhere in that area, but Van Dusen wasn't sure if Oicha was the best location for it.

The Africa Inland Mission presently had two hospitals in Belgian Congo: one at Aba in the far north, and one at Rethy, 200 miles south, where an eventual school for missionaries' children was evisioned. Some 200 miles farther south—not too far from the U.A.M.'s stations at Kitsombiro and Katwa—were two new A.I.M. stations which had just been opened up: Oicha and Ruwenzori. It made sense to have a string of hospitals 200 miles apart, not only to reach the Africans, but also to serve the missionaries themselves.

"If you decide that the area can use full-scale medical work," Van Dusen continued, "then you'll have to decide between Ruwenzori and Oicha as the best site."

Ruwenzori, Van Dusen explained, was located six miles from the nearest road on the base of 17,000-foot-high, snow-covered Ruwenzori, the third highest mountain in Africa. A stone's throw from the Ituri forest, it was still untouched by civilization although the government was hoping to build a new road soon. Fifty miles east of Oicha and only a dozen miles from the Uganda border, it gave the mission an opportunity to reach nearly 40,000 Africans who had never before heard the Christian message. Scenic and favored by a resort-style climate, it was at the edge of Albert National Park and was a magnet for naturalists who wished to study jungle life.

Oicha, however, was quite the opposite. It was hot and teeming with malarial mosquitoes. There were no hills, only trees, trees, trees. Food was scarce and vegetables struggled to grow there. To tell the truth, Van Dusen said, there was hardly room for a mission station there. Immense trees shot straight up 100 to 150 feet in the air and then spread their branches. The trees grew so closely together and the lower branches were so closely hung with vines, that a person beneath them felt trapped in a maze of vegetation. At eye level there were only grand columns of smooth-trunked trees and a wall of green.

Through this tangle of vegetation in the Ituri forest, the Belgian government had sliced a road. Though it was no superhighway, it was still a remarkable achievement, considering what they had to overcome. At the small spot on the road called Oicha, the road builders had made a mistake. After going about 100 yards in one direction, they decided that if they took another direction instead, they could avoid crossing a stream. So they changed their minds, left a dead end road of 100 yards and proceeded on their road construction chores. Jim Bell considered the mistake providential. At the dead end he built his mission station.

"You won't find it very pretentious, Doctor," Van Dusen concluded. "Last time I saw it, it consisted of only one mud-and-wattle hut, and you can pierce the roof with your hand. But Jim Bell sees in those Pygmies a race that no one has ever reached before with the gospel of Jesus Christ."

"But there are more than just Pygmies around Oicha."

"Oh yes; other tribes who are dependent on the Pygmy for meat have clustered around them too. From what I hear, Bell is having more success in reaching them than he is in reaching the Pygmies."

Carl Becker didn't care at all to leave Aba. He loved the Christian fellowship which it had afforded, and he wasn't sure how he would react to isolating himself in the jungle. The children were even unhappier; they had a pet cheetah that would have to stay behind.

But regardless of their personal reservations, a few days later the Becker family climbed into the Buick, packed to the roof, and headed south. Helping them make their 400-mile move was another young missionary, Earl Dix, who hauled their household goods and medical equipment in his truck.

All along the way the bridges were out, but the big Buick and the hefty truck managed to ford the streams. When they finally came to a river, Mary and Carl Jr. jumped out and collected rocks to build a foundation for a bridge, and Carl and Earl Dix engineered a bridge of poles. The Buick made the crossing safely, but as Dix's truck edged across, the bridge began to dip and sag. The Beckers heard the loud cracking of bamboo almost simultaneously with the racing of the truck motor. Just as Dix pulled safely across, the bridge fell lifelessly into the river.

At Oicha, the Beckers went back to living in mud huts again, but this time the children seemed to enjoy the rough and rugged surroundings. Young Carl built dams in the stream and constructed soapbox-derby racers. Both of them found plenty of time to read from the family library. At the supper table, their father always made sure that there was not only food for the body, but also food for the soul and food for the mind. Almost as frequently referred to as the Bible was their handy set of reference books.

Oicha was deceptively peaceful. During the day, even the sunlight was soft, diffused through the trees' foliage. There was an illusion of tranquility. The bees were constantly buzzing and monkeys were constantly chattering and romping through the branches. Swarms of butterflies invaded the area and tiny birds flitted around in brilliant hues. Even the African's sing-song Swahili language seemed to add to the easygoing quality of the day.

But the Beckers soon learned that the night was different. The wail of the jackal, the bark of the bushbuck and the screech of the owl came with frightening unexpectedness. And the living things that made no noise were even more dreaded: pythons, lying in wait on low-hanging branches, driver ants that moved like small glaciers devouring everything in their path, and malarial mosquitoes that ruined more missionaries than all the beasts of the jungle combined.

Dr. Becker knew too of the Anyota, the leopard men, who were terrorizing the forest villages around Oicha. It was no secret that the Anyota ate human flesh. Though the society of leopard men had been outlawed by the Belgians, and though soldiers had rounded up all the members of the Anyota that they could find, the Anyota and their new counterpart called the Kitawala were still making frequent attacks.

The Kitawala said that the white man had destroyed the Anyota because they wanted to kill the Africans, and they blamed much on the white doctors and their hospitals. Hospitals, they said, were centers of sorcery where white men practiced cannibalism themselves. Wearing leopard skins, making the noise of the leopard, jumping from trees like a leopard upon their victims: these were the marks of the leopard men around about Oicha.

At Oicha, Dr. Becker treated some who had been scarred by leopard's claws, but whose assailant had obviously been human.

Pygmies, however, seldom came to the dispensary under the trees at Oicha. The one who finally came represented a victory for Dr. Becker and Jim Bell. They determined to handle him especially carefully, because the way he was treated would determine their future success with these little forest people.

The case was a herniotomy, and afterwards the Pygmy was ordered to stay in bed for ten days. At the edge of the station alongside the massive Ituri trees they built a special little hut for the little fellow to recuperate in. Well aware of the nomadic tendencies of the Pygmies, Dr. Becker used a few extra sutures and, remembering his first surgery patient at Kitsombiro, he assigned an African medical boy to sit at the door of the hut and guard the Pygmy with his life.

But only a few hours after the operation, hardly long enough for the anesthesia to wear off, the medical boy came running to the doctor. "That old Pygmy has escaped. He just got out of bed and ran off."

"We'll have to find him," said the doctor. And with the medical boy he began to search the forest area near the convalescent hut.

The Pygmy hadn't gone far. After catching him, Dr. Becker talked to him severely. "You promised me that you were going to stay in bed. Why didn't you keep your promise?"

"But *Bwana*," the Pygmy said innocently, "I did stay in bed, and I was just lying there and looking out my little door and then do you know what I saw?" The Pygmy waited for a response but the doctor said nothing. "*Bwana*, I saw all those monkeys out in that tree, and I just looked at them and they looked at me, and my heart just went like that." He tapped his chest vigorously. "And you know, there was no one else anywhere around to shoot them. So, *Bwana*, I just had to get up and do it myself."

Though Bell spoke highly of the prospects of a hospital at Oicha, Dr. Becker remained dubious. Occasionally, he would go out into the Ituri forest to the villages with Jim Bell; on weekends he would preach and teach to small groups of Africans. But while he appreciated Bell's concern for the work at Oicha, he couldn't picture anything more than a small dispensary there. There were certainly no long waiting lines of patients. In fact, the very people that Bell wanted to reach the most—the Pygmies—seldom came to the dispensary at all. But Jim Bell was always optimistic.

"Praise the Lord, praise the Lord," he exclaimed one day. "It's another token of the Lord's blessing on this place."

"What are you talking about, Jim?"

"A check for $700 just came. I've been praying for that amount so we can build a chapel and an operating room for you." Jim Bell had it all planned in his mind. He would build the chapel of burned brick and roof it with sheet iron.

Carl Becker looked at the huge trees that surrounded the station. Would Oicha ever be anything more than a little hole in the forest? He doubted it.

"Listen, Jim, I don't know how long I'll be around Oicha. When Dr. Trout goes on furlough next year, I'll probably fill in for him at Rethy. Besides"—he shook his head as he spoke—"I'm not very optimistic about the possibilities for medical work at Oicha."

Late in 1934, after less than a year at Oicha, they were indeed summoned to the A.I.M. hospital at Rethy, to substitute for Dr. C. L. Trout.

Set on a hill 7,000 feet high, cool and invigorating, Rethy is in the center of the A.I.M. field. Opened originally in 1920, it took on increasing prominence in the A.I.M. picture as Rethy Academy was launched for missionaries' children. Because of a lack of dormitory space, the school had only a small enrollment until 1933, when the Congo Council of the A.I.M. voted to build a brick building to meet the needs of children of missionaries throughout the territory. And the following year it was ready.

Because of her background, Marie Becker was asked to teach fourth and fifth grades, and became one of the first teachers of the enlarged school. Carl Jr. and Mary were both experiencing their first formal school training.

When Dr. Trout changed his furlough plans and decided to stay in Rethy, Dr. Becker spent much of his time in itinerant medical work visiting stations throughout the area, revisiting Oicha, trekking to Ruwenzori, traveling up the escarpment to Bogoro and Blukwa, and visiting the Kilimoto mining region.

A year later the Beckers returned to the United States for their first furlough, after six years in the heart of Belgian Congo.

Just before they returned to the States, Van Dusen asked Becker for his opinion of the medical needs in the southern part of the field.

"Between Ruwenzori and Oicha combined, there's certainly enough to keep a doctor busy."

"And where do you think the doctor should have his headquarters?"

"Jim Bell will be disappointed, but there seem to be too many drawbacks at Oicha. I think I'd have to vote for Ruwenzori."

8
Go Down the Mountain

A little sparkle-eyed mulatto girl named Alice first invaded Dr. Becker's life when he was serving at Greenlawn Hospital in Aba. She was all of ten years old at the time. Observing Dr. Becker's need for experienced nurses, she volunteered her services.

Spindly-legged Alice had arrived at Aba to have her tonsils out, but Dr. Becker soon put her to work cheering up a patient who desperately needed someone to lift his spirits. Little Alice took the job seriously.

Having performed her first nursing assignment successfully, Alice thought she should stay on as Dr. Becker's special assistant nurse. Her persistence required a tactful reply. Dr. Becker explained that she was still a little bit young and that nurses had to have some more schooling than she had.

"What do you have to go to school for, just to be a nurse?" she asked indignantly.

He pulled a chair over and sat beside her bed. "For one thing," Dr. Becker patiently responded, "you have to learn some arithmetic."

"What do you need arithmetic for?"

"Well, you need to be able to give a quick gauze count," he said. He knew she didn't know what that meant, but it didn't matter right then.

She cocked her head to one side and said, "You know, Dr. Becker, maybe you're right. Maybe I will have to wait another year or two."

Alice, the daughter of a Belgian father and an African tribeswoman, was an outcast like most mulattoes in Africa, unwanted by either Europeans or Africans. Fortunately for Alice, Harold and Doris Wentworth, first-term A.I.M. missionaries to the Kilimoto mining district, spotted her and took her to their hearts. After her adoption, she became Alice Wentworth. She looked forward to the regular

77

visits from the traveling doctor. Whenever Dr. Becker arrived, he was surrounded by crowds of people clamoring for attention, and yet he always took time to recognize her.

And there was one time when a young man came crawling on his hands and knees to Kilimoto. The Wentworths could do nothing for him; his condition seemed hopeless. But Dr. Becker was coming the next day.

Alice watched with big eyes as the doctor put the cripple in the back of his car and took him away. A few weeks later, the doctor came back; the poor cripple was on crutches now, and could run as fast on his crutches as she could without them. Besides that, the doctor said that in a few more weeks he wouldn't need to use his crutches at all.

Alice hoped that he would give her some crutches. Maybe she could run faster if she had some.

The Wentworths opened a new mission station at Maitulu in Congo. Five months later, 1200 Africans were coming to church each Sunday. Crowds would stay afterwards and ask how they too could become Christians. One Sunday morning, when Wentworth concluded his sermon, the front of the church was jammed. When the Wentworths finished counseling they counted up the number converted. The total was 319.

But in 1936, Harold and Doris Wentworth, due to go on furlough, were concerned about what to do with Alice. If the Beckers hadn't also been scheduled for a furlough soon, Alice would have joined them; instead Dr. Becker found another missionary to watch over Alice until the Wentworths returned.

But the Wentworths never came back, due to Harold Wentworth's poor health. Alice was again virtually an orphan.

Meanwhile, Carl and Marie Becker used only seven of the allotted twelve months of furlough, and then booked passage back to Africa. Furloughs were not at all satisfying to the doctor. He felt ill at ease in a pulpit or traveling from place to place showing missionary slides. However, one of his big burdens, financial support, was lifted when congregations within the Evangelical Congregational denomination pledged to take over the Beckers' support.

After returning to Africa in November, 1936, the Beckers were scheduled to begin their medical work at Ruwenzori and to investigate the possibility of developing a hospital there. But since Ruwenzori was not as yet ready to receive them, they returned to their little grass-roofed mud house at Oicha, fifty miles away. The "house" was a three-room, mud-walled affair, built for Africans, not much of an improvement on their home at Kitsombiro seven years earlier.

Not long after they had returned to Oicha, Alice was brought to the forest settlement to stay with them. Thus began a new phase of life both for the Beckers and for Alice Wentworth. A teenager now, she was added to the family without commotion.

"Dr. and Mrs. Becker gave me a personality," Alice Wentworth recalls. "Up to this point many missionaries found it very difficult to relate to me. They didn't know if I was an African or, because I had been adopted by a missionary family, if I was a part of A.I.M. But Dr. Becker never batted an eye about the problem; neither did Mrs. Becker; neither did Carl or Mary. I just moved right in as another human being; and that gave me status throughout the mission."

"I remember how Mrs. Becker made such wonderful meals out of the little old forest mushrooms, called plantains. We had them fried, many, many times. The larder was often bleak, and it took all the ingenuity of a Pennsylvania Dutch housewife to get nourishing and tasty meals on the table in those days." But Marie always seemed to manage.

One day not long after Alice joined the Becker family, Dr. Becker marched in and told his wife, "Marie, you'd better get ready because we're going to have a guest for a few days."

"A guest? In this place?"

Dr. Becker explained that a Belgian colonel, a cultured, elderly gentleman who was the curator of the Albert National Park, had had an accident at Mutwanga. "There is no other place for him to stay; he will have to stay here until he can return to his post."

Marie was speechless.

"But Marie," Dr. Becker explained, "his eyes were burned with battery acid and they will be bandaged. So he won't be able to see the place for several days anyhow."

That made Marie feel better. For three weeks the colonel crowded in with the others in the three-room, leaf-thatched mud hut.

In gratitude for the family-style convalescence, the colonel later sent a mahogany dining-room suite, too big for the three-room house. But shortly thereafter, the Beckers received word that they were to move permanently to Ruwenzori to begin their hospital work there. At Ruwenzori, Dr. Becker decided, "we'll have to build a dining room big enough to hold the mahogany suite."

Alice was thrilled with the idea of going to Ruwenzori—all except the six-mile walk to the station at the end of the trip. But even that wasn't too bad—fording mountain streams, smelling the invigorating mountain air, seeing the elephants and baboons that roamed the Ruwenzori area unmolested, admiring strands of tall, slender eucalyptus and bamboo, pleasant meadows and farms of tea and coffee shrubs.

Marie Becker planted her garden and helped to make the family self-sufficient. Alice Wentworth started her nurse's training under Dr. Becker's watchful eye, and Carl and Mary continued their education at Rethy Academy.

Dr. Becker looked forward to establishing his hospital at Ruwenzori. An ideal resort setting, it was a place where sick missionaries could come and rest for a week or two until they regained their strength. High enough to be out of the malarial mosquito zone, its climate seemed ideal.

So when they moved to Ruwenzori, Carl told Marie, "I think we're finally settled now—after eight years on the missionary field." Kitsombiro, Katwa, Aba, Oicha, Rethy, Oicha again and finally Ruwenzori—seven family moves in eight years. "We're over forty now. I suppose it's time we settled down."

But for Carl Becker it wasn't settling down. He was continually driving back and forth between Ruwenzori and Oicha, with occasional side trips to the leprosy camp he had started years before at Katwa. He wanted to build up the work at Ruwenzori, but Oicha wouldn't give him the time to do it. Only a few years earlier, Oicha didn't seem to have the potential to develop into a hospital station. Yet now, almost every time he turned around, he was receiving an emergency call from that forest station.

Occasionally, he was able to squeeze out enough time to drive up to Rethy to visit Mary and Carl Jr. But it wasn't often—not often enough, he felt. Marie sometimes prodded him.

"All right, Marie, we're going up to Rethy," he said one evening. "I've two days absolutely clear."

They left the dispensary and made the six-mile trek to the parked car. As he opened the door, he heard a frenzied wailing down the jungle trail. He stood still as the wailing came closer. Then a group of Africans appeared around a bend on the trail. On an improvised stretcher lay a little girl. He walked hurriedly to them.

One of the Africans explained that a forest branch had broken off and fallen on the girl's head. The villagers laid the stretcher down in front of the doctor. Dr. Becker stole a glance at Marie in the car, looked at the wailing women, one of whom doubtless was the girl's mother, and then down at the suffering girl. Quickly, he knelt on the ground beside her, feeling her pulse, looking at the trickle of blood from her mouth and noticing the flick of an eyelash.

Dr. Becker felt Marie move in beside him as he carefully touched the African girl.

Dr. Becker looked up at his wife. He didn't know what to say. He had failed his children so many times, and he knew how much Marie was looking forward to this trip. "Well, Marie," he finally spoke, "fractured skull, brain hemorrhage—really there's very little hope, but I suppose there is a chance surgically. What shall we do?" He did not wish to make the decision himself.

Without hesitation, his wife responded. "We'll stay, of course, and operate."

There were times of family fun, a time for a vacation in the Kivu area with its glowing volcanoes and lava beds, but these were rare occasions.

Ruwenzori presented Dr. Becker with a wide variety of cases and a fascinating assortment of patients. One thin, emaciated African, burdened by a tumor weighing 75 or 80 pounds, almost as much as he did himself, trudged to Ruwenzori requesting an operation. He was dressed in his Sunday best, an odd assortment of garish clothing. When the operation was successful, the patient was so jubilant that he insisted that Dr. Becker return with him to his village.

"I want you to meet all my friends," the African clotheshorse begged. He also wanted to be Dr. Becker's personal valet, and assured him that he would provide for him the rest of his life. Dr. Becker turned down the offer.

One Wanandi tribesman was brought to the dispensary porch by his long-suffering wife. They had walked for more than 100 miles to come to Dr. Becker; the trip had been tedious, for they could accomplish only a few miles a day. The man, Dr. Becker discovered, had been blind with double cataracts for fifteen years.

After a delicate operation and a two-week convalescence at Ruwenzori, the man was pronounced cured, and sent on his way home. His eyes were filled with tears as he bade good-bye to the doctor and the nurses. As payment for his operation, he gave his *Bwana Munganga* a scrawny little Congo chicken.

Dr. Becker watched the Wanandi couple leave. Now the husband no longer had to be led by his wife. This time he strode off while his proud wife followed meekly in the rear carrying their possessions on her back and on her head.

Another husband brought his wife to Ruwenzori, explaining that her jaw had slipped out of joint a few days earlier and had locked. When Dr. Becker found out that they lived only a few miles from the dispensary he was shocked. "Why," he asked, "did you wait so long before bringing your wife for treatment?"

"*Bwana*," said the African calmly, "she talks too much."

Yet, despite all his efforts to make something of Ruwenzori, the pleasant station on the side of a mountain seemed destined to remain a good dispensary, but no more. It was that hopeless little jungle station of Oicha which was claiming more and more of his time. An additional problem in building up a hospital at Ruwenzori was that of assigning forest patients to a mountain hospital. While its height made Ruwenzori nonmalarial, yet it also provided a climate that induced pneumonia and other respiratory illnesses in patients accustomed to life at lower altitudes.

Over and over again, as he returned to Ruwenzori after the fifty-mile trip from Oicha and began the six-mile trek up the mountainside to the dispensary, hulking Claudon Stauffacher, Ruwenzori missionary, would be standing there, hands on hips, a broad smile on his face.

"Doctor, I just got a call from Miss Smith, and she wants you again. There's another strangulated hernia at Oicha."

Usually he was tired out, as were Alice and Marie. But all he would say was, "Where are my bags?" And he would turn around, get in his car and return to the little hole in the forest called Oicha, leaving Alice and Marie to go up the mountainside to get some rest.

Late at night he would return the second time from Oicha. The six-mile trail from the road to the station would now be dark. A herd of marauding elephants might be raiding the banana patches, as Dr. Becker with quick, short steps would stride up the trail. It was not that he was oblivious to danger. It was just that he was confident that if he were in God's place, God's hand was on him and there was nothing to be feared from Ruwenzori elephants, nothing to fear at all.

Nor was there any need to fear the Oicha leopards. And month by month, he seemed to be spending more time at Oicha.

Oicha was still simply a hole in the forest. The hospital itself consisted of ten leaf-covered mud huts, each with a room and a porch and each furnished with two or four frame beds. When a patient registered, banana leaves were cut to make a mattress. Most patients, except the very poor, brought along a grass or bark mat to put on top of them as a cover. Back of the row of ten hospital mud huts, separated by a banana grove, were three small huts housing ten leprosy sufferers.

Although Oicha's dispensary was small, Dr. Becker made sure it operated efficiently. Nurse Zola Smith, assisted by several African medical boys, handled the work. Before seven each morning, between 50 and 100 Africans lined up outside the dispensary to listen to a short sermon which explained what God had done for them through Jesus Christ. Then one of the African assistants would take temperatures and record them on an individual chart. Two assistants would be stationed in the ulcer room ready to handle the dressing of ulcers and sores. Another stood at the dispensing table where medicines and injections were given.

Zola Smith wrote the prescriptions down on cards and passed them through a window to the assistant in charge of dispensing medicine.

Dr. Carl Becker had devised the system carefully, and it was working well. He depended heavily on African help, counting on them to do a conscientious job. Sometimes they disappointed him, but usually not.

By 1938, Edna Amstutz, a third-term missionary nurse with an indomitable spirit, replaced Zola Smith as the Oicha R.N. Dr. Becker, who had hoped to train Africans to serve in the pharmacy, finally handed the exacting job to Marie, who was able to master the metric system that seemed to mystify the young uneducated Congolese.

Another person in training was Alice Wentworth, now a rambunctious teenager with a habit of expressing herself graphically on almost any subject. Dr. Becker liked the zest with which she tackled most tasks and her quickness in comprehending intricate procedures; however, many rough edges would still have to be sandpapered to smoothness before she would become a mature Christian nurse.

One day had been particularly strenuous. Patients seemed to come through the walls and emergencies appeared at the most unwanted times. Alice lived a continuous ordeal in the operating room. Between operations she had to wash all the instruments, put them up in packs and autoglaze them, because they were in short supply. It was like washing dishes all day long. At the day's end, all Alice wanted to do was to crawl into her bed at the Becker hut and fall sound asleep.

"I guess that's it, Alice. You can clean up in here and put everything away. By that time, it will be close to supper," Dr. Becker said with disgusting cheerfulness, as he left.

She dragged through the final procedures, putting the surgical instruments in their proper places, and cleaning—Dr. Becker insisted on strictest hospital sanitary standards even in the midst of a jungle —the operating room with drudgery.

She was just closing the door of the operating room, when two of the African aides brought a filthy, reeking old forest tribesman to her.

"What's wrong?" she asked. She turned her face away, hoping to avoid the odor of the old man.

"We don't know."

"You get the information on him and I'll get Dr. Becker."

She ran to the Becker home as quickly as her tired legs could carry her and told the doctor. He returned hurriedly and examined the old man.

Alice was at his side, looking on curiously. "What is it?"

"Strangulated hernia, I think." The doctor continued his examination. "He's not in very good shape. I really don't think he's going to make it, but there's a chance, just a slim chance."

Alice looked down at the unpleasant sight. The man looked like a pig that had rolled through the mud. Accustomed as she was to dirt and grime, she had never seen a more abhorrent mess. And he was already half-dead. The corners of her mouth turned down.

Dr. Becker broke into her reverie. "Alice, get the operating room ready."

Her head flew back, her mouth opened in amazement and then in pain. "Oh, Doctor, for that dirty old man?"

A look of disappointment swept over his face. His brown eyes seemed to bore deeply into her own, but he said nothing. She wanted to say something, something like, "But you don't know how tired I am." But now she knew he had been working just as hard as she had all day long.

And then she remembered something that he had said more than once to her, something that she could never forget: "Any person is precious in the sight of the Lord."

She broke away from his gaze and looked into the stupor of an expression on the face of this miserable tribesman. Even this man? she wanted to ask. But she knew what his reply would be, so she turned silently and quickly into the operating room to prepare for surgery.

The workload became heavier and heavier. At times Alice Wentworth thought she could take no more. Sometimes everything about the hospital seemed inadequate. She complained that the facilities weren't big enough to handle the crowds of patients; the staff wasn't large enough; the bandages weren't plentiful enough; and the medical supplies were somewhat like the widow's cruse of oil—always on the verge of running out. And once when this mood struck her, Dr. Becker noticed it, took her aside and counseled quietly, "Alice, whenever you start getting that feeling, just go out, drop everything, take ten deep breaths and then come back and tackle one job at a time—one at a time. That's all you have to do."

Dr. Becker and Alice continued to travel back and forth between Oicha and Ruwenzori, still calling Ruwenzori home, but realizing more and more that God wanted them at Oicha. Sooner or later a decision would have to be made.

Dr. Becker wanted a clear sign from the Lord before taking a definite step away from Ruwenzori. He had been assigned to it by the Congo Field Council after he had testified of the difficulties in trying to launch a hospital work at Oicha. He had certainly made enough plans to develop a hospital in Ruwenzori and in many ways it would have been ideal. Even the Belgian government had officially approved their request to operate at Ruwenzori, which they had been doing for several years on a concession from a local tribe chief. And now a road was being constructed up to the station, removing the ordeal of a six-mile trek. To cap it off, a medical building had just been erected as a first building in Dr. Becker's proposed Ruwenzori hospital.

Dr. Becker, whose philosophy of divine guidance was summed up in his dependence on the Lord to control circumstances supplemented by his belief that "God cannot steer a parked car," kept trying to work out of Ruwenzori, until he was shown otherwise.

His guidance came in January, 1939, when lightning struck the newly completed Ruwenzori medical building. The ensuing fire com-

pletely destroyed it along with all the drugs, supplies, furniture and
equipment. Only a few bottles and a microscope were saved. The
house was also burned to the ground.

"Pray for him in this great loss and handicap," beseeched the
editor of *Inland Africa* in an appeal to all friends of the Africa
Inland Mission.

But Dr. Becker regarded it neither as a great loss nor a handicap.
It was an answer to prayer. The following issue of *Inland Africa*
stated, "The burning of the dispensary at Ruwenzori, Congo, was not
without a harvest of spiritual gain." Perhaps the hospital at Oicha
was erected on the ashes of Ruwenzori.

Oicha's ministry now expanded rapidly as Dr. Becker spent more
time there. In two years, the average number of patients at Oicha
grew from 70 to 300 per day. The number of operations for the first
full year was 1,000, 200 of them of a major nature. Instead of only
10 lepers Oicha now cared for 175. Ambulatory patients brought
their own food, and cooked their own meals on the fires in front of
their hospital huts. Sometimes they would roast a whole monkey; one
of their delicacies was a soup made out of elephant intestines.

To the Beckers, on the other hand, the food supply at Oicha was a
problem. They had no affection for elephant intestines and monkey
meat, and besides, they craved vegetables with their meat. The
Stauffachers at Ruwenzori were generous with their garden products,
but the Beckers never liked to be dependent.

Marie told Carl one day that she thought vegetables could be
grown at Oicha just as successfully as at Ruwenzori, provided they
were given a little sunlight. Encouraged by her husband, she began
experimenting with traditional American-type vegetable seeds and
nurturing them with elephant manure. Amazingly, it turned out to be
a winning combination. From the start, the problem of an adequate
food supply—one of the big drawbacks in thinking of Oicha as the
site of a hospital—was soon conquered.

The problem of the Oicha insects didn't lend itself to a ready
solution. Former Belgian Red-Cross nurse Betty Russ wrote home in
disgust. "The insects here are a plague. They eat clothing, papers,
books, curtains and all they can get hold of. Huge, fat cockroaches
come out at night. Tiny little black ants get into the food. . . . Please
pray for us."

"If this is where God wants us," Dr. Becker told Marie one day,
"we'd better start fixing the place up." His idea of a hospital was not

a few mud huts. It didn't have to be chrome-lined or ten-stories high, but at least it had to be clean and able to be kept clean. In addition, the hospital would have to be constructed economically with both local labor and materials.

But there was no budget for the construction of a hospital. Whatever was built had to come out of their $60-a-month income, which they sometimes had to stretch to include the purchase of medical supplies as well. Their monthly support arrived more regularly now, as the Evangelical Congregational denomination was taking an increasing interest in their financial backing. But the support wasn't enough to build a hospital.

Dr. Becker's building plans also included the construction of decent houses. Edna Amstutz was living in a little two-room log cabin, and the Beckers were in the small house which had been built for her.

One visiting missionary suggested that he make an appeal for funds to build up the hospital. A medical facility with more than 300 patients a day, a growing leprosy colony with a TB sanitarium and 1,000 operations a year, the visitor argued, deserved some support. "If people in the States knew more about your needs—your financial needs," he counseled, "I think you could raise enough money to build a good hospital."

Dr. Becker shook his head. "No appeals for money. We'll let the Lord take care of that."

"Couldn't you just let the need be clearly known? You don't have to come out and ask for the money."

Dr. Becker broke into a broad smile. "We'll let the Lord take care of that too."

He knew that some of his workers had their faith strained by shortages of supplies and provisions, but his was unshaken. Yet, once he wrote home in one of his rare letters. "Indeed, we have been sometimes tempted to despair over the prospect of finding accommodations for these folks, food for those who must have it, and drugs and supplies for all. In many unexpected ways which remind us of the way Elijah was fed by the ravens, the Lord has been providing for us from here and from there."

And indeed, the supplies always came when they were needed. Then Dr. Becker would say with tears in his eyes, "That's the way the Lord has always done it."

A visitor asked him once, "But don't you have big dreams for this forest hospital? Don't you have a goal of a huge work which would be known and recognized as a lifesaving institution throughout this section of Congo?"

Dr. Becker merely shook his head then, but a few weeks later he found his answer in a quotation:

"The ultimate goal is not our problem; it is God's. Our problem is the recognition of the divine initiative and purpose. The laborer does not grasp the full purpose of the architect. The soldier does not enter into the whole plan of the general. There is an intelligence, a design, an activity, a power, working behind every obedient life."

He had no great dreams for Oicha, merely a humble desire to be obedient to the will of God. For that purpose, he had left the mountain of Ruwenzori for the jungle of Oicha.

9

The Deaths and Lives
of Chief Kisobe

*"God made the sea, we make the ship; He made the wind,
we make a sail; He made the calm, we make oars."*—SWAHILI PROVERB

Carl Becker Jr. later described Oicha as a conglomeration of buildings that expanded like a rabbit warren.

Probably, if his father had been a visionary instead of a doctor, he would never have taken a second look at Ruwenzori, but would have devoted all his time to Oicha from the start of his second term in Africa in 1936. Had he not been a down-to-earth, day-by-day workman, he might have built with a comprehensive plan of development in mind, calling for a new wing to be added five years later and a new building ten years later, with other appropriate facilities scheduled in between. Had he been public-relations-minded, he might have raised a large sum of money by promoting it as a memorial hospital in honor of some dear-departed saint whose memory would call forth devotion and donations.

But Dr. Carl K. Becker wasn't that sort of a man.

A.I.M. General Secretary Sidney Langford puts it this way. "They put up a building because they needed it. There has been no overall general plan. Some money came in and they put up a building; some more money came in and they put up another building. Thus it grew."

The story of Oicha, however, has to begin with an African chief or head man named Kisobe. Like most mission stations, Oicha sits on ground that originally belonged to an African chief. The procedure in obtaining land was to apply to the government, which approached the paramount chief of the district who, in turn, consulted the chief of the local area. Kisobe, the local chief at Oicha, had the final say.

When Jim Bell first saw the dead-end road at Oicha, he knew that

89

Kisobe, a cannibal chief with a savage reputation, was the man to see for permission to start a mission station there. Kisobe's village consisted of only a few mud huts, hardly an impressive domain, but throughout the jungle he was feared and revered.

Whether Kisobe was still plying his cannibal trade in 1928 when Bell first met him is unknown; Bell wasn't interested in finding out. But it was no secret that Kisobe had eaten Pygmies, who weren't considered human anyway, as well as others who had crossed him. He had pronounced that the thighs and chest were the tastiest.

Kisobe was sitting idly outside his hut when Bell approached. The palaver lasted most of the afternoon. The missionary argued his case, over and over again. They would build a chapel where they would teach Kisobe about God, they would build a dispensary where they would heal Kisobe's body when he got sick and they would build a school where they would teach his children to read.

The chief sat quietly, grunting occasionally to indicate he had heard and shaking his head vigorously to show Bell that he wasn't going to be easy to convince. He wasn't interested in having another God to worship; he didn't need the white man's religion. Nor was he interested in a dispensary; he had a witch doctor who could frighten away the most persistent of evil spirits. But the school for his children? He nodded slowly. The missionary had won.

Chief Kisobe watched the missionaries work. His eyes followed the fall of huge timbers as they thundered to the ground. The brush was gathered and burned in big piles. Now unfiltered noonday sun poured down its brilliance.

He watched as Jim Bell built a row of log cabins and a bigger house for himself. Then he saw the missionaries chop large trees, saw them up in sections and burn out the huge stumps that remained. And he watched as poles were linked together with a strong twine, then pitched with mud and sealed with whitewash. A small chapel was erected where the missionaries worshipped their God. But Kisobe wasn't interested. He became much more interested, however, when the little school building went up and when his son Benjamina began to show him the scratchings in a book and say that they meant something to him.

Bwana Bell often came to talk to Kisobe. At first he listened to the white missionaries, but then he turned away. "Those sayings from the Book of God are too hard for me," he explained. But that wasn't what bothered him. What bothered him was that *Bwana* Bell not only wanted him to believe in God, but also to live as God wanted him to live. And as Kisobe understood it, this meant no more all-night dances, no more banana beer, no more eating of men's flesh.

Perhaps Kisobe could have forgotten those hard sayings from God's Book if some of his own village people hadn't gone to the little chapel and come out with smiling faces and with words of "accepting Yesu," who they said was God's Son. Perhaps he could have forgotten if his own children had not gone to the school and had come home singing songs about Yesu and saying that they too had believed.

Troubled Kisobe wended his way back into the jungle to the witch doctor's hut. The missionaries had talked about Jesus' dying for their sins; the witch doctor said that the blood of a chicken would cover his sins. The missionaries said that God's forgiveness was free; the witch doctor always asked for a goat. But the witch doctor never said he must live differently. That was the kind of religion Kisobe liked.

Sometimes the missionaries told him when they didn't like what he was doing; this irked Kisobe. He had given them his land; why should they now tell him that what he was doing was all wrong? They told him that he shouldn't kill twins when they were born, but he knew that twins came because there was a curse. And the only way to remove the curse was to kill one of the twins.

Then a doctor came to Oicha. He had a thin face and a slight smile, but Kisobe soon learned that he could be just as forceful as Bwana Bell. Before long, people were coming from far away to see this Dr. Becker. From Kenya, from Tanganyika, from Uganda, from Azandeland people came to be healed. And Benjamina, his own son, was training to be an assistant.

Before the doctor came, only a few people had believed in Yesu; but now as hundreds thronged into the mission station every day, and as Africans themselves began to tell the story, many of his friends believed in God's Book.

But Kisobe wouldn't believe.

Kisobe had a physical problem, a hernia which was worsening steadily. Benjamina told him he should see Dr. Becker. Dr. Becker was removing hernias every day, he told him. The doctor had a skillful knife and the operation would be simple. Kisobe didn't listen. Instead he went to the witch doctor as the pain grew more severe. It was a curse, said the witch doctor, which an enemy had cast upon him. A chicken was sacrificed, but it did no good. The witch doctor

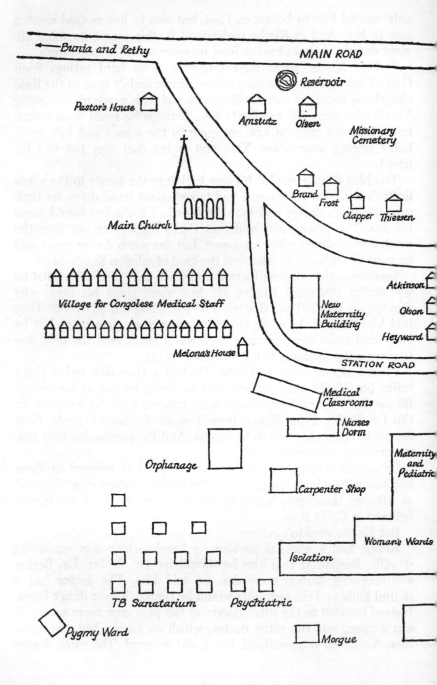

← Bunia and Rethy

MAIN ROAD

Reservoir

Pastor's House

Amstutz

Olsen

Missionary Cemetery

Main Church

Brand

Frost

Clapper

Thiessen

Village for Congolese Medical Staff

New Maternity Building

Atkinson

Olson

Heyward

Melona's House

STATION ROAD

Medical Classrooms

Nurses Dorm

Orphanage

Carpenter Shop

Maternity and Pediatric

Isolation

Woman's Wards

TB Sanatarium

Psychiatric

Pygmy Ward

Morgue

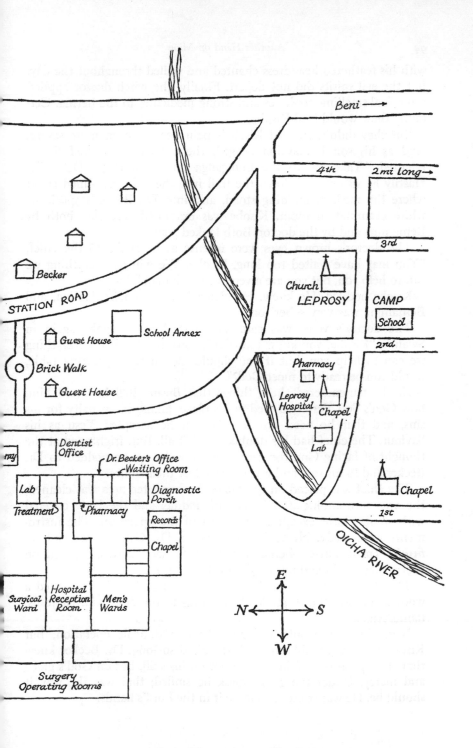

with his feathered headdress chanted and wailed throughout the day, but the evil spirits did not depart. Finally, the witch doctor applied some foul-smelling poultices and strong medicines to the hernia. Certainly these would heal Kisobe.

But they didn't. Instead Kisobe's pain became even more severe. And as his son Benjamina begged, the old cannibal chief finally relented. "Take me to the *munganga mukubwa* ("Big Doctor"). Hastily he was carried down the trail into the palm tree-lined street where the medical building stood, and into Dr. Becker's spotlessly white examination room. Kisobe was examined carefully, both by Benjamina and by the doctor. Both looked grave.

The doctor's brown eyes were intense as he spoke to the chief, "You may have waited too long, Kisobe. We will do everything we can to help you, but you are a very, very sick man."

Kisobe nodded. He knew. He glanced at his son Benjamina, and Benjamina was very sober too.

The doctor's voice was calm and restful as he spoke again in Swahili, "Kisobe, you know that Benjamina and I will do everything we can to help you, but if you should die on this operating table, would you be ready to meet God?"

Kisobe remembered those things that *Bwana* Bell had told him, how God's Son Yesu had died in his place, taking the penalty for his sins, and that he need not fear God if he accepted Yesu as his Saviour. The chief had his doubts about it all. But, frightened at the thought of facing God the next time he woke up, he nodded to Dr. Becker and to his son, and was rewarded by their smiles.

The chief was placed on the table, the herniated area was cleaned, the area surrounding it painted with iodine, and the body covered with sterile cloths except for the area of the operation. The instruments were ready. Nurse Edna Amstutz, Dr. Carl Becker and *infirmier* (male nurse) Benjamina Ndakote had all washed, tied on their gauze masks and put on their rubber gloves.

The three huddled over the cannibal chief and Becker breathed a word of prayer, "Lord, guide these hands to do Your will. In Jesus' name. Amen."

Normally, this would not have been a difficult operation, but Kisobe had been stubborn; he had waited so long. Dr. Becker knew that this operation would depend not on his skill, but on God's grace and mercy. Under the gauze mask he smiled; that was the way it should be. He was content to leave it in the Lord's hands.

Yet he couldn't deny the importance of the operation before him. Here was Kisobe, the archenemy of the gospel in the area and yet oddly enough the benefactor of the mission station itself. Would the superstitious forest people accuse the mission of foul play if Kisobe should die on the operating table? Would they think that, just as the chief had killed many people and perhaps some white men, the doctor was seeking revenge?

So it was good to have Benjamina at his side. Benjamina would understand that, come what may, the missionaries were trying to do everything they could for his father. But was it fair to the young infirmier to ask him to assist in such a crucial operation? Wasn't this too much to ask? This too was in the Lord's hands, which was enough for Carl Becker.

He glanced down at Kisobe. The patient was well anesthetized by now; the operation could begin. He looked out of the corner of his eyes at Benjamina; Benjamina appeared stoic, but the doctor recognized it as fear, bordering on terror. "Ready, Benjamina?" the doctor asked calmly.

Benjamina knew how serious it all was. He had been an infirmier long enough to know both life and death. He knew the doctor's skill, but he also knew that some patients did not leave the operating table alive. He had also observed many patients with strangulated hernias; the forest seemed full of them. If they came to the doctor in time, there was a good chance that they could be handled. But if they had dallied with the *mufumu*, the witch doctor, it was often too late. If this patient on the operating table in front of him had not been his father, he would have judged that it was too late.

Maybe he shouldn't have suggested that his father come to the hospital at all, Benjamina thought momentarily. But it was a self-centered thought. He thought of the accusation that would be flung at him if his father did not recover. "My whole tribe will accuse me of bringing my father to his death." He shook his head to dislodge the thought from his mind. He had done the right thing; he had done the only thing he could.

"Ready, Benjamina?" The doctor's voice was a bit more penetrating this time, and Benjamina realized that it was the second time he had heard the question.

"Muzuri," Benjamina replied, indicating that he was prepared to begin. He stole a glance at the doctor and was reassured. The doctor looked calm and confident.

The doctor applied the scalpel and made the incision; there was bleeding and Dr. Becker's stubby fingers, clothed in rubber gloves, seized the catgut held by the nurse and formed non-slipping knots with elegant economy. Three Spencer-Wells forceps were applied to stop the bleeding. Benjamina's retractors pulled apart the edges of the incision. The silver gleam of the peritoneum became visible. The doctor's hands worked with speed and precision performing the surgery. A part of the intestine was removed to relieve the obstruction and then the loose ends were anastomized together.

Benjamina was sweating profusely now. He was amazed at what the doctor could do and wondered if he ever would be able to perform surgery like that. Usually, when he was assisting the *munganga* in the operating room, time flew quickly. Today, the operation seemed to drag, though Dr. Becker was working as rapidly as ever.

Then, Dr. Becker was tightening the suture and the operation was finished. He pulled down the gauze mask and smiled at Benjamina, who immediately erupted in a wide, relieved grin.

But the elation was cut off at once by Edna Amstutz. "Doctor, no pulse!"

Benjamina looked at the body on the table. "He's dead," he sobbed.

The doctor stepped quickly in front of Benjamina and bent over Kisobe, massaging his chest vigorously. The doctor still appeared calm, unexcited. "Get ready for an adrenalin injection," he ordered the nurse. She moved quickly.

His father was dead. Benjamina was convinced. His breathing had stopped; his heart was no longer pumping. Why was the *munganga* still working? The nurse stepped back and placed in Dr. Becker's outstretched right hand an adrenalin syringe. The surgeon pushed the needle boldly into the wall of the heart.

There seemed to be no response. Kisobe lay unmoving, lifeless. Benjamina wished there was something he could do, but there was nothing—except to pray as the *munganga* had taught him.

"Artificial respiration," the doctor said quietly to the nurse and they tried to coax breath back into his lungs.

Still no response.

Benjamina glanced back and forth between the doctor, the nurse and his father. There was no sign of life. If the adrenalin was going to work, it certainly would have by now.

And then Nurse Amstutz said, "I think I detect a faint pulse, Doctor."

"We'll keep working on him." The respiration continued. "I think his breath is returning, too."

His father was going to pull through, after all.

"Thank you, Lord," he heard the *munganga* whisper, almost too low to be heard. Benjamina didn't know what to say or whether he could say anything.

Finally in good Congolese idiom he said, "At last my heart is resting again in my stomach."

In a few minutes old Kisobe began to stir his way out from under the anesthetic. Half-drugged, he complained, "Don't just stand around; get on with it and finish the job. I want to get back to my warm hut."

Dr. Becker was smiling. "The operation is all finished now, and you are going to be well."

It soon became evident that it wasn't all over as far as Kisobe was concerned. His physical problems had been cleared up, but his spiritual problems remained. In fact, like Pharaoh of old, every time he saw a miracle his heart hardened. The adrenalin had only reactivated a very physical heart. His spiritual heart was obdurate as ever. Kisobe had not become a Christian on the operating table.

Now he discouraged his subjects from going to Dr. Becker, and eventually he imposed a ban on any of his villagers consulting anyone except the witch doctor for medical treatment. His son, Benjamina, became the family outcast, though he lived only a stone's throw from his father's village.

Yet dispite Kisobe's persecution, the hospital grew. Most of the growth came from villagers and tribes from beyond Kisobe's domain. But the chief's orders were often disobeyed when a sick villager found that the witch doctor could do no good.

One day two badly mauled women who lived in Kisobe's village were rushed to Dr. Becker. They had been cooking supper in their smoky banana-leaved hut, when a hungry leopard crept in behind them. Ignoring a goat which was also in the tiny hut, the leopard leaped upon one of the women. When the other woman tried to drive it away, the leopard turned savagely on her.

One of the women had more than fifteen wounds; the other had received a blow which crushed her skull and left her brain exposed.

None of their families thought of the witch doctor with a case like this. For hours Dr. Becker labored over the woman with the crushed skull, and was saddened when she died the next morning. The other woman recovered.

Most of Kisobe's villagers came to the doctor only as a last resort. Only after they had tried the witch doctor and had gone home waiting to be cured; only after they had finally lost all hope; only when they were so weak and emaciated that all resistance was gone, did they come to the hospital. And when the doctor leaned forward across his little table and asked, "How long have you been ill?" they would reply, "Just a couple of days."

Yet no matter how ill they were, they expected that the *Munganga Mukubwa* could heal them. Often they had to be fed intravenously until they were strong enough to take an operation. Sometimes Dr. Becker prescribed some of his "strength-building" medicine for them. The strength-builder was simply eggnog which Marie had mixed. It had to be labeled *"Dawa"* (medicine), for in the forest area raw eggs and milk, associated with the life cycle, were taboo. No woman could touch eggs or milk; in fact, she could not even touch a pot in which eggs were cooked. Since Africans had been known to die upon hearing that they had inadvertently eaten raw eggs, Marie Becker's eggnogs were liberally flavored with vanilla extract to make them taste medicinal. Often the Beckers went without eggs and milk in order to provide eggnogs for starving patients.

But eventually the tide turned. The Africans heard rumors that even the witch doctors were coming to the hospital. One *mufumu* (witch doctor), long declared an enemy of "the *munganga* who has been stealing my people's hearts," came secretly at night. He had a personal ailment, he explained, that he'd been unable to "enchant away."

The examination revealed a large hernia in an advanced stage, which led the *mufumu* to pose some penetrating questions.

"When you put the blood of a man from one tribe into a man from another, how can you tell what tribe he belongs to?"

"When you cut off a leg or arm, how do these parts find the man again after his death?"

Becker patiently explained to the witch doctor, in simple Swahili, question after question. Finally, after he had explained how malaria is transmitted, the witch doctor's face brightened. "Aha, but what makes that particular mosquito bite that particular man?"

When the doctor paused to consider his answer, the witch doctor pointed a shaking finger at him. "This is what is caused by the evil spirits."

Leaving Oicha, the witch doctor went back to his mystic profession, but nevertheless ceased his attacks on the doctor, and occasionally even referred difficult cases to "his friend," *Mufumu* Becker.

This one did not become a Christian, though three or four other witch doctors did turn to Jesus Christ and did bring all their paraphernalia to Oicha in order to renounce them publicly. And there, as Kisobe watched the public ceremonies, the converted witch doctors would lay down bird claws, lion's teeth, lizard skins, snake skins, horns full of mysterious medicines, hollow gourds and their elaborate headdresses, before casting them into the fire.

But old Kisobe did not respond as easily as some of the witch doctors. He sat in front of his little house, watching more trees being chopped down and more buildings going up at the nearby hospital. He saw hundreds of families walk by him every day on their way to visit the *Munganga Mukubwa*.

According to African custom, whenever patients come to stay at the hospital, their relatives came with them, to cook and help care for them.

Marion Cribbs, who arrived at Oicha during the Second World War described the hospital interior as she first saw it. "The patients lie on wooden beds—just planks nailed together and set on four legs. They are rickety with age and black with many soakings of old motor oil which help to keep out the 'livestock'. The mattresses are broad banana leaves, and over these there may or may not be a mat. We supply a blanket for cover.

"Under the beds are bunches of banana, mohogo roots, clay pots and pans and the family mattress of leaves. You see, the whole family moves in with the sick one and sleeps under and around his bed at night. Nursing in the homeland is fascinating but it cannot be compared with this."

In one way the coming of families helped the missionaries; in other ways it complicated their tasks. But it certainly meant that the facilities at Oicha had to be rapidly enlarged.

Dr. Becker built slowly, only when necessary, but it seemed that it was always necessary. The tiny clearing in the forest had to be continually enlarged.

Another reason for beating back the great forest that hedged in the

small clearing was the need to let in more sun. Sunlight was important to the recuperation of many of his patients, and in the forest all
sunlight was heavily filtered. Even more important, with the forest
too close, Becker feared that he would lose as many patients from
wild animal attacks as from disease; more than once leopards had
invaded the mission station.

But extending the clearing was a mammoth task. The giant trees
were so thick that a chopped tree, instead of falling, would merely
lean against its neighbor—or if not felled properly, would crash
down upon the little huts.

To provide sturdier structures than the native mud-and-leaf variety, as well as better defense against marauding wild beasts, snakes
and insects (such as the murderous armies of driver ants that occasionally swept through the villages destroying all life in their path),
Dr. Becker experimented with making bricks from native soil, as was
done on many other A.I.M. stations.

Aided by New Zealander Bennett Williams and by Harry Hurlburt, youngest son of the A.I.M. pioneer, the hospital expanded
rapidly. But perhaps the biggest assistance came as male missionaries
brought their expectant wives and awaited the arrival of a child.
They usually arrived two to three weeks early and waited a week or
two after the baby was born to begin their trip back to their home
station.

The doctor figured that if he didn't charge them anything for his
obstetrical services and if Marie provided food and lodging, he
should be able to put them to work. And this he did. Most of the
A.I.M. Congo missionaries as well as many from other missions have
done their share to build Oicha.

Patients in the leprosy colony were also put to work. "Self-respect
means a lot to these people," Dr. Becker told Nurse Edna Amstutz.
"If they are kept busy, they will feel better." So they too were hired
for a modest sum, to work in the building of the hospital.

One building was put up for patients with pulmonary tuberculosis.
A small maternity ward was constructed. Twenty houses were constructed in the leprosy colony, a special leprosy dispensary was completed; the foundation for a new chapel was laid. And still the work
expanded.

Carl Becker and his infirmiers went out every weekend into some
of the 300 villages which surrounded the Oicha station, and as soon

as villagers were converted, little chapels and schools were built in those villages as well.

Owen Brand, station superintendent at Oicha for many years, described the work at one small village several miles from Oicha. "Here at Rutama, we are building a new church, a teacher's house, and a small missionary rest house, all with shingle roofs. The buildings are built out of poles, with mud walls, but they are laid up straight with even corners and then are whitewashed.

"The work of clearing sites in this forest is enormous. Water for mud is brought by women who carry waterpots or saucepans on their heads. I brought with me an empty forty-gallon gas drum, and this is rolled as near to the source of water supply as is practical. Then it is filled by the women and rolled back to the place where the mud is being mixed. About twenty boys get in the sticky mud and puddle it with their feet until it attains the right consistency. Then it is used to plaster the house.

"The shingles are split from a tree in the forest and nailed to small poles, but the rest of the house is tied together with native string."

Though the construction was literally dirt-cheap, yet each building did cost money. In 1940, Carl Becker explained to the American Leprosy Mission, which assisted financially in the leprosy program, "I hoped to be able to build the patients' houses for $10 per hut, but because grass was not available for roofs, wood made into hand-split shingles was used for the roof. But nails cost money." And apologetically he added, "It now looks as if the huts will run about $12."

Every year there were new buildings to erect. Every time a missionary brought his wife to have a child, Carl Becker found for him more construction work to be done—X-ray buildings, a pharmacy, kitchen, carpenter's shop, women's wards, men's wards. Nothing was fancy, but it was all efficient.

Disgruntled Kisobe watched the development of Oicha. "Why did I ever allow my land to be used for such purposes? Why did I ever allow my son to go to school there?" he would complain.

But he couldn't deny that miracles were performed in those operating rooms. He had been a miracle himself. And he had seen others whom the witch doctor could not heal, but whom the God of Dr. Becker did heal.

Like many Africans, Kisobe was wracked with fear. Though he had a reputation as a fearless chief, he lived in constant fear of the evil spirits. It was this ingrown dread that kept him returning to the witch doctor. But there was another fear in his heart now. He knew that he had lied to Dr. Becker's God and to Benjamina's God when he lay upon that operating table. Many times he feared that the Christian God would strike him dead for having lied to Him.

Then one Sunday Kisobe heard that there would be a special meeting at the Oicha church. Hundreds of Africans would be there to hear an evangelist from America named Bill Rice. Kisobe watched the crowds walk by his hut on their way to the church, but he would not go.

And then a car stopped in front of his house. It was *Bwana* Jim Bell, back from Biasiku.

"*Hodi,*" said the white missionary.

"*Karibu,*" responded the African chief.

"*Habari,*" said the white missionary.

"*Muzuri,*" replied Kisobe. But everything wasn't *muzuri* with him.

Then Bell spoke firmly, almost severely to the old chief, "Come on, Kisobe, you have heard the good news for many years and have never really accepted it. All your children are Christians and here you are, old and broken in body, and still you are an unbeliever. You come with me right now to the meeting in the church and get right with God."

Kisobe had frequently been invited to church by Bell, but had always turned him down. He wanted to refuse this time also. But for some reason, he couldn't.

This time Kisobe nodded his head. He would go to the church, he said, if *Bwana* Bell would drive him in his car. When they arrived at the large, orange-brick church, Kisobe asked the missionary for permission to stay in the car and to hear the sermon through the church's open windows. Besides, he pleaded with Bell, if he went inside his presence would surely disrupt the service. Bell consented. Together Bell and Kisobe sat in the car listening carefully to the evangelist's message, spoken in English, then translated into Swahili.

Finally Evangelist Rice called for anyone who wanted to become a Christian to walk down the aisle to the front of the church. Nervously, Kisobe began to rattle the handle of the car door.

"What's the matter?" Jim Bell asked.

"I want to go," replied the chief.

"You want to go home now?" asked Bell.

"No, I want to go to the front of the church."

"I'll go with you," Bell volunteered. He helped the infirm chief out of the car and the two walked the long aisle between the rough wooden benches to the front of the church where the evangelist stood. There were whispers at first, and then the throng of Africans was hushed as they saw this old antagonist of the gospel finally respond to Jesus Christ.

Later Kisobe gave this testimony. "I went with *Bwana* Bell to that meeting because I thought that God was giving me one last chance. God had spared me once from death and was patient to me when I lied to Him, but the second time I said yes to Him I really meant it. I am old now and death will come soon, but now I am prepared to meet God."

After that, the old cannibal chief couldn't get out to the church services very often because of his health. This disappointed him deeply, because he wanted to show everyone that he had now become a Christian. But as he watched the missionaries construct another new ward for the hospital, an idea flashed through his mind.

The next time he saw *Munganga* Becker, he asked, "Could you build just one more building?"

"What kind of a building, Kisobe?"

"Could you build a chapel for my village right next to my house?"

And so Kisobe had his own chapel and the building of Oicha continued.

10

How to Measure a Pygmy

One thing stumped Dr. Becker. How could the Oicha hospital reach the Pygmies? They certainly had as many physical needs as anyone else and yet they shied away from the hospital. Although Oicha was solidly planted in Pygmy country and had been founded specifically to reach these little forest people, Carl Becker had to admit that the hospital hadn't been very successful at it.

One of the complications was that the other African tribes—the Babila, the Wanandi, the Walesi—never thought of the Pygmies as human beings. When the population of a village was counted, it was always reported as "47 people and 23 Pygmies."

Even the African converts found it difficult to cast aside old prejudices against the Pygmies. When Dr. Becker sent his African staff out regularly to preach on Sunday afternoons, they would shun the Pygmy villages as though these creatures did not even belong to the human race. Dr. Becker recognized that before the Pygmy could be effectively evangelized, either in the villages or at the hospital itself, this prevalent African attitude would have to be changed.

He had reminded his African staff repeatedly, just as he had reminded Alice, that "any person is precious in the sight of the Lord." And he had also told them repeatedly, "God measures the soul, not the body."

But while they nodded their heads, this Christian principle didn't seem to reach their hearts.

One hot and extremely busy morning as Dr. Becker stole a quick glance out the window, he noticed a little copper-colored Pygmy carrying his embwa (dog) and followed dutifully by his wife, hurrying towards the registration desk at the next building. The doctor waited a minute wondering if he should check on how his infirmiers handled the Pygmy. He didn't like to intrude when his helpers had been given specific responsibilities. But this case was different. He knew that at the registration desk the Pygmy would be asked to pay an annual registration fee (the fee had been initiated by Dr. Becker to give the Africans a sense of self-esteem, as well as to pay the wages of his infirmiers), and while the fee amounted to only a few cents, most Pygmies didn't handle such sums of money. Although he had left instructions at the desk that nobody should be refused, even if they didn't have the fee, he wasn't certain that his aides would extend the privilege to a Pygmy.

"Haw, haw, haw." Raucous laughter came from the direction of the registration desk. As the laughter continued, and other infirmiers seemed to be joining in the merriment, he stepped abruptly out of his office and headed quickly toward the registration area. He didn't like the idea of such laughter being at the expense of the Pygmy.

As he rounded the corner of the building, the scene confronted him. A Pygmy with his *embwa* in his arms, and clad only in his bark cloth, stood forlornly in front of the small registration desk. His little wife stood to the side and slightly behind him.

The registrar behind the desk slapped his sides, then hunched over, then threw back his head in peals of laughter. Other infirmiers were in various phases of convulsive laughter. But as the doctor's presence became known, a sudden pall fell on the festivities.

"What's the trouble?" he asked.

Loud laughter suddenly broke loose again.

He strode to the side of the Pygmy and reached under his white jacket into his trousers' pocket. He spoke sternly to the registrar, "If he can't pay, I'll pay the registration for him."

"Oh, that isn't the trouble, *Munganga*," the registrar replied, still having difficulty controlling his hilarity. He pointed to the coins on the registration desk.

"What's the trouble then?"

The contagious smile erupted again on the infirmier's face, and Dr. Becker could hear uncontrolled snickers behind him. "This—this thing here," the infirmier pointed to the Pygmy, "doesn't think you have enough work to do looking at people." Laughter again behind him. "And so he brings his *embwa* to you." Once again the laughter broke out.

Becker knew he was no veterinarian, but on the other hand he wasn't going to stand there and see a Pygmy humiliated. He looked at the pathetic Pygmy, who seemed more frightened than embarrassed, and hugged his dog more snugly than ever. Then he looked back at the registrar and ordered, "Write up a card for him."

He reached over and opened his arms to receive the embwa from the Pygmy. For the first time the Pygmy looked up, his eyes widening suddenly, his mouth falling slightly open; then responding almost automatically he handed the embwa into the doctor's outstretched arms.

There was no laughter from the infirmiers now. All was instantly quiet.

The doctor knelt on the grass with the dog in his arms and the Pygmy and his wife on their haunches on the other side. A crowd of Africans, summoned by the noise, had gathered in a huddle around them.

"How did it happen?"

The Pygmy explained that he had been hunting, when an enraged monkey dropped out of the trees and attacked his dog. He thought of chewing up leaves and applying them to the wounds, but he was afraid that his dog was much too seriously injured to be healed by leaves. So he came to the doctor.

The doctor listened patiently to the story. Then he asked, "Would you bring your embwa into my office?"

The Pygmy tenderly scooped up his dog. Then, proudly erect with almost a trace of a swagger, he walked by the doctor's side toward the private office, going to the front of a line of waiting African patients. Carl Becker was tempted to look back to survey the expressions on his infirmiers' faces, but it was a pleasure he did not need to indulge in.

In the following days he felt that the incident had at least some effect on the attitudes of the infirmiers. But he had also hoped that the Pygmy would pass along the word to others that he was treated with dignity and respect by the munganga. He had hoped that henceforth the Pygmies would know that they would be treated as human beings at Oicha.

But the Pygmies remained aloof. Of course, they came from time to time for treatment, but it was rare for one to be willing to be hospitalized. In such a case, he had to be bribed with promises of meat or chicken.

Carl Becker was fascinated by these little people. To him it was amazing how different they were from their neighboring African tribesmen. The Pygmies averaged about four feet in height. Their legs seemed very short in proportion to their bodies. Their round heads, widely set-apart eyes, broad flat noses and thin-lipped mouths were other noticeable features. Besides this, they were hairier than most Africans and were much more quick and nimble.

Carefree and friendly, they seldom saw the sun, did no work and lived on game they speared and trapped. They wore nothing but a scrap of bark or liana tied around their waists. The children often had swollen stomachs with navels jutting out in the shape of small pears.

While most of the African tribes lived in fear of the forest and dreaded the evil spirits which were said to inhabit it, the Pygmies felt at home in it and were completely happy-go-lucky in their attitude toward life. The forest was their world.

Born hunters, they lived and slept with their bows and arrows. When they came to the hospital at Oicha, their bows and arrows rested alongside their beds.

Because Pygmies were constantly on the go, missionary work among them had always been difficult. The traditional style of missionary approach had historically been centered around the mission station. A compound was built and the "natives" were invited in to hear the missionary's message. Evangelistic forays were made into the bush, but essentially the work was centered around the station with its large church, school and dispensary.

At one point, Jim Bell managed to recruit eight Pygmy boys and eight Pygmy girls—all eight to ten years old—for the Oicha mission school on the compound to be taught reading and religion. The children were also given appropriate small chores such as tending gardens, cooking and sewing. After a few months, all sixteen of them vanished without a sound into the night. They had gone back to their hunting groups. Jim Bell had learned his lesson. The traditional method of reaching Pygmies through a mission station wouldn't work.

Since the Pygmies wouldn't come to them, the Bells began living in the forest, spending weeks in the middle of the dense vermilion vastness. And when Carl and Marie Becker and others came to Oicha, Jim and Agnes Bell could spend more and more of their time out on safari. Day after day, they trekked through the jungle, winding through narrow paths, wading across streams, climbing over slippery logs, grabbing for vines to keep from falling and reaching thorn trees instead, crossing rivers of fallen trees made slippery by moss growth, and finally coming to a Pygmy village.

Upon arriving, Jim Bell would announce, "Listen, I have come to tell you some very good news. I want to live with you a while and teach you the words of *Mungu* (God). If you will clear a place in this brush and build me a house, I will pay you and give you salt and candy."

Camp groups, ranging anywhere from 30 to 100 in number, found it hard to sit still for Bell's sermons, but loved to sing choruses where they could act out the words. Though they were reluctant at first to memorize Bible verses, Bell found them excellent memorizers if the incentive was enticing enough. Soon they were chanting "Jesus loves me," and quoting over and over again, "Christ died for our sins according to the Scriptures."

But as Oicha's hospital grew and the station became more civilized, individualist Jim Bell moved his headquarters farther into the jungle to a Shangri-la named Biasiku, about 150 miles west of Oicha and closer to nowhere, in order to reach other Pygmies.

Taking the Bells' place at Oicha was Margaret Clapper, from an Evangelical and Reformed denominational background and trained at Chicago's Moody Bible Institute. At first, she too was at a loss as to how to best reach the Pygmies and what to do when she had reached them.

"I began," she explained, "by asking the village people where the camps were. They would tell me about those nearby. When the Pygmies learned that I was going to be their missionary they began coming to the station and asking me to come to their village, and every week I was finding new camps.

"Then I was faced with the problem of how to find the camps the second time, because when I would go back I found they had moved. No one could help me much because I had failed to get their names."

So she began to compile a veritable census of all the Pygmies she had talked to. When a name was written down, the Pygmy was asked if he had ever heard the gospel before and if he had accepted the Lord Jesus Christ as his Savior.

Roaming through a dense jungle of 16,000 square miles, Margaret Clapper recorded 4,000 names in her book and visited 140 different Pygmy camps. By this time, nearly one-third of the Pygmies had professed to accept Jesus Christ as their Savior, either as the result of Bell's preaching, Margaret Clapper's witness or the ministrations of the Oicha hospital. Throughout the Ituri forest, six Pygmy chapels were started and in each a school was begun.

While the frontier of the Pygmy work was in the jungle itself, the supply base was at Oicha. The healing ministry of Dr. Becker and his staff was of continual value to the effectiveness of the evangelistic outreach of Margaret Clapper and Jim and Agnes Bell.

Because of their dangerous outdoor life, Pygmies were frequently rushed in for emergency attention, gored by a forest buffalo, trampled by an elephant or fallen from a high tree. The record Pygmy stay at Oicha was six months when Bakaiku, hospitalized with tuberculosis of the spine, had to be operated on. Dr. Becker had taken a bone graft from his leg and put it into his back in a rare and delicate operation, requiring him to be placed in a stiff body cast for several months. Six months later Bakaiku could walk again, and the news of his recovery stirred the Pygmy world.

Most diseases the Pygmies tried to treat in their own way. If a Pygmy had a fever, the men of the camp would join together in digging a shallow grave. After lining it with leaves and herbs, they placed the ill person in the hole and covered him with more herbs and dirt, burying him completely except for his face. Sometimes even the face was covered loosely with twigs and leaves. In serious cases the treatment was continued for seven days. At the end of the period, the patient was either healed or dead. Those who came to the hospital were given special treatment by the *munganga*. Oblivious to his schedule, he sat beside his Pygmy patients and talked quietly, asking about their lives, their problems, their customs, their relatives and even about the Africans with whom they had working agreements.

"Tell me," the doctor asked one Pygmy, "why do you work for him?"

The Pygmy's eyes brightened. "Oh, *Bwana*, because he gives me salt and clothing and candy and food."

"Is he a good overlord?"

"Oh, yes, he is."

The doctor was thoughtful for a moment. He checked the walls to see if they needed to be whitewashed in the near future, and then returned to the Pygmy. "If you ever did something wrong and were arrested and put in jail, what would your overlord do then?"

The Pygmy raised his hand off the bed and pointed toward the doctor. "Do you know what he would do? He would go to that jail, and talk to the police and pay my fine and take me home with him."

It was the answer Dr. Becker was hoping he would receive. Now it was time to speak seriously to the patient. "Did you hear what Melona, the evangelist, said this morning?"

"I heard, *Bwana*." And then the Pygmy shook his head sadly. "But he spoke so fast and my head went so slow."

The doctor smiled. "He was saying that you have broken God's law and you will have to be punished because you are a sinner. But just as your overlord would pay your fine, so the Lord Yesu has paid your fine for breaking God's law. And just as your overlord intercedes with the police for you, so the Lord Yesu intercedes for you; and just as your overlord will take you out of jail to go home with him, so the Lord Yesu wants to take you home with Him."

The Pygmy's hand reached out to touch the hand of the doctor. "Do you have time to tell me more about this?"

Carl Becker thought of the footsteps he had heard in the hall and recognized them as those of one of his nurses. She undoubtedly had a question to ask. And probably some of his infirmiers had problems too. There were other patients to see, an inspection of the leprosy camp to make, several letters to write.

"Yes, I have time," the doctor said, "I have plenty of time to talk to you."

The trouble was there weren't enough Pygmies who stayed in the hospital long enough to talk to.

So Dr. Becker dispatched his nurses to the Pygmy villages on Sunday afternoons to tell them flannelgraph lessons of Bible stories. This not only was effective in proclaiming the gospel, but also in enabling the Pygmies to become better acquainted with the hospital staff.

Then Dr. Becker developed the idea of a special hospital ward just for Pygmies. If they could have an area all to themselves, maybe they wouldn't be so bashful about coming. Margaret Clapper was doubtful of the wisdom of it: the Pygmies might consider themselves herded off like animals rather than being treated like people. But she was willing to go along with the experiment.

Off on a hill, the hospital for Pygmies would be by itself so that the patients would not feel inhibited by the regulations of the rest of the hospital and could live their lives somewhat as they did in their Pygmy camps.

Dr. Becker knew the dangers of "segregating" patients just as well as Margaret Clapper. The Pygmies were as important as anyone else. "God measures the soul, not the body," he had said often enough.

But since the Pygmies certainly weren't flocking to Oicha with the present "integrated" plan, Dr. Becker could afford to experiment. Maybe it would work out better to build them a separate ward. So in early 1956, a three-room Pygmy dispensary was constructed.

The first disappointment came when only seventy-five Pygmies attended the dedication services, a disappointing turnout in view of the fact that Margaret Clapper had spread the word to as many Pygmy camps as she could. But then, after a short period of Pygmy indifference, the little dispensary suddenly became very popular. One boy was brought in trampled by an elephant, another was seriously ill with pneumonia, a third had fallen from a tree.

Through the first few months Pygmy interest came in spurts, and then gradually faded away. After a year of such sporadic attendance, Dr. Becker talked with Miss Clapper. "See if you can find out why they aren't coming."

Margaret Clapper did. She brought back the news that the Pygmies wanted to be treated like everyone else and with everyone else.

That settled it; the Pygmy dispensary was abandoned. Converting it into a TB sanitarium, Dr. Becker was more mystified than distressed. Yet he still deeply regretted that so few Pygmies felt at home at Oicha.

One of those Pygmies that did feel at home at the hospital was dwarf-sized Bingula. Dr. Becker took a personal concern for Bingula, and Bingula responded with a deep regard for the doctor. A strange Pygmy, he seemed always to show up at the most surprising times, peering through a window, jumping through a door, peeking around a tree, or as Dr. Becker himself put it, "like a dwarf who had hopped out of the pages of a storybook right into our home."

Bingula was a natural clown who had learned that his talent could be a profitable avocation. Nimble-tongued and a born mimic, he seemed always to produce laughter in any audience. He sounded more like a monkey than a monkey did, and he could imitate an elephant or a dog with surprising accuracy. One of his masterpieces was his imitation of a white man, an act that never failed to bring gales of laughter from the African villagers. And by the time he had completed his comedy routine, everyone seemed eager to give him a piece of food, rock salt, a bit of cloth or some other small gift.

Carl and Marie Becker spent hours trying to teach Bingula to read, instructing him in verses of Scripture, and explaining to him the simple facts of the Christian message.

Dr. Becker recalls: "As we saw him grow older and older and grayer and grayer, our desire increased accordingly. But it seemed as though no serious word or thought could enter that heart. If we said to him, 'God loves you,' or 'Christ died for your sins,' immediately like a parrot, he would say, 'God loves you' or 'Christ died for your sins'—until we almost despaired."

It seemed that Bingula had spent so many years filling his heart with foolishness that he had no room for anything else. His dark brown eyes were continually flashing; his mouth seemed always ready to break into a broad grin.

Could it be, Dr. Becker wondered, that he doesn't understand Swahili well enough to comprehend the gospel message? Like the African villagers, the Pygmies were usually conversant in two languages, the tribal language and the Swahili language of trade. The tribal language of the Pygmies was dependent upon which African tribe they were near; the Pygmies took the language and managed to corrupt it to their own usage. Bingula, for instance, knew both Swahili and Kibila, the language of the Babila tribe. The doctor surmised that Bingula could understand the Swahili language well enough to communicate, but not well enough to think philosophically.

The next time a missionary who spoke Kibila came to Oicha, Dr. Becker introduced him to Bingula the clown. For about an hour the two sat together under a huge date palm tree and talked about the Bible in the Kibila language.

At the supper table that evening the missionary told Dr. Becker, "I think he understands well enough."

"That's good to hear," responded the doctor, "but do you think he has put his faith in Jesus Christ?"

The missionary looked away. "I wish I could say for certain. But I do not know."

After that day Bingula went back into the forest, hunting, fishing, roaming, or tracking down beehives, and for several months he was not seen at the mission hospital. Then one morning as Dr. Becker was walking with swift, quiet, small strides to the dispensary, one of the African staff came running to him. "The clown is back."

"Oh, is he? I haven't seen him yet."

"That's because he's in the hospital."

The doctor raised his eyebrows.

"Pneumonia. But it doesn't seem too serious."

The doctor found him securely tucked between two warm blankets on a soft bed. Sulfa drugs were prescribed from the pharmacy.

Dr. Becker recalls: "In a few days he was begging me to permit him to return to his little leaf hut to *ota moto*" (warm myself by my fire). For Bingula this was a far greater luxury than sleeping under blankets in a comfortable bed.

But Bingula was aging and soon the word came to Oicha that he was rapidly failing in strength. Dr. Becker dispatched Melona, his hospital evangelist, to Bingula's Pygmy camp. Day after day, Melona returned to teach Bingula the Word of God and to teach him how to pray.

One afternoon Melona returned to the doctor's house and said, "*Munganga*, I feel quite sure now that Bingula is trusting in the Lord Jesus. He says that he is, and I believe him. But he is not well at all; in fact, Doctor, I don't think he will be alive tomorrow."

And it was the very next day that two young Pygmy boys came asking for Melona.

"What is wrong?" asked the doctor.

"Bingula has died."

The doctor was saddened. He had faced death frequently through his years of hospital work, but Bingula had come to be a friend.

"But before he died, *Munganga*," one Pygmy boy blurted out, "do you know what he said?"

Dr. Becker shook his head.

"Before he died he said, 'My soul is going to God.' "

"Thank you for telling me that, *mutoto* (little one). Thank you very much. But tell me, why do you want Melona?"

"We want Melona to come out and help us bury his body, and we want him to preach to us at the grave."

The doctor looked up. His eyes had begun to moisten. Never before had a Pygmy requested a Christian burial; never before had a Pygmy requested a sermon to be preached at his graveside. Bingula, the clown, was making him happy even after he died. Dr. Becker summoned Melona and soon the evangelist was hurrying off into the jungle trying to keep pace with the nimble Pygmy boys.

Late in the day, when Melona had returned from the funeral, Carl Becker asked him to tell him all about it.

Melona, with his Bible still tucked under his arm, said, "When I arrived at the camp, the grave still hadn't been dug. They were trying to dig with twigs and branches and it was taking them a long time. So

I ran to a village and borrowed a shovel to help them, and then it didn't take long."

"But tell me, Melona," Dr. Becker asked, "what kind of message did you give that those Pygmies could understand?"

Melona, with deep-set eyes and penetrating gaze, replied, "I took some dry kernels of corn along to the grave, because Pygmies know all about corn. And I asked them, 'When you bury this corn in the ground, what happens to the outer shell?' "

"And they all answered, 'It decays.' "

"Good, I said, and what happens to the inside of the kernel, the heart of the seed? Does that decay too?"

" 'No,' they shouted in unison, 'no, it doesn't die; it lives and grows and becomes big and good and turns into many kernels of corn.'

"Good, you have learned much about corn; and it is just so with Bingula. His outside, his body, will decay in this grave, but the inside, the spirit of Bingula, will live on and on and on and will continue forever because he believed in the Lord Jesus. He will have life forever, a full life, a happy life, a bigger life in heaven for ever and ever."

Carl Becker thought about the sermon long after Melona had gone, and he remembered another Pygmy who was asked, "If you die tonight, are you sure you will go to heaven?"

And the Pygmy looked up boldly into the missionary's face, slapped his heels together and replied, "When I die, I will go to God's village." Then raising his hand stiffly but militarily to his forehead, he continued. "And at God's village I will salute and say, 'Greetings, God, I am come to my house in Your village.' "

"And when God asks me what permission I have to enter, I will tell Him that His Son Jesus Christ died for me and washed my heart clean in His blood. And then He will tell me, 'Enter, your hut is waiting for you.' "

Carl Becker felt certain that for Bingula as well, a hut was waiting.

11

When Blood Types Match

"God . . . hath made of one blood all nations of men . . .
that they should seek the Lord"
PAUL, THE MISSIONARY, AS RECORDED BY LUKE, THE PHYSICIAN

Some smiled when Dr. Carl Becker first started a medical training course for Africans in 1933 at Aba. Was he foolish enough to think that he could train these Africans to become doctors in "ten easy lessons?"

There wasn't a medical college anywhere in Belgian Congo at the time—not even in the relatively civilized cities of Leopoldville, Elizabethville or Stanleyville. And here Dr. Becker was in primitive northeast Congo.

Actually, Carl Becker wasn't training Africans to be full-fledged doctors, but to be male nurses. He felt confident that Africans could be trained to relieve doctors of at least the more trivial matters that occupy so much of a medical missionary's time. He even envisioned the day when these Africans could be dispatched to outlying dispensaries and take charge of those visited only periodically by the doctor.

"Wishful thinking," said some of the more cautious missionaries. The African couldn't be trained like that. How could you take a boy from the forest with only three or four years of spotty grammar-school education, with a record of being irresponsible and undependable, with no disposition toward a scientific mind and make him perform without constant and careful supervision? It would be more trouble than it was worth.

And it was true that the training program was plenty of trouble. When Dr. Becker finally settled at Oicha in 1939 and resumed his medical training course again, most of his students had only a third-grade education. Classes were held in the afternoon, with the doctor teaching laboratory methods, the dressing of ulcers and how to diagnose and prescribe for the more common ailments. A careful teacher, he took time to explain details and had considerable patience with an African's inexperience.

Soon promising young men were sent from other A.I.M. stations to take Dr. Becker's training course. At the conclusion of it, they underwent examinations from the Belgian colonial government; those who passed received certificates as *Aide Infirmier.* Having finished their schooling at Oicha, they could handle nearly half of the cases which came to the hospital for help. Later, Carl Becker acknowledged the obvious when he said, "Without the help of these infirmiers it would have been impossible to carry on the ministry of Oicha."

Not only did he teach medical practice and procedure, but he supplemented the on-the-job training with an entire liberal-arts education as well. This he delighted in doing. His medical crew spent many evenings with him discussing subjects ranging from the ecumenical movement in religion to the philosophy of communism. In addition, he met regularly with them for intensive Bible study. But Carl Becker knew that the best teaching was done in life situations.

And an extremely disagreeable patient named Lazaro provided an excellent life situation.

Before the days of penicillin, tropical ulcers were particularly serious in the moist hot climate of central Africa, because they were extremely painful and extended rapidly with accompanying gangrene of the tissues. Lazaro was brought to Oicha suffering acutely from these ulcers.

Dr. Becker discussed the case carefully with the trainees. He stressed how serious it was. Indeed, Lazaro seemed destined to die. It was only a matter of time.

In one of their informal sessions a medical trainee asked, "Why do you show so much interest in Lazaro? He certainly is a most ornery patient, and since he will die anyway, we wonder why you spend so much time with him?"

"Is that what you are wondering?" the doctor responded quietly. "Or maybe you think I spend too much time with Lazaro since he comes from a low-caste tribe, a tribe you all despise."

There was no reply and the doctor knew he had scored a direct hit.

Two days later, Edna Amstutz brought word that Lazaro was sinking fast. His life was hanging by a thread. After examination, Dr.

Becker told his nurse to round up the medical students and check to see whose blood matched Lazaro's. He would need a transfusion.

Later, as the trainees lined up in Dr. Becker's office, he explained the situation to them. "Miss Amstutz will take blood samples from each of you to determine who will have the honor of giving blood to Lazaro."

He walked out the door to check again on Lazaro. On the way he saw Edna Amstutz and told her the boys were ready to have their blood samples taken. But minutes later, his nurse returned to him. "Where are they? They weren't in your office."

He had been afraid of that. He rounded them up again, said nothing about their evasion, but merely sat at his desk and looked at them while Edna took blood samples. He was keenly disappointed in them.

From the group, only one had blood to match that of Lazaro. He dismissed the others and spoke to the prospective blood donor. "Are you willing," he asked in almost a whisper, "to give your blood to save Lazaro's life?"

The African put his hands behind him, feeling the white-washed wall, groping for an exit. "You can't expect me to do that, *Munganga*. Maybe for someone else, but not Lazaro, not Lazaro."

The doctor sat with his head bowed a minute. Then speaking softly, "I can't force you to give your blood, but the patient is getting weaker every minute."

The infirmier shifted his weight uncomfortably to the other foot. He avoided the doctor's eyes and would not answer.

After an awkward silence, the doctor finally said, "We can't wait any longer. My blood type matches Lazaro's too." He took off his white jacket and began rolling up his sleeve. "You know how to take blood, don't you?"

The African nodded.

"Then I want you to take mine for Lazaro."

The medical boy seemed frozen to one spot. Then finally he almost exploded, "No, Munganga, no. You don't have to give your blood; I will give mine." As he walked to the doctor with his arm outstretched, he continued. "But I'm giving it for the Lord and not for Lazaro."

As his blood flowed into the bottle, he almost broke down in tears. "Oh the shame of it—for me, a Christian, to refuse my blood to a man of my own race when you were willing to give yours for him."

For several years the only African trainees were male, with one exception—the once-unwanted Alice Wentworth. Under Dr. Becker's training Alice rapidly took her place beside the qualified R.N.'s, such as missionaried Edna Amstutz and Lois Uhlinger. Then in the early 1940's Dr. Becker began training other girls for nursing.

At first, he took girls from the tribes surrounding Oicha, but for some reason these girls, while quick and bright, did not have the endurance needed for the duties of nursing. So he asked A.I.M. missionaries farther north if they could furnish him with some good prospects.

It was from a cattle-herding tribe north of Bunia that the hardiest girls came. Unlike the girls from the forest area, they were tall and husky. One of the girls in the first group was a six-footer, who provided quite a contrast to the Pygmy women of the area. But these girls were also characterized by stubbornness. When they were told that they would have to sleep under mosquito nets at Oicha because of the prevalence of malaria, they paid no attention. And one by one they succumbed to malaria, which sometimes evolved into deadly blackwater fever.

One of the girls was clinging to the edge of life for several days. During that time she was given eleven blood transfusions, as one by one the hospital staff volunteered to try to save her life. Dr. Becker spent hours at her side in attempts to improve her condition, to no avail.

One morning, seven or eight European cars were driven to the Oicha hospital, some driven by Belgian officials who had come to the doctor for his expert medical attention. Not wishing to be attended to by the African infirmiers, they decided to wait a few minutes until the doctor could see them. But it stretched on longer than just a few minutes.

The Belgians who ruled the Congo, were not accustomed to waiting, and they asked a missionary nurse, "Where is Doc-tor Beck-air? What is keeping him so long?"

The nurse replied apologetically, "I am sorry, but there is an African girl who is very ill, and he is trying to save her life."

Hour after hour went by, and the temper of the Europeans escalated. But the doctor was not to be disturbed. The infirmiers and the nurses, going about their duties, watched with amusement the growing aggravation of the Europeans. And all the time their admiration for Dr. Becker was expanding.

Dr. Carl K. Becker visits the Africa Inland Mission headquarters at Brooklyn during his short furlough in 1963. *Gene Phillips, American Leprosy Missions*

Congolese men chanting and beating a stick to keep time near A.I.M.'s Rethy Station in Congo. *David Hornberger*

But there were more serious complications too. The missionaries understood very well what they were. The medical-training program had to be approved by the Belgian colonial government. Didn't the doctor realize how important it was to stay in the government's good graces? So they dispatched an infirmier with a note reminding the doctor that the Europeans were becoming impatient. And the doctor replied somewhat curtly, "They can wait; this girl cannot."

The infirmier started to leave, but was called back by the doctor. "See if there is anyone else whose blood matches that of this girl. She needs another transfusion immediately."

Alice Wentworth returned with veteran missionary Olive Love, who had labored for years at the Blukwa mission station from which these nurse trainees had come. She had taught them how to read, how to write and how to pray; one by one she had introduced them to Jesus Christ. And now she lay down at the side of one of them; slowly her blood coursed into the veins of the dying African girl.

The doctor waited patiently by the bedside, finally noting improvement in the girl's condition. The tide had turned at last. The girl began to recover. And it was a day that the African infirmiers and girl nurses could never forget—a day when bwana munganga made the Europeans wait for hours so he could watch over an African girl, and a day when the twelfth pint of blood from a veteran missionary had brought a stubborn nurse-in-training back to health.

As a teacher, Dr. Becker was a strange amalgam of infinite patience, inveterate optimism and nearly impossible standards. At times he seemed utterly unrealistic in giving repeated "last chances" to an African trainee who had proved totally incorrigible, irresponsible or completely immoral. Missionary nurses who found an African helper to be completely substandard would go to Dr. Becker to have the African fired, but the doctor instead would advise them to give the boy one more chance, or to pray about it some more. As a last resort the nurses deviously arranged to have the boy transferred to work directly with the doctor. It was here that his exacting medical standards clashed with his infinite patience and inveterate optimism. In such cases, his medical standards usually won out. For to Dr. Becker, there was no excuse for practicing a brand of medicine in Oicha that he would be ashamed of practicing in Philadelphia.

When the Beckers went on their second missionary furlough in 1944, Alice Wentworth—along with Edna Amstutz—was left at Oicha to carry on the medical work, while Jim Bell and Owen Brand looked after other areas of the Oicha ministry. With 400 to 500 Africans coming daily for help, Alice often went out and took ten deep breaths and then came back to tackle one job at a time, as Dr. Becker had previously counseled her.

She described her reactions thus: "When I was a few years younger, I loved to catch those big, blood-sucking buffalo flies on the windowpanes, decapitate them, and let them loose to fly about crazily. They would zoom about upside down in a gremlinesque manner and finally tailspin into a landing.

"That's the way we are without Dr. Becker—flying around upside down, leaping the loop, tailspinning, and going through all the blind gyrations of a doctorless medical work.

"One of the front-porch infirmiers, who diagnoses and does simple operations, came in with a handful of cards. 'Some of these people are ready to be discharged,' he announced triumphantly.

"Any little tropical ulcer or stubborn case of yaws that responds to treatment these days seems like a reward from heaven. In the old days while the doctor was here, anything too hard for us we took to him. But now we must get our heads together, not to mention all the books, and try by ourselves.

"The other day the Lord called home the small son of one of our medical boys. As we followed the little coffin to the grave, you can understand how our weak minds had the thought: 'If Doctor had been here, Mika might not have died.'

"But even as the thought took shape, we recalled those other two who said, 'Lord, if thou hadst been here . . .' and we know the Lord was here and is here. Even though we are doctorless at present, we still have the Lord. He has been and ever will be very, very good to us in a thousand ways."

Not long after Dr. Becker's return from his second missionary furlough, troubles with his African medical-training program began to mount. The Belgian colonial government, imposing more stringent standards and stiffer examinations upon the Oicha graduates, threatened the very existence of the school. Always before, a graduate of Oicha would receive a government-approved certificate as a licensed *Aide Infirmier,* recognized anywhere in Congo. Now, as the government began boosting its standards, many of the Oicha graduates were flunking the tests.

The fault did not lie in Dr. Becker's standards, which were exacting, but in the previous education of the trainees, who were all products of A.I.M. schools. The mission's educational policies were being drastically challenged at the time because of a new Belgian colonial policy. In earlier days, the Belgian government had subsidized only the Roman Catholic schools in Congo. But shortly after the Second World War, a progressive Belgian minister of education suddenly ruled that Protestant schools, which were educating about half the Congolese, should also receive government subsidy. The action caught the missions by surprise, and while most Protestant missions accepted the subsidy without question, the Africa Inland Mission and others strongly influenced by American church-state separation concepts refused and held out against subsidization for several years. Limited to unsolicited donations, the A.I.M. education could not keep pace with the rapidly escalating government standards.

Indirectly, Dr. Becker's medical-training program at Oicha felt the sting.

As the government began closer inspection of hospital education, another problem loomed. Provincial medical officers became arbitrary and officious. One of these, if he was opposed to Protestant missions, could devise even stiffer regulations or switch the language of the examination from the native Swahili to the official French.

Oicha and the Conservative Baptist missionary work directly south of Oicha (in 1943, the Conservative Baptist Foreign Missionary Society had taken over the mission stations and several of the missionaries of the Unevangelized Africa Mission) were both supervised by a district medical officer who was pronouncedly anti-Protestant. To the north, the A.I.M. hospitals at Rethy and Aba, as well as the Plymouth Brethren Immanuel Mission hospital at Nyankunde were supervised by a district medical officer who was much more favorable to Protestants.

Concerned by the problem, Carl Becker called together at Oicha other doctors from the Conservative Baptist Mission, the Immanuel Mission and the A.I.M. for a weekend conference late in 1953. The problem of certification for Congolese medical trainees was on top of the agenda.

Since Nyankunde was supervised by an unprejudiced medical officer and since a second doctor was scheduled to join the staff there in the near future, A.I.M. and Conservative Baptist doctors decided to send their medical trainees there until the situation improved in their district.

Discussion of this issue led naturally to the next item on Dr. Becker's agenda—the need for better cooperation among the three missions. He suggested that the ideal solution to the problem would be to launch an inter-mission medical-training school, with joint control as well as cooperation from all the missions involved. No doubt, other missions serving in northeast Congo would also be interested in such a project.

While he eagerly explored the possibility and the other doctors agreed with him about the value of such an inter-misson hospital, they did not all share his optimism. Would any mission board relinquish one of its own hospitals, and allow it to be operated by men of various denominations, boards and missionary philosophies?

"Impossible," said one man vigorously.

"Watch out when you say the word 'impossible' in front of Dr. Becker," another cautioned him.

To all but Dr. Becker, an inter-mission medical-training school for northeast Congo was a forgotten figment of his imagination.

Not only did some missionaries challenge Dr. Becker's views on training Africans, but others did not see eye-to-eye with him regarding what they saw as his "exaggerated role of medical missions."

They said, "Our job is to preach the gospel, to get the heathen saved. Education and medicine are only means to the end—the end is the salvation of the heathen. Certainly, we need doctors. Doctors can take care of the missionaries who are engaged in evangelistic ministries. Doctors can sometimes soften the hearts of pagans in totally unreached areas and prepare the way for the evangelist even as John the Baptist prepared the way for the Lord. But it is Biblically wrong to give medicine such a prominent role in the missionary enterprise. We should be training our young men for evangelism; instead, all of them seem to be running off to Dr. Becker's medical-training school. They should learn how to be Bible teachers, not doctors. How many souls can an African male nurse save anyway?"

Without formal Bible education in a mission which required it of its candidates, Dr. Becker often felt inferior to other missionaries in this area and their charges bothered him greatly. Maybe they are right, he thought.

Yet he knew how his infirmiers witnessed daily to the patients they served. He knew also of the spiritual results from the faithful preaching each morning by Melona, the hospital evangelist. And he delighted to hear their testimonies when they returned late on a Sunday afternoon from their speaking engagements in surrounding villages.

Thin, angular Melona, for example, tucked his well-worn New Testament and a hymnbook under his arm every Sunday afternoon and marched jauntily to some small village in the Ituri forest. On the way he heard the continuous drumbeat and the hollow-sounding Pygmy whistles, signaling a native beer dance. He pushed aside branches that threatened to slap him and leaped from rock to rock across small streams.

Finally he reached a thatched-roof village. In front of the houses, women were pounding out the acrid-smelling manioc, a mainstay of their diet. In the round-roofed palaver house, men were smoking their hemp pipes. He waved to them, trying to collect them for a church service. Some looked disinterested, but one by one they came around him and squatted on the ground. When most of them had gathered, Melona bowed his head to pray and his audience copied him. Then enthusiastically, they joined in a hymn.

After singing, Melona lifted his hand for silence; all eyes were riveted on his intent face. He spoke slowly, deliberately, searching out the eyes, seemingly looking into the hearts of the villagers. "My mother and my father worshiped Satan. One day I woke up very sick. I was too sick to carry water, so my father called for the mufumu. Into the door of our one-room house came an old wizened man. Feathers were stuck into a band about his head. Animal horns and claws dangled from his neck and waist. Bells clinked and he had a leather bag full of many different things."

The men squatting on the ground nodded. They too had such experiences.

The evangelist paused briefly, looked over his audience and then continued. "A small hole was dug in the earth. Stones were placed around it, and each stone was given the name of someone in the village. Now the mufumu would find out who was causing my sickness. The mufumu chopped off the head of the chicken, and the chicken's body ran crazily around the hole, bleeding heavily and finally it collapsed on one of the stones. The mufumu called out the name of the man whose name had been given to the stone. And that man was very, very much afraid. That man spit into a leaf which the mufumu mixed with chicken blood and he applied it to my forehead and heart. Then they did the same thing over again and finally the

124 Another Hand on Mine

mufumu threw the chicken over his shoulder. This is the way that the mufumu thought he could save me from the power of the evil spirits." Melona paused again. The men of the village were more serious now and the evangelist breathed a prayer, asking that God's Holy Spirit would touch the hearts of these villagers. He began fingering his New Testament before he began again. A few women were still pounding away at the manioc, though most were now listening. Babies were squalling, and in the jungle trees brilliant little birds chatted irreverently back and forth. Thumbing through his New Testament, the young evangelist began speaking again.

"One day a Christian teacher came to my village. And all of my friends were gathered around him; just as you have gathered around me this afternoon. And he opened the Book of God, just as you see me opening my Book of God. Then he read this verse—listen very, very carefully." His eyes looked up from his Bible and dug deeply into the throng around him. They were waiting for his next word.

"Listen, because this is what the Book of God says: 'Neither by the blood of goats or calves' "—he looked up quickly and added— "and neither by the blood of chickens"—the villagers stirred somewhat uneasily—"No, not by the blood of any animals but by the blood of the Son of God, Jesus Christ, can we be delivered from the power of Satan." He closed the Bible again.

"That day I believed in the Lord Jesus Christ as my own Savior." The intense evangelist went on, sometimes motioning swiftly toward heaven, and sometimes pointing deeply into the earth. Within a few minutes his African sermon was finished and he asked, "How many of you will do what I did? How many of you will stop trusting in the blood of chickens and the dawa (magic) of the mufumu and put your trust in the blood of Jesus Christ to take away your sin?" One hand was raised in front of him, and then he spotted another off to the side.

"And I know some of you, some of you who became Christians the last time I was here. What have you been doing? Have you been living as a Christian should? Have you been living as the munganga mukubwa has told us?" It was the only reference to a missionary in his entire presentation.

Slowly, two men rose to their feet, quietly slinking away to their huts and then returning in a few seconds. One brought a pipe, the other an animal skin and some fetishes purchased from the witch doctor. Solemnly they handed these symbols of their paganism to Melona.

They knew what came next. Melona built a bonfire, and amulets and fetishes and the witch doctor's dawa (magic) were thrown in. Once the fire was started, others went back to their huts and returned with their symbols of backsliding.

As the fire died down and the twilight threatened, Melona was on his way back to Oicha. Others of the hospital corps had gone in other directions that day; the nurses to the Pygmy village and the "Big Doctor" a few miles north of Oicha. On his hike back Melona wondered what spiritual victories they would share together tonight as they all gathered at the Becker home and rehearsed the events of the day.

Dr. Becker too had been evangelizing a village. Not fashioning himself as a polished public speaker, he often took a blackboard with him and drew crude stick drawings on a board to illustrate a Bible story. He made no claim to be an artist either, but was concerned about communicating the gospel to the African. Women were often distracted by crying babies; the diseased were often more concerned about their own maladies than about the gospel. And he was all too well aware that the traditional sermon by an American missionary often went over the heads of many Africans. It wasn't merely a matter of the proper choice of Swahili words; often it was the way that western imagery beclouded the Bible stories. So Dr. Becker adapted the details to make more sense in an African context.

In the story of the rich man and Lazarus, he depicted the rich man smoking his long pipe and sitting with crossed legs on a chair in front of an African hut. The African understood that only a very rich man would own a chair; his crossed legs indicated his boorishness.

At first the doctor had experimented with traditional Sunday-school story pictures from the United States, but these usually confused the African more than they helped him. When he began drawing his own crude stick figures, the response was gratifying. After the meetings, Africans requested copies of them so they could remember the story. And soon Dr. Becker acceded to their requests, mimeographing his drawings and distributing them to the Africans who came to the meeting. Because most could not read the Bible for themselves, the stick-figure Bible story served as a potent reminder of the Biblical message. Eventually, the doctor had stick-figure drawings that illustrated most of John's Gospel, the Acts and the stories of the first books of the Old Testament.

To the older people of the area who could not read and had no hope of ever learning to read, the doctor's innovation was exciting.

They took the mimeographed pictures into neighboring villages and "read" the picture stories to their friends.

One day as Dr. Becker was walking through the town of Beni, he spotted a crowd around a Congolese soldier in the middle of the road. As the doctor joined the crowd to see what was going on, he recognized that the soldier was using one of his mimeographed Bible picture stories. Several months earlier, he had used the pictures at a nearby military camp. This particular soldier, chagrined that he could not read, had been eager to obtain a set of the doctor's pictures. And now months later, he was still reciting the story accurately and enthusiastically to an African gathering in the middle of the road.

But despite such successes in sharing the gospel with others, Dr. Becker knew that he was primarily not a Bible teacher but a doctor. Certainly there was tremendous need all about him—thousands afflicted with leprosy, major emergency operations daily, diseases of all kinds that needed skilled medical attention—but above the busy schedule Dr. Becker was continually asking himself the question, "What is the spiritual value of all this?" It was a question he had not asked himself during the first years of his missionary service. He had come to Africa because of a boyhood promise he had made to God and because he had been impressed with the great need for missionary doctors. Never before had he troubled himself with the question, "What is the spiritual value of all this?"

So he studied his Bible more diligently. After having poured over the latest medical journals, counseled an African family or perhaps listened to a Penn-Cornell football game on short wave until nearly midnight, he would rise at 5 A.M. the next morning and spend an hour in Bible study and prayer.

As he sought guidance from the Lord, his eyes spotted James 2:15-17, verses that took on fresh meaning for him: "If a brother or sister be naked, and destitute of daily food, And one of you say unto them Depart in peace, be ye warmed and filled; notwithstanding ye give them not those things which are needful to the body; what doth it profit? Even so faith, if it hath not works, is dead, being alone."

It would seem, thought Dr. Becker, that evangelism alone is not enough. Like faith, it was dead without the needed services to meet the physical needs of the people. He was not saying that educational and medical missions were essential in every place, but in many places—and northeast Congo was one—it was "an essential outworking of love," as he called it. "Medical work and that of secular education," he wrote, "are to be governed by the necessities of life for those to whom the missionary is sent."

Yes, after praying about it, Dr. Becker felt strongly that there was spiritual value in medical work. In fact, far from imagining that medical work was only the soil-breaker for the seed—only the John the Baptist for the Messiah—he came to see it was a complete missionary ministry. It was an opportunity for mass evangelism, for where else could he find several hundred needy Africans each day, coming from distant places to one site where the gospel could be preached? It was also an opportunity for Christian nurture. With the in-patients he had a chance to help young Christians grow in their Christian life, to provide a sort of hot-house climate for young plants. And Dr. Becker felt, too, that it was an unparalleled opportunity to build a responsible African church.

It was perhaps in this last area where the doctor incurred the most opposition. A progressive in his dealings with Africans, he encouraged them to do their own thinking, to stand on their own feet. A co-worker said, "He welcomed their growing maturity. He gave them jobs to do and expected them to work. He didn't sit over them watching. Some responded to this and some didn't. I'm not denying that Dr. Becker had his share of failures, but his successes were remarkable."

One day, as a visiting mission leader was walking down the station road with Dr. Becker, one of the African infirmiers approached them. "I think I recognize that fellow," the visiting missionary commented. "He had a bad reputation up North—insolent, surly, and you couldn't trust him out of your sight."

"Maybe so," said the doctor with a shrug, "but he's one of our most trusted staff members now." Then he called the infirmier over.

The mission leader boldly asked some questions about the infirmier's former life and then asked him, "Why has your life changed since coming to Oicha?"

The African looked at Dr. Becker a second and then back to the mission leader before replying. Finally he said, "Many missionaries had preached Jesus Christ to me, and many missionaries had taught Jesus Christ to me, but in the *munganga* I have seen Jesus Christ."

12

Conquering
Public Enemy Number One

*"My greatest experience on the mission field is meeting
impossible circumstances with Someone who makes them possible.
It is the deep thrill that comes from facing something you know you
can't do—and finding your weakness suddenly turned into strength.
That's something exciting."* DR. CARL K. BECKER

When Dr. Becker first set foot in Africa in 1929, the incidence of
leprosy in Africa's equatorial belt was the highest in the world, in
some areas infecting as much as 40 per cent of the population. To
Africans, no words were more dreaded than "You have leprosy."
Once these words were pronounced, they became outcasts, left to die
alone in the forest or at best to join other outcasts eking out a bare
existence awaiting their fate—gradual disintegration and finally
death.

Nearly every African mission station carried on some kind of leprosy program. It seemed inevitable. Here were people who had no
place else to turn for help; furthermore, the sufferers often responded
readily to the gospel because the mission station was the only place
in their dismal world where they found love.

Sometimes there wasn't much the mission station could give them
besides love. And sometimes the leprosy asylum was scarcely anything more than an isolation area where the patients could be shut
away from the world's gaze.

Carl Becker often recalled the statement of a Belgian prospector,
shortly after he had arrived in Africa: "My men tell me you have
medicine for everything but leprosy."

Everything but leprosy. In 1930 this was not quite true: there
were other diseases for which there were no known cures, but none
that so ravaged Africa as leprosy.

When he had first come to Belgian Congo, sleeping sickness had swept through whole villages and decimated entire populations. Now, because of his ministrations and those of others like him, sleeping sickness had been virtually wiped out. Epidemics of yellow fever and smallpox, which could take thousands of lives within a few weeks, were now largely plagues of the past. And yaws, those acutely painful raspberrylike sores that eat away flesh like fire and result in mutilation and horrible disfigurement, could be treated by modern medicines. Pneumonia, that periodically swept through village after village thinning out families and tribes, had been stopped in its tracks again and again. When Dr. Becker arrived in Congo, nearly 50 per cent of the babies died at birth or shortly thereafter, and the mortality rate for mothers was also startlingly high. But at Oicha the mortality rates at childbirth had been cut virtually to zero. Even the ravages of malaria and blackwater fever had been radically reduced.

But leprosy was different. Dr. Becker pored over the medical journals in hopes of finding a breakthrough for treating this disease. He subscribed to several medical publications and each month experimented with some new treatment that had been discussed in them. In fact, his nurses always feared what would happen the day after a medical journal arrived. His whole procedure might suddenly be changed. To Dr. Becker, if Oicha could become more efficient and effective, it would be worth the trouble to change the procedures every day.

But though he worked closely with the American Leprosy Missions and other leprosy societies, he could discover no startling cures for leprosy.

Among Dr. Becker's earliest patients were many with the telltale signs of leprosy's onset. Usually the rash appeared as a red raised flush, frequently on the face. In the more contagious cases, a thickening took place in the skin, producing smooth, rounded nodules. The disease, apparently not the same as Biblical leprosy, attacked the skin and peripheral nerves. As the nerve endings of the hands and feet lost their feeling the muscles tended to atrophy; the limbs themselves, injured repeatedly because there was no feeling in them, often became mutilated.

Dr. Becker saw many of these cases come to him with clawed hands, mutilated stumps where fingers or toes had once been, with

furnished food at one time for more than ten to twenty seriously sick or crippled."

The cripples were the ones on whom Edna Amstutz showered her love. "My poor," she called them, and she parceled out flour and fish, rice and salt, and palm fat to each one.

The only medicine available was chaulmoogra oil, supplied in quantity by the American Leprosy Missions. While treatment with chaulmoogra oil offered some help to the sufferers, it was a long and tedious process, requiring a course of painful injections. The percentage of leprosy cases arrested by this means was relatively small.

"There is no cure for leprosy," the tropical-medicine books said. But Dr. Becker, not believing anyone who said "It can't be done," experimented with various dosages of the medicine, often exceeding the amount recommended by leprologists. He knew from his reading in the subject that patients in Asia differed from those in Africa, so he thought by experimentation he might develop a process that would improve the effectiveness of chaulmoogra oil in Congo. Keeping careful records of the reactions among various patients, he found that he could restore pigmentation with his own formula and could reduce even the more severe cases of leprosy.

By exchanging notes with other medical missionaries around the world he learned what advances they had been making with their experimentation. His own African infirmiers were trained in recording the research information. Leprosy was a tricky and trying disease to treat. Some cases seemed to cure themselves. Others cleared up under treatment and showed no bacillus in the blood, only to relapse later. Others were negative for years, while still others remained heavily positive after long treatment.

Although Dr. Becker seemed to have lower rates of relapse than most medical missionaries with whom he corresponded, he wasn't happy. Why should this disease be so reluctant to yield to treatment?

Then during the Second World War came the exciting news that Promin had been tried with encouraging results at the U.S. Public Health leprosarium in Carville, Louisiana. Shortly thereafter other sulphone derivatives became available at low cost.

Immediately after the war Dr. Becker received word that the American Leprosy Missions had selected his Oicha medical work for experiments with the promising new drugs. The mission was sending him $1000 worth of diasone, as well as money for the construction of ten new leprosy houses.

Becker was thrilled. Faithfully he kept notes on the progress of the new drugs, which he gave by mouth as well as by the usual injection. During the next few years his results were dramatic. In many cases leprosy lesions cleared up rapidly; bacilli disappeared; relapses were few.

Becker's notes were made available to other medical missionaries and leprologists in Africa, India, Britain, and America. In 1950 he asserted that "leprosy is both arrestable and preventable." Better still, he was able to assure patients that if they would stick conscientiously to their treatment, their chance of being rid of their leprosy was very good indeed.

As Oicha's amazing successes in the healing of leprosy became known, the population of the leprosy village doubled, then tripled in size. Patients poured in, even from more than 700 miles away, coming from Uganda, Rwandi, Burundi, Tanganyika, and all parts of the Congo. By 1951, Dr. Becker had at Oicha more than 4,000 leprosy patients who with their families comprised a village of more than 10,000—the largest leprosarium in Africa, second largest in the world.

The 1,100-acre leprosy village expanded much more systematically than did the main hospital center itself. Laid out almost as a planned suburban subdivision, there were fifteen streets, each ranging from one-half to one mile long, lined with neatly spaced native huts. Each street had its own water supply and each family its own shamba. From seeds supplied by the Beckers, villagers grew three crops a year of lush vegetables and made their surroundings gay with colorful flower beds. Because one of the prominent tribes in the area had a rule that a man must pay in goats for his bride, the village was overrun with goats.

Dr. Becker set the village up as a self-governing community. It had its own community council composed of ten elders, that settled the affairs of the camp. If someone's goat got into another's field or garden and caused damage, the problem was brought to the African court. There were sometimes cases of assault and battery or arguments about dowry or bride prices. Sometimes there were more serious matters such as adultery. Cases judged were put on record and signed by the missionary nurse to become valid. Difficult cases were brought to Dr. Becker.

"Why in the world," asked a visitor in Oicha, "has everyone come to this place? Are the results that spectacular?"

The doctor tried to reply as objectively as possible. "I think that's only part of it," he said, sinking his hands deeply into his side pockets as he spoke. "Certainly when they saw that results were taking place, they began coming in droves. But that wasn't all. The leprosy work grew because leprosy patients are treated like people here. Self-respect means a lot to them, and when they are growing their crops, living in their own houses, and paying at least partially for their own medical treatment, they feel like human beings."

As the leprosarium mushroomed, the Belgian government, taking further notice of the work there, began helping with expenses. Late in October, 1953, two Belgian administrators questioned Dr. Becker as they strolled through the leprosy village. By the time they had seen half of it, they were so impressed that they said, "Dr. Becker, we are planning to recommend that the colonial government grant you $25,000 for the work of your leprosy camp."

Twenty-five thousand dollars? That was nearly his annual budget for entire medical work at Oicha, and the leprosy program was only a small percentage of the whole. But while the major medical facility was in dire need as usual, the leprosy camp, thanks to the support of the American Leprosy Missions, was in satisfactory financial shape. So in candor he finally replied, "To be honest, I don't know if we really need $25,000 for our leprosy program."

"You can't be serious. To handle those thousands of leprosy patients you must have a tremendous budget."

"No," contradicted Dr. Becker. "Our leprosy budget is rather small. You see, we don't feed and clothe the patients; they provide for themselves."

"Ah, but how wonderful it would be if the government could help them."

"They don't need help. They can take care of themselves." Dr. Becker could see that the Belgian administrators didn't comprehend his policy. At length he concluded, "Let us think it over, and we will write and tell you what we think we could use."

With veteran nurse Edna Amstutz on furlough, her niece Vera Thiessen, a second-term missionary nurse from Detroit, substituted at the leprosy camp, and the doctor consulted her.

They agreed that they didn't want the government permanently to provide food and clothing for the lepers. Not only would subsidization tend to make the leprosy patients wards of the state and thereby be detrimental to their psychological welfare, it would also tend to make the mission's leprosy program dependent on the state. And Becker wanted no part in such a dependency. There was only one Person on whom the doctor wished to be dependent.

Finally they agreed to accept a grant from the government to construct a little hospital at the leprosy camp. Until then, the leprosy patients had to go to the station hospital for any treatment not directly related to their leprosy. Besides that, some additional money could be used to supply food, supplies, and clothing to those whose cases were so serious that they were unable to make gardens for themselves. The government insisted on sending them fish also; Dr. Becker countered by accepting it only on the condition that "we be allowed to sell it at a reduced rate rather than to give it outright."

Vera Thiessen, competent, hard-working and efficient, handled a double load during Edna Amstutz's furlough. She described her initiation at the leprosy camp in a letter to her parents:

After the first week, I am just beginning to realize what a tremendous job I have gotten into. Doctor has so little time he can spend over at the leprosy camp that much falls on my shoulders. The mornings are completely filled just writing up treatments for the leprosy patients whom I see only once a month when they get their prescriptions rewritten. In the afternoon, there are a variety of things to do. Yesterday it was measuring locations for new houses and seeing that the empty ones were occupied and sold to their new owners at a proper price.

Today is the day Doctor makes his weekly visit over there. He is playing with cultures trying to grow leprosy bacillus, and I have been sort of willed the job of carrying it on. At the same time he presented me with a camera to take pictures in a microscope, so you can see that any evenings I have will be filled. Thursday afternoon is baby clinic and Friday I am going to take the wives of the medical boys for Bible study and personal work in the leper camp. Saturday I have to spend going with one of the boys to see if all the lepers have outhouses and are working on their houses, keeping them repaired or else finishing the building of them. I had to stop and laugh to myself wondering how it would look in writing to say I spent the afternoon inspecting outhouses.

As organized by Dr. Becker, the leprosy camp was guided by Nurse Thiessen, his trusted African infirmiers, and some eighteen leprosy patients trained to assist in passing out medicines and applying dressings. Pills were handed out three at a time to 700 patients a day.

For a while they dispensed pills in larger quantities, but when it was discovered that patients saved their pills and sold them, making a healthy profit from them, the more rigid system was instituted. Thereafter the leprosy patient, on being given the pills, had to swallow them in full view of an infirmier. Actually, three infirmiers were used in the pill-dispensing production line. One infirmier handled the records, another gave out the pills, and a third supplied a water tube, squirted a stream of water into the patient's mouth and observed whether the patient swallowed or not. For sanitary reasons, drinking glasses or cups could not be used.

Hardly had Vera Thiessen learned her way around the leprosy metropolis than Dr. Becker was asked to present a paper to an international Christian Leprosy Conference in Lucknow, India. The doctor had corresponded with some of the world's outstanding leprologists, but now he had a chance to meet them and discuss his problems with them. Among these problems were the care of children of patients, the prevention of deformities, and the rehabilitation of arrested cases.

In his paper, which dealt with the question of financial support for leprosy work, he discussed how the work was carried on at Oicha—nearly self-supporting except for a modicum of help from the Congo government and medical aid from the American Leprosy Missions. "With little help the patients have provided themselves with good housing and clothing," he reported. "Available resources of money and time have been concentrated on spiritual ministry and medical care."

But Dr. Becker felt a bit uneasy in the company of so many men who had devoted their lives to leprosy. He didn't consider himself a leprologist. He was not a specialist. He was almost ashamed to mention that he spent only one day a week at the leprosy camp; the rest of the time the work was handled by his nurse and his African infirmiers.

Not considering himself an authority, Dr. Becker had gone there to learn. What fascinated him most were the new techniques of surgical rehabilitation of leprosy victims through nerve operations, skin and tendon transplants, and plastic surgery. In the past it had been assumed that leprosy sufferers would inevitably lose the use of hands and feet, and that once the disease had done its damage nothing could be done to restore the limbs to usefulness. Dr. Becker knew that leprologists now were challenging this assumption.

Day by day he jotted down notes for new procedures and practices to be tried at Oicha. When he returned, the staff, both American and African, gathered in the Becker living room to hear. They knew what was coming. It was bad enough when he read medical journals and decided to employ a new medical tactic. "But just think," said Yonama, an African infirmier who always had a comment on everything, "he has been with seventy-five doctors for a whole week. Everything is going to be changed."

Not everything. But the leprosy program was certainly drastically altered. Vera Thiessen, still swimming in the ocean of detail that Aunt Edna had learned to float in, wrote home to her parents the next day: "I feel almost breathless after having spent the afternoon with him at the leprosy camp. As I feared, we are having one grand revolution beginning tomorrow. In some ways some of the things we have been doing will be simplified but in their place are a dozen and one new things that will take teaching and supervising. We are going to try to train as many leprosy patients as possible and thus eliminate the need to draw on as many infirmiers, but there will be so many new records to keep and all the old ones brought up to date with the new data he wants to include."

The doctor increased his visits to the leprosy camp to three times a week and initiated new treatments. Immediately Vera Thiessen began working with patients with deformed hands, massaging and exercising them.

The leprosy patients couldn't understand what the purpose of the hand exercising was. "We hope that we will be able to restore your hand so that it will be normal again," explained Miss Thiessen.

The newer patients laughed. It was ridiculous to think that a leprosy patient would be able to regain the use of a hand. But the older patients had seen too many miracles at Oicha to laugh. They remembered when leprosy sufferers came to Oicha to stay. Now there were almost as many who were discharged as were admitted for treatment, although Dr. Becker was beginning to have difficulty getting his cured patients to leave the premises.

After a series of hand exercises which lasted for several weeks, the leprosy patients were ready for their hand operations.

The first attempt was on a middle-aged Munandi whose ulcerated feet had been deeply infected. His fingers had curled into a completely useless claw. It seemed impossible that this African would ever be able to use his hands again. But according to leprologist

Robert Cochrane, the tissues of leprosy patients are capable of responding to surgery despite the destructive action of the disease. Dr. Paul Brand had proved this in Vellore, India; now Dr. Becker had to prove it in Oicha, Belgian Congo.

Muscles would have to be taken from elsewhere in the hand and transplanted. Following the same technique Paul Brand had demonstrated, he made a midlateral incision on each side of the finger, baring the lumbrical tendon. Then freeing the healthy sublimis tendon, he split it into two parts. One part he put back in place; the other was retunneled in the fingers and substituted for the paralyzed muscles. After closing the wound and applying the dressings, he put the fingers in a light plaster splint.

The first such operations took him nearly two hours to do, but soon he cut his operating time down to forty-five minutes. It still seemed too long to him.

One of the problems was the lack of proper instruments. Unwilling to wait out the long delay in ordering them from a supply house in America, he began looking for a substitute. That night after supper, he had an idea; turning to his wife, he asked, "Marie, do you still have some crochet hooks around?"

When she brought them to him, he inspected them carefully and then said, "I think you have just solved a big problem." Because all the structures in the hand and fingers were so small, the crochet hooks seemed the ideal surgical instrument. The next week he experimented with them; his operation was further reduced to thirty-five minutes.

After a succesful hand operation, the patient reported to Vera Thiessen for more hand exercises. Gradually, after nearly two months of physiotherapy, fingers that had long before been pronounced dead came back to renewed life and usefulness again.

About five months after he began repairing hands, Dr. Becker decided to venture into another new area of corrective operation for leprosy patients—nerve surgery. The results were remarkable. Leprosy patients who said they had not slept for weeks were much relieved. One patient who had one arm operated on one week pleaded with the doctor to do nerve surgery on the other arm the very next week.

Then came foot operations and delicate eye operations and plastic surgery—operation after operation. Scores of them.

On furlough Vera Thiessen took special courses in physiotherapy and on her return was greeted with a government-supplied therapy building equipped with a nerve stimulator and diathermy machine. After she initiated a program of making simple prosthetics and corrective shoes for the patients, the government decided to send polio cases as well to the jungle station for physiotherapy.

And thus the leprosarium grew like a huge suburban housing project—wooded lots, half-acre gardens, and the meandering Oicha stream, a community of 10,000 in a corner of Congo which had only one major city that was any bigger.

But Dr. Becker was not interested in building a metropolis. He was more interested in spiritual results.

When Edna Amstutz had seen that the Oicha station church was too far away for many of the patients to hobble to, she had inspired them to build their own House of Prayer, which dominated the village. And on the center block of each street in the sprawling community was eventually constructed a chapel where those who lived on the street could gather each day at sunset for a vesper service.

For many years the chief pillar of the main church of the leprosy camp was a former *mufumu* named Vubisi. A victim of the horribly disfiguring nodular type of leprosy, he came to Oicha in 1940 and was cured after years of treatment. Free to return to his own village, he asked to stay on and eventually became a Christian, publicly burning the paraphernalia of his witchcraft. At this time he changed his name to Lazaro, "after him who was raised from the dead."

For years he lived alone in his little hut, exerting a powerful influence by virtue of his past position and his dramatic conversion. After he had learned to read the Bible and comprehend its teachings, Lazaro was asked to take the responsibility for preparing Christian converts in the leprosy camp for baptism. Those who indicated a desire to become Christians were enrolled in a two-year "catechumens" class, where they were taught the Bible and Christian doctrine and where they memorized a variety of Bible verses. Those who successfully completed the course were eligible for baptism and church membership.

The church in the leprosy camp brought more encouragement to the missionaries than the much larger Oicha church on the mission station.

One day, for instance, in 1954, several of the leprosy patients came to Vera Thiessen and commented, "Zefania is the pastor of the big church at the mission station, isn't he?"

"Why, yes, he is," replied Vera. She knew that in typical African fashion they were driving at something, but she didn't quite know what.

They asked her one question after another about the Oicha church and about Zefania, until one leprosy patient with a swollen face and a bandaged leg finally blurted out, "We want our own pastor." The others murmured "Yes, yes, yes" in agreement.

"But if you have your own pastor, you will have to pay him a salary." She wondered if they thought the mission would provide the money for a pastor's salary.

"Our leper village has been prospering. We will be able to pay the salary of our own pastor."

Then another patient interrupted. "And not only that, but we also want to send some teachers to other villages. There are many who suffer from leprosy in other villages who need to know about Jesus. We will have enough money to pay for these teachers too."

Vera Thiessen was pleased. And God seemed pleased too. Week after week there were conversions in the church at the leprosy village. The catechumen class taught by Lazaro was well attended and the annual baptismal service was slated for Christmas Eve.

The Christmas Eve festivities began early in the morning with Dr. Becker taking his public address system to the leprosy village and playing carols to call the patients to the service. As the music began, hobbling forms appeared from everywhere, some almost crawling, some leaning on others as crippled as they, some with babies on their backs, some with huge ulcers on their legs, some recently operated on who could use their fingers again.

Soon the chapel was jammed with hundreds of brown bodies tight against each other on crude benches. The chapel was decorated for the occasion with strips of green crepe paper which Vera Thiessen had given the leprosy patients a few days earlier. Paper ornaments were dangling from the most unlikely places. Added to all this were palm branches and brilliant red cannas in front of the church.

The high point of the worship service was a choir of leprosy patients who sang a Swahili version of "O Holy Night." The choir was trained by Yonama, the indefatigable infirmier from the mission station who loved gaudy clothing, flamboyant ties, and loud singing. Some of the missionaries closed their eyes in a vain attempt to shut out some of the discordant singing. Everyone else, and certainly the choir itself, seemed to enjoy the music immensely.

Melona's message was short but forceful. Toward his conclusion, tears rolled down his cheeks as he pleaded that no one reject the Savior.

That afternoon Lazaro led a line of fifty-eight baptismal candidates who had confessed Jesus Christ as their Savior and who had completed his two-year instructional course. It was a strange collection of people: some wizened, elderly people, some young pregnant mothers, many with scarcely anything left of their hands, some who came on crutches because they had only bandaged stumps which served as feet.

Carl and Marie Becker were among the spectators.

What did it mean to have 4,000 leprosy patients and a village of 10,000? What did it mean to have long lines at the dispensary? What did it mean even if hands were raised in an evangelistic meeting? Dr. Becker knew how often Africans raised their hands, but not their hearts. But these fifty-eight who were now being baptized, these were his reward.

But his alone? No, he thought, these were just as much the reward of Marie and of Edna and Vera and of Africans like Melona and Yonama and of leprosy patients like Lazaro. Each had played a vital role; his was no greater than that of any of the others.

And then he recalled the question that had plagued him years before. "What is the spiritual value in medical missions?" He smiled to himself.

13
The Doctor Takes a Vacation

Daylight was scarcely trickling through the towering trees of the Ituri forest as long streams of the sick and halt came surging into the mission compound.

The kerosene lamp in the doctor's study had already been glowing an hour, but finally he blew it out and moved silently away from his desk, out of his modest brick home, down the walk, and across the paths of the incoming patients. A little African woman, bent beneath the load of her infant on her back, reached out and touched him as he passed. He smiled briefly at her; no doubt he would be seeing her again in another two hours or so.

He felt as if he were swimming across an overwhelming tide, a tide of brown-skinned bodies whose paths crossed his every day. On and on the tide came, some on crutches, others deformed, bent, babies with watery fevered eyes cradled in crinkled arms, faces old beyond their years.

He walked into a room where both African infirmiers and missionary nurses had already gathered. After he spoke briefly, sharing a thought he had gleaned from his Bible study earlier in the morning, he asked for prayer requests.

A missionary nurse spoke up. "We had better ask the Lord to supply us with some aspirin mighty soon. Last night I prescribed the last that we have." For a hospital that used up to 2,000 aspirins a day, this was a serious matter.

"Not only that," someone else spoke up; "the Lysol is all gone too."

"And we have just enough sulfa to last for two weeks."

All was quiet for a moment. Then a nurse spoke. "Shouldn't the order for all of that have been delivered long ago?"

"Yes, I thought so," said the doctor simply, "but apparently the Lord didn't, and He knows far better than we do. We have received no word on that order whatever."

"Isn't Owen Brand bringing in three boxes today from Bunia?" asked a nurse.

"Those are the new lighting fixtures," the doctor responded. "Are there any other matters for prayer this morning?" He paused to give the staff a chance to voice any personal problems they were facing, but there was no response. "Let us talk to the Lord about our needs, then." He paused again. "But remember, the Lord knows our needs better than we do; sometimes we get our wants mixed up with our needs. If He wants us to have some aspirin today, He will get it here." It was childlike, almost naïve faith. And they prayed, not beggingly, not prolongedly, but trustingly.

To Dr. Becker it seemed an ordinary day at Oicha—except for the fact that they had no aspirin to give out and no Lysol to use in the sterilization of the operating rooms. In the morning Owen Brand brought the three boxes of lighting fixtures, which were set in a corner until the doctor had time to open them. That seemed the only unusual event.

The dispensary handled the usual number of cases as best it could. Melona preached a powerful sermon to the gathered throng on the necessity of faith in God. When Dr. Becker saw him, he wondered if Melona was preaching to himself as well as to the outpatients.

After lunch and before a heavy schedule of operations, the doctor decided to examine the new electrical fixtures. Nurses Vera Thiessen and Lois Uhlinger stood behind him eager to catch a glimpse of these symbols of Oicha's modernization. After tearing open the top of the box, the doctor peered inside. With his head halfway in the carton, he muttered, "There aren't any fixtures in here!"

"What's in it?" asked Lois Uhlinger.

"Let me see," said the doctor, pulling out a small box with his sturdy fingers. It was marked ASPIRIN. Excitedly, he pulled out the other boxes as well. Before he was finished he had pulled out 50,000 aspirin, 50,000 sulfa tablets, and a drum of Lysol.

He turned to Vera. "Find Owen Brand, will you?"

Shortly Owen was brought in front of the doctor and was asked for an explanation. "I don't understand it. These boxes were clearly marked *Electrical Fixtures*," he apologized. "Shall I return them?"

"No," said the doctor without hesitation. "This is our order, all right. And I think the Lord knew what He was doing."

Several years later it was Owen Brand himself who lay deathly sick on an Oicha hospital bed in need of a missing drug. Once again the staff had been praying for a shipment of drugs to arrive. A shipment of fifteen crates was reportedly at the port of entry but tied up in the red tape of government papers and permits. As Owen Brand's condition deteriorated, a special prayer meeting was called. The next day the fifteen crates arrived. Dr. Becker personally unpacked each crate until he finally came upon the special drug needed for Owen Brand.

Bandages were usually provided by women's missionary societies in the United States, but once when a shipment was delayed, Dr. Becker ordered his nurses to cut up old sheets and scraps to make bandages. Then one of his nurses came and said, "We don't have any more old sheets to cut up, Doctor. I don't know what we'll do."

"There's only one thing we can do," responded Dr. Becker, and shortly after the prayer meeting a large shipment of bandages arrived at Oicha.

Art Buchwald, the American syndicated newspaper columnist, traveling through Congo, stopped at Oicha and wrote home, "In all of Congo, the man who made the greatest impression on us was an American missionary doctor named Carl K. Becker." Becker, however, refused to let his staff see a copy of the article when it was published, saying that it was "grossly exaggerated." He was especially embarrassed by its concluding sentence: "We couldn't help thinking as we left Oicha that America had its own Dr. Schweitzer in Congo."

What Becker feared most from such publicity was a descent of American tourists to the jungle outpost; he could do very well without tourist interruptions. Besides that, publicity was obnoxious to him, and fame and prosperity were feared more than welcomed. He remembered how easily they had dimmed his spiritual eyesight at Boyertown.

Despite his dislike of publicity, his fame spread, stretching hundreds of miles not only into East Africa but throughout Central Africa and even to Europe. Europeans in Congo—government officials and those employed in the rich mining districts—came regularly to Oicha, many traveling great distances. A Greek, formerly employed in Congo, returned from Athens to undergo surgery in the forest hospital. Another man came from the island of Cyprus. A woman of high birth flew in from Brussels to have her baby delivered by Dr. Becker.

Through the years he found himself forced to perform operations of the most intricate kind, yet he had had only the scant introduction to surgery given the general practitioner at medical college. "I'd be a fool to attempt some of these operations if I didn't know there was another Hand on mine as I operate," he once said.

Although he tried to be supplied with the best surgical equipment and spent every dollar he and Marie could spare for the purchase of better tools for his craft, sometimes a seldom-performed operation caught him unprepared. Faced one day with a man dying with a badly diseased prostate gland and lacking suitable instruments, he remembered an old motorcycle a tourist had abandoned on the station. Station manager Bennett Williams removed its mudguard and gave it to the doctor, who forged and fashioned the part into a set of retractors. Then, after carefully sterilizing his new instrument, he used it to save the patient's life.

In the early days he traveled around with a small library of medical books, including several on surgery. At first Africans were wary about undergoing surgery at the mission hospital, for many had seen canned goods from the United States with pictures of people on the outside. They felt certain that medical missionaries cut their patients up and canned them.

So Dr. Becker had to educate the Congolese about surgery. Once, after saving an African's life through an operation, he was asked by the patient who was just coming out from under the anesthesia, "Where's my gift?"

The doctor apparently looked surprised, for the African quickly added, "I let you take out my tumor, didn't I?"

But when the doctor, reaching for his scalpel, replied calmly, "Very well, I'll put it back," the patient hastily canceled the debt.

Thenceforth Dr. Becker told every patient, "If you consult the witch doctor, you bring a chicken as a fee; my price is the same." Later he changed the system slightly to make an annual registration: for 50 francs (about a dollar) or its equivalent, a family got a card entitling each member to medical care, including medicines for a year. For minor operations such as hernia repair the charge was 100 francs (two dollars); for major operations, 200 francs (four dollars).

(The Belgian government in Congo, after trying out free medical care, later switched to Becker's system; government hospitals and dispensaries charged 160 francs per family per year before Congo independence in 1960.)

While such fees did not begin to cover the cost of treatment, they did increase African self-respect. They also insured that patients, having invested in their own health, would follow through with Becker's prescribed treatment. And they helped pay the wages of the African staff.

More adequate fees from European patients helped a great deal as well. But such patients got no preferential treatment for their higher fees. They had to wait their turn. As one infirmier said, "The *munganga's* rigid rules for patient care are as scrupulously observed for the poorest Pygmy as for a Belgian countess."

Every patient was certainly equal when it came to spiritual matters. Dr. Becker affirmed, "There is no hesitancy in earnestly trying to bring every man, woman, and child into direct contact with the Lord for acceptance or tragic rejection."

The first contact a patient had with Christianity was in the 7 A.M. dispensary service, usually presided over by Melona. In earlier years all the patients could be reached at one time, but as the volume swelled from 300 to 500 patients a day, then soared upward to 1,000, 1,500, 1,800, and occasionally 2,000 per day, Melona was forced to add a midmorning sermon and occasionally an afternoon message too.

Other hospital services included a general hospital service each evening, special services each morning in both the men's and women's wards for the hospitalized patients, a special women's service once a week, and services during weekly baby clinics conducted by the hospital's missionary nurses.

But even this proliferation of services did not satisfy Dr. Becker. Hospitalized patients needed spiritual counsel and personal attention. Dr. Becker well knew how easily a new convert slipped back into animistic practices and reverted to the ways of the *mufumu* once he had returned to his village. But one day as he read a Scripture portion in his morning devotions, he had a fresh idea. All hospitals maintain charts on a patient's physical progress; why shouldn't a Christian hospital maintain charts on a patient's spiritual progress as well?

The "spiritual health chart" idea had been germinated by Acts 26: 18: "To open their eyes, and to turn them from darkness to light, and from the power of Satan unto God, that they may receive forgiveness of sins, and inheritance among them which are sanctified by faith that is in me."

On the basis of this verse, Dr. Becker developed seven symbols for the spiritual health chart: (1) A closed circle—indicating a person unaware of his need of Jesus Christ and not yet interested in the gospel; (2) An open eye—symbolizing the first four words of the text and indicating a person who seems interested in the Christian message; (3) An arrow—symbolizing "to turn them from darkness to light," indicating that the Christian message has been understood and received, and that the person is in the process of "turning"; (4) Two linked circles and a third circle withdrawn from it—symbolizing "from the power of Satan unto God," indicating that a person has broken with the devil and has made a profession of faith in Jesus Christ; (5) A simple cross—symbolizing "that they may receive forgiveness of sins" and indicating one enrolled in a catechumen's class to become better acquainted with the doctrine he has professed to believe; (6) A cross with the numerals one and two under it—symbolizing "inheritance among them which are sanctified"; and (7) A cross with the numeral one under it, indicating a baptized believer no longer in fellowship with the church because of a wayward spiritual condition.

As the medical staff members made the rounds of Oicha's 250-bed hospital, they knew at a glance not only the physical condition of the patient, but by means of the spiritual health chart, his spiritual condition also.

As one African nurse described it, "Dr. Becker wasn't just interested in converting people; he wanted to take them beyond conversion. He came to help free the Christian from the shackles of the old life, even more than to convert them. He took them a step further."

If Dr. Becker had one eye always on the spiritual side of the medical ministry, the other eye was certainly never closed to hospital carelessness or indolence. Nor was any lack of clcanliness permitted. The uniforms of the girl nurses were spotless, and the male infirmiers had both efficiency and proficiency drilled into them.

Not a man to shout in rage, his keen disappointment was felt rather than expressed. His nurses would much rather have endured an angry outburst, however, than undergo his quiet displeasure. If an instrument were not in its precise location, he seemed to take it as a personal affront.

He trusted others to perform their duties as conscientiously as he did his own. When they didn't, he was hurt. He especially couldn't understand missionaries who took their task lightly or who revealed a lack of love for the African people. On furlough he once told an American audience, "If you would not be willing to live at the side of a colored person in the United States, don't go to Congo."

He was also perturbed when missionaries looked forward too eagerly to diversion. Some of them had become excellent hunters in Africa. Becker had gone hunting once and had come back disappointed. He didn't mind when missionaries went hunting for needed fresh meat, but when hunting became an inordinate preoccupation instead of a secondary matter, it perturbed him.

Relaxation and recreation were another matter. He loved to tinker with a tape recorder or a stereo set, to listen by short wave to the World Series, or to read *Time*, a book by C. S. Lewis, or a nonfiction best seller. But one of his missionary co-workers said facetiously, "Dr. Becker doesn't know what a holiday is. It even hurts him not to operate on Thanksgiving, Christmas, and New Year's, and he often seems to manage to get an emergency in so that we have to anyhow."

Yet he encouraged his nurses to take the vacations to which they were entitled. Quite often, though, they felt—as one nurse commented—"Because the doctor never took one, I'd feel conscience-stricken if I did."

Once he remarked casually to a newcomer to the Oicha staff, "I think it's about time for my vacation." The newcomer took him seriously. Becker's vacation, however, was his monthly seven-day whirlwind safari to the A.I.M. dispensaries under his care. And there was nothing he liked better than to sit behind the wheel of his Plymouth or Ford, successors to the Buick, and bounce merrily along the dusty Congo roads. On a trip there was time for him to think and plan. If he was accompanied by a friend, this was the rare time when the reserved and introverted doctor opened up and recounted the stories of the past. There was something strangely therapeutic about those safaris.

Bright and early, at six in the morning, as light catapulted itself over the primeval foliage, Marie would hand her husband a cup of coffee and his medical bags, which she had packed for him. It was Marie who, despite increasing trouble with arthritis, was not only the pharmaceutical assistant, the charming hostess for the seemingly endless stream of tourists, notables, and missionaries who found their way to the jungle outpost, and the efficient manager of the evangelistic teams which left the hospital grounds each weekend to preach in the neighboring villages. She was also the head cook, the supervisor of the work crews, the gardening expert, and the teacher of a fruitful woman's Bible class of 200 at the Oicha church.

With his cup of coffee downed, Becker strode to his car, started the motor, restrained himself past the point where the mission-station road merges into the main dirt highway, and then gradually stepped more heavily on the gas pedal until he was well on his way to the first dispensary.

Because there were no other A.I.M. stations in that direction, the fifty-mile trip to Ruwenzori in the Mountains of the Moon was a trip by itself. Sometimes he tried to squeeze the Ruwenzori leg of his safari into a long afternoon. During the rainy season the side road up the mountain was a distinct challenge both to the doctor and to his vehicle. If he got stuck, throngs of Africans inevitably sprang out of the elephant grass like magic genii to push the *munganga* out of his mucky ditch and back onto the main path, getting mud-splattered in the process by the churning wheels. If the trip was made in the early morning or at twilight, wildcats, monkeys, elephants, and other forest creatures graced the roadside. Just before coming to the station, a fork of the meandering Semliki River had to be crossed by pontoon. Here the danger was bumping into a hippo.

Similarly, the treacherous trip to Bell's Shangri-la of Biasiku was an independent journey, and the doctor didn't always make it over Bell's homemade road every month. A visit to Biasiku took two days not because of the mileage but because the road was a constant series of curves through the dense jungle, and the law of averages said that at least one tree would be blocking the road during the trip. Trees 150 feet long were not easy to move.

But these were side trips, one to the east and one to the west of Oicha. His main monthly safari was north out of the forest area to visit A.I.M. dispensaries at Bogoro, Blukwa, Kasengu, Linga, Aungba, and Rethy. In order to keep to his schedule, he worked into the late evening hours. One afternoon and evening at Rethy he performed thirty-three operations, prepared systematically and according to a strict time schedule by the missionary nurse stationed there. Still going strong at ten-thirty that evening, he glanced at his medical crew and asked brusquely, "What's next?"

Not hearing an immediate response, he observed how haggard they were. "You're tired, aren't you?"

Sheepishly they nodded one by one, completely exhausted. He couldn't understand why until he glanced at his watch. "Hmmm, I didn't realize it was so late."

After an afternoon like that—or more commonly after performing twenty-five to thirty operations over two days at Rethy—he would jump back into his car, speed down the escarpment on his way home, arriving at Oicha at dawn the next morning. After sleeping through the morning, he was ready to resume his Oicha schedule in the afternoon. Thus ended his vacation.

At the end of such a trip his nurses felt sorry for him and often tried not to schedule any operations on the afternoon of his return. Vera Thiessen told of one typical experience in a letter home:

"Dr. Becker left Rethy about eleven last night and drove all night, weary as he was, and then today insisted on doing his usual day's work. He slept between six and ten this morning, but I just now left him after doing our leprosy cultures after supper. Jewell [Olson] and I had thought we would spare him and not schedule any operations this afternoon, but he would have none of it, so we hunted up three patients in place of the usual four or five and then had to add a Caesarean, so he did four after all.

Part of the reason for his energy was his ability to relax completely, and to fall asleep no matter how many problems were to be faced the next day. Probably it was because he was confident that what he had done during the day was the best he could do. Others might have done differently or might even have done better, but he knew that God didn't hold him responsible for others, only for himself. "I simply try to do my best," he said; "from there on, I leave it to the Lord."

Always on call, he felt hurt if the nurses failed to call him for an emergency in the early morning hours. "Don't spare me," he'd repeat.

Two operating rooms were necessities for the doctor's feverish schedule. When Oicha had only one operating room, it had to be thoroughly sterilized after each operation. But with two, the doctor could move back and forth; while he was operating in one, the other would be in process of preparation for the next surgery.

Major operations performed by Dr. Becker totaled well over 600 during the course of a year; minor operations topped the 3,000 mark.

In a normal year there were some 500 babies born at Oicha. Pre-natal clinics were an opportunity for the missionary nurses to share their Christian faith with the mothers as well as give hygienic advice. Sometimes the classes contained as many as 120 expectant mothers. One nurse commented wryly, "The population is not going to die out very rapidly at that rate."

When a baby was born in the jungle, the villagers felt uneasy until they could examine the child for any abnormalities. If the child was born with a cleft palate, a deformed hand, or a club foot, it was thought that a curse had been cast on the entire tribe. To remove the curse, the baby was allowed to die of slow starvation.

In one of these tribes a baby born to a Christian couple had a cleft palate. Frightened by the attitude of the neighbors, the parents fled to Oicha to see if anything could be done for the child. Dr. Becker operated successfully, and after a short time the family returned to the village, and the child was fully accepted into the tribe.

Dr. Becker, even at Boyertown, had done well in gynecology, partly because he treated women as people and not merely as objects. At Oicha he had new problems: wives came to him feeling worthless because they could not bear children: childless marriages in Congo were doomed to failure since the society was basically polygamous. Even Christian husbands were sorely tempted to take a second wife if their first wife seemed unable to bear them children. Nothing made Dr. Becker happier than to be able to help the couple have children and thus save a threatened marriage. After careful examination, treatment, and counsel, he would send the couples on their way with new hope and new self-esteem. In a year's time many of them returned for the delivery of their baby.

A sick woman was regarded as of little value since she could not go into the fields and work. Sometimes Dr. Becker had to convince a husband that his wife was worth bringing to the hospital.

One day the doctor heard that in a nearby village an expectant mother was dying. She had gone to the witch doctor and to the midwives for help, but when their clumsy manipulations did not bring about the delivery, the woman was left in the forest to die.

Finding the husband, Dr. Becker demanded, "Where is your wife?"

"Oh, *Bwana Munganga, wapi, wapi, wapi* [woe, woe, woe]! She cannot work; she cannot bear children. She is of no value to me any more. What is the use?"

"But you can't just let her die in the forest," the doctor began to argue. Then, realizing that the superstitious villagers didn't value human life and especially a woman's life as he did, he switched his argument. "How many goats did you pay for your wife?"

"Oh *Bwana*, I paid many, many goats for her." The African seemed eager to impress the doctor with the cost.

"Yes," said the doctor, "and if she dies you will have to pay many, many more to get another wife."

The man looked at the doctor with surprise. He had never thought of this financial aspect. "You are right; you are right. I will bring her to you as soon as I can."

The woman was brought to Oicha in desperate condition. While the baby's life could not be saved, the woman's life was spared, and her husband did not have to part with any more goats.

The doctor often was brought the cases the forest midwives had bungled. Sometimes, too, the doctor was brought the cases that the government doctors were afraid to handle. Although these doctors often gave other excuses, the reason usually was that they felt the woman would probably die anyway and they didn't want her to die in a government dispensary. Africans had little confidence in government dispensaries. If a relative died there, the Africans were enraged and suspected foul play; if the loved one died at Oicha, it was "the will of God."

Becker's maternity specialist was tall, blonde Carolyn Saltenberger, who had come from an Evangelical Congregational church in Philadelphia. When Becker was on his seven-month furlough in 1951, the second longest of his stays in the States since 1929, he met Carolyn, who had already been accepted by the A.I.M. and who had been pledged financial support by the denomination; only a question of passage money prevented her from joining the ranks of the active missionaries. Becker cut through the red tape with two long-distance phone calls and in a matter of days she was on her way to Congo. After a first term at Rethy, she joined the Oicha team and took primary concern for maternity, though like other nurses she sometimes served as a general stenographer to Dr. Becker as well as a general-purpose nurse.

As it became known as a place of love and compassion, Oicha began to be an orphanage. It was not planned—any more than any of the buildings at Oicha were planned—it just happened: there were orphaned children around the forest with no one to love and care for them; there was enough love at Oicha to handle them.

In the marriage counseling he frequently did in the evenings, Dr. Becker encouraged African couples to adopt children if they were unable to have children of their own. Yet the hospital still seemed always to have a dozen or two orphans to be cared for.

One Sunday word came that a little girl was very sick in a nearby village. Dr. Becker sent missionary Nina Smith, who handled the girls' work at Oicha at the time, to find the girl. In a small hut that had almost collapsed upon her, Nina found the little four-year-old. For more than a week she had been there uncared for, ever since the last family with whom she had stayed had abandoned her. When her own parents had died she had been taken for a while by another couple who eventually tired of her and passed her on to another family. No one knew exactly how many different African parents had had her in their homes.

Africans who passed by the collapsing hut had dropped food on the ground for the little tot to pick up; these had been her only bits of nourishment. She was too weak to walk. As the four-year-old was carried out into the sunshine, missionary Nina Smith counted fourteen ulcers on the tiny body. Brought into the hospital for doctor's care, the girl was nursed back to health, joined the Oicha orphanage, and was nicknamed "Our Treasure."

Dr. Becker had not planned on having a special ward for mental patients either. But mental illness, he had learned, was far more prevalent in Congo than generally supposed. He had been told that primitive minds were peaceful and that only the civilized know mental disorders.

It wasn't so. Congolese society was riddled by fear, he discovered, and in such a society even the mildly ill may lose their mental balance when told their ailments were caused by evil spirits.

Within his tribal group the African seems to lead a fairly stable and secure life. He works in conjunction with his group and does not normally set individual goals for himself, as a person in Western society does. He consequently doesn't have as much frustration in failing to meet these goals. It is only when the African loses his sense of belonging to the tribe, when he is cursed by an evil spirit or when he is forced to compete in a Western-type civilization, that his stability and security begin foundering.

On the other hand, the African faces certain strains Westerners don't face. Cursed by the witch doctor, the African may become totally deranged and fall into a state of frenzied anxiety before blacking out entirely. His neighbors, regarding him as demon-possessed, will have nothing to do with him. Taken to Dr. Becker, such a mentally ill patient needed special care. More than once a hospital patient went into a frenzy, climbing the roof and having to be restrained by a nurse or an infirmier with a tranquilizing hypodermic.

To cope with mental illness, Becker established a mental ward and later a small psychiatric clinic. Purchasing an electric-shock machine and studying the techniques carefully, he became the first doctor in equatorial Africa to use shock treatment successfully on African villages. Yet despite his use of shock therapy, he remained convinced that simple Christianity was the soundest general therapy for the mentally upset, that "the gospel of love and hope alone can banish superstition and fear."

By 1957 Becker's Oicha hospital was composed of a vast leprosy program, a tuberculosis sanitarium, well-equipped operating rooms, a maternity ward, a psychiatric clinic, an orphanage, a smoothly efficient dispensary and pharmacy handling well over 1,000 patients per day, a 250-bed hospital, a staff of competent missionaries and well-trained African infirmiers, and one doctor who took a week's vacation each month to cover 25,000 square miles, oversee eight dependent dispensaries, and perform twenty surgeries or more a day.

"Really," his wife spoke fervently to him one evening after he had returned from a whirlwind safari, "we are both going to be sixty-five very soon, and we should think of slowing down a bit."

He nodded, but he hardly heard her. He was thinking about those test tubes over in the laboratory and the strange things that were happening in them.

After all, a doctor had to have something to do in his spare time.

14

What's Going on in Those Test Tubes?

"I look on that man as happy, who, when there is question of success, looks into his work for a reply." RALPH WALDO EMERSON

"What's going on in those test tubes?" asked the visting British doctor as he passed a row of them in Dr. Becker's small laboratory.

"We don't know exactly," commented the Congo doctor somewhat apologetically. "Something is happening, but we don't know where to go from here."

The questioner was Dr. Robert Cochrane, widely acknowledged to be the world's foremost authority on leprosy. Formerly a medical missionary at Vellore Christian Medical College and Hospital in India, he was now director of the Leprosy Research Unit of London. He had met Becker at the leprosy conference in India in 1953 and had later asked him to be host to an institute on leprosy at Oicha.

So in the fall of 1954, Carl Becker had invited fifteen other medical missionaries from East and Central Africa to his station to discuss leprosy problems with Cochrane.

Like Becker, Dr. Cochrane seemed to possess boundless energy. The day after he arrived, he asked to see other dispensaries in the area, and Dr. Becker chauffeured him to Ruwenzori, fifty miles east, and on the next day to the Conservative Baptist Katwa dispensary, fifty miles south, to see the leprosy programs of these stations.

On the third day, eager to get down to business, he told Carl Becker, "I will need some leprosy patients for demonstration purposes at the lectures tomorrow. Would you mind if I selected some from your leprosy camp?"

To make certain he had the best examples for his lectures, he asked to have all of Oicha's leprosy patients parade before him. Dr.

Becker questioned him, but seeing that Cochrane seemed convinced that such a thorough inspection was necessary, he assured him, "Miss Thiessen will have the leprosy patients lined up for you at 9:00 A.M. sharp."

The next morning at nine a double line formed outside the leprosy dispensary and snaked its way along the roadside, stretching almost interminably around the corner at Second Street. Cochrane mopped his brow. "My word, I never imagined you had that many." One by one they passed in review; occasionally the British doctor would speak to Vera Thiessen, singling out one or another as candidates for his demonstration. As he finally saw the end of the line coming into view, he straightened up in the hard wooden chair and gasped, "That certainly was far more than I thought you had."

Vera Thiessen tapped Dr. Cochrane on the arm and pointed out the window in the other direction. "What I've been trying to tell you, Dr. Cochrane, is that you have only seen the contagious patients thus far, and they're the smallest group. The non-contagious patients are in a double line in the other direction." Dr. Cochrane looked to his right and there stood another double line winding down the road waiting for his review.

Although Dr. Becker thought that his work of being the host exempted him from further obligations during the institute, Dr. Cochrane pressed him into service, asking him to demonstrate techniques of hand and nerve surgery to the other physicians.

After the meetings, Cochrane jotted in his private diary, "I never cease to marvel at Dr. Becker and his staff. They are all frightfully busy, but always find time to assist and cooperate. The whole atmosphere is one of quiet efficiency, based on complete confidence in the Lord. . . . Oicha is the only institution in Africa besides Kano [Nigeria] where eyes [delicate operations in which eyelids are turned inward or outward] and hands have been done. . . . He is called the doctor who works miracles, and with it all he is an intensely humble man and somewhat diffident."

Toward the end of Cochrane's visit, as Dr. Becker was strolling with him down one of the long lanes of the leprosy colony, the Oicha doctor queried his guest as to his suggestions for improvements.

Cochrane responded, "The biggest problem I see in your work is that you allow children of contagious patients to remain living with their parents. When one permits this to go on, 50 per cent of the children living in contagious homes contract leprosy."

Becker doubted that Cochrane's estimate would hold up at Oicha.

"You must remember that this is Congo, and leprosy here reacts a bit differently from leprosy in India."

"Would you mind checking on it? If my estimate is not accurate for Congo, I would like to know."

Vera Thiessen took a spot check of 300 children living in contagious homes; approximately 150—Cochrane's 50 per cent—had already contracted the disease. Of some 600 in the homes of non-contagious leprosy patients, only 47 had the disease.

Vera returned shamefacedly with the figures. "We're going to have to do something," she commented. "What, I don't know."

Dr. Becker jotted down a note to figure out a solution as quickly as possible.

Cochrane also suggested that there be more inter-mission medical cooperation in the area. Dr. Becker told him of his dreams for the medical training school at Nyankunde, at present thwarted, but still being prayed for. And then, as they walked into the little room that served as Becker's laboratory, the leprosy expert noticed those test tubes.

"It's sort of a hobby," Dr. Becker explained. "In our reading on leprosy several years ago, we noticed that no one has ever been able to grow and cultivate the leprosy bacillus."

The leprosy bacillus was first discovered in 1873 by Armauer Hansen, after whom the disease is technically known as Hansen's disease; although the *mycobacterium leprae* was the first bacterium to be reported as the cause of a human disease, it had never been successfully grown *in vitro* or transmitted to animals. As a result, leprosy research had been severely hampered. If the leprosy bacillus could be cultivated on an artificial medium or transmitted to animals, the effectiveness of drugs could be checked rapidly. Experiments could be made easily.

"With all the cases of leprosy around here, we thought it was a shame to neglect research. We certainly have enough raw material for diagnosis," said Becker.

At first Cochrane seemed amused and Becker was a bit embarrassed that he had mentioned it. No doubt Cochrane was wondering what business he had in research. He was single-handedly running a hospital treating 500 to 600 patients a day at the time, managing the largest leprosarium in Africa, circuit-riding to a half-dozen outlying dispensaries for which he was also responsible, handling a medical-training school for nurses and infirmiers, and performing as many as 3,000 surgeries a year, yet he had an interest in devoting his spare time to leprosy research. He had no research equipment, no proper facilities. Cambridge or Oxford, or even large well-staffed mission hospitals like those at Kano or Vellore would be the place for leprosy research. But Cochrane seemed ready to listen.

"We've been interested in the tuberculosis bacillus for some time. Since the leprosy bacillus is rodlike, like the tuberculosis, we thought that we might do some experimenting. So we've been testing different culture media trying to grow some *mycobacterium leprae*. It's been an on-again, off-again project for us, and we haven't devoted a lot of time to it, but ——"

"How's it coming? What results have you had?"

It was hard to tell if the leprosy expert was impatient or intrigued.

"A couple of months ago we thought we had something, and we took some pictures that we can show you. But we don't really know. Would you care to take a look?"

The gray-haired Britisher peered intently into the test tubes for a moment and then straightened. "Would you mind telling me what medium you are using?"

Dr. Becker rattled off the formula: "Lactate Ringers with 2½ per cent dextrose, serum, penicillin, and thiamine."

"And you think you're growing the leprosy bacillus in it?"

"I can't say for sure, but at times it certainly looks that way."

"Hmmm." Cochrane looked at the test tubes again.

That afternoon Dr. Cochrane went to the leprosy camp and excised some nodules from several leprosy patients. Returning to the simple laboratory, he placed the nodules in some fresh samples of Becker's special medium.

Early the next morning, Becker and Cochrane checked the experiment. Cochrane shook his head in amazement. "Fresh leprae bacilli growing on these nodules already. Dr. Becker, you may have stumbled across a formula that leprosy experts have pondered over for years."

Becker was pleased but reserved. Other researchers had cultivated the bacillus on living tissue; the next step would be to cultivate the bacillus on an artificial medium.

"I can't get over it," Cochrane continued. "Your laboratory consists of one little room half exposed to the open air, certainly not sterile, and yet your results are better than those of the experts at the universities."

Dr. Becker stopped listening. He thrust his hands deeply into his pockets. "Our trouble is that we don't know where to go from here with these experiments. What would you suggest?"

The British doctor squinted into the microscope again, then straightened up and asked, "Would you mind if I took some of these test tubes back to England with me to determine what is occurring in there? I'm not that much of a research bacteriologist myself, but I might find specialists at Cambridge who could pursue this further." A few hours later, with test tubes taped securely to his body under his armpits to insure proper temperature, he boarded a plane back to London.

Two months later Dr. Becker received a letter from Cochrane asking for tissue specimens from one hundred new leprosy cases. Cochrane explained that he had caught the interest of Dr. Howard Brieger, pathologist on the staff of the Strangeway Medical Research Unit at Cambridge and an expert in tuberculosis. Brieger had requested more clinical material.

At Oicha, Becker continued to "fiddle around" in his laboratory with new solutions to cultivate the leprosy bacillus, while Brieger at Cambridge checked Becker's findings with the latest electron microscopes.

Then, nearly a year after Cochrane's first visit to Oicha, Becker heard that he was returning, this time accompanied by Dr. Brieger. Cochrane had warned Brieger that he might be disappointed, but after spending a week there the Cambridge researcher commented, "The outcome has exceeded expectations; there is no other place where the circumstances are so favorable for this work."

Cochrane and Brieger, with Vera Thiessen at their side, spent a vigorous week taking photographs, doing biopsies, examining slides. Cochrane wrote in his diary:

"Some strange things are happening. After three weeks when the acid-fast [color-fast in an acid solution] bacilli have been in Becker's culture medium, they seem to lose their acid-fastness and show up as blue balls. The other week Becker was experimenting with a slightly different solution, more on the alkaline side, and at the end of three weeks he found acid-fast rods. "Does this mean that acid-fastness depends on the acidity or alkilinity of the tissue?" I discussed the matter with Brieger and we are going to try to get Professor Knox, Dr. Riddell and Dr. Brieger together on my return to discuss this matter.

All this is very intriguing and it would be wonderful if the Lord permitted one of His servants to learn the trick of cultivating the M. Leprae. This makes life decidedly interesting.

Though Cochrane continually encouraged him in his research, Becker frequently became discouraged with it, wondering if it was worth the effort. On the surface it looked like an insignificant piece of scientific research; but, as Cochrane said, to medical bacteriologists around the world it might prepare the way for the complete defeat of leprosy. Each little research discovery, however small, was of great significance in the time-consuming, frustrating, trial-and-error cultivation of a strange bacillus, and time after time Carl Becker seemed on the verge of achieving success.

Cochrane, who had visited mission stations around the world, was increasingly impressed by the entire Oicha team: "The more I see of this work, its excellence, the marvellous teamwork, the close co-operation between Africans and American staff, the initiative in research, the more tragic does it appear that Dr. Becker has to work alone. The Lord has set His seal on this place in many ways, and it would be a tragedy if this work could not continue at the high level of efficiency because of poverty of staff."

Before he returned to London, Cochrane talked seriously to Becker, urging him to recruit another doctor to assist him at Oicha. Becker, now sixty-one, told him how he had tried during his last furlough, in 1951. In fact, this had been the main purpose of his trip to the States.

"Couldn't you find any doctors?" asked Cochrane.

"Oh, we found plenty of doctors, all right. But they seemed concerned primarily with how much salary they would receive, and what the pension provisions were. We told them that our allowance was eighty dollars per month, and they all turned away. There wasn't a single one who volunteered to come."

Cochrane shook his head sadly.

"But then," Becker shrugged his shoulders and threw out his hands, palms up in helplessness, "thirty years ago we might have said the same thing."

There was a break in the conversation. Then Cochrane spoke again, "Frankly, Dr. Becker, you might be on the brink of a real breakthrough in leprosy research. I don't know; at this point Brieger doesn't know either. But I think you ought to consider the possibility of devoting all your time to leprosy research; your age would indicate that you can't take the busy, hectic life of hundreds of surgeries and hundreds of thousands of patients every year for very much longer."

Dr. Becker, saying nothing, only stared at him.

Cochrane went on. "Do you realize what it would mean to medical missionaries around the world if you could solve this research problem?"

Cochrane and Brieger then left Oicha to study under the Cambridge electron microscope the reaction of live leprosy bacilli to Becker's culture medium. And they left sixty-one-year-old Carl Becker to ponder whether he should slow down and devote his time to leprosy research or try to maintain his crazy pace at Oicha. Becker saw no easy answer to the dilemma. Certainly he could not even consider it until another physician was found to assist him at Oicha. Then, maybe—but only maybe.

In his spare time Dr. Becker continued experimenting, assisted by Vera Thiessen and African personnel. There seemed to be little doubt that he had the leprosy bacillus growing, but "it always stops when it gets to a certain point," he wrote Dr. Cochrane. "Our problem is to find what makes it stop and what there is in that medium which is not conducive to growth. According to us it develops into a blue ball which under proper conditions bursts and expels millions of bacilli. We have caught some of them in the very act, but we don't have enough of them to have conclusive proof. We get the blue balls consistently, but to get them changing into bacilli is much rarer."

If he had some of Brieger's Cambridge equipment at Oicha, maybe he could solve some of those problems himself. A research microscope, of course, would be a boon to his research, but that was out of the question. It was foolish even to think of it.

The following September Dr. Brieger appeared again, this time accompanied by a research scientist from Kampala, Uganda. The British Colonial office had become interested in Becker's leprosy research, had made a grant to Dr. Brieger to implement Becker's research, and had authorized him to make as many trips to Congo as he felt necessary.

With the British government showing interest, the Belgian colonial government feared the British would take a medical discovery out from under its nose. So in mid-1957, after inspecting the Oicha leprosy colony, two Belgian officials asked Dr. Becker to list all the equipment he would like for his research laboratory. One of the items Dr. Becker listed was a $900 research microscope.

A few weeks later, Becker received a large grant for the construction and furnishing of a large leprosy ward, even to foam rubber mattresses and bedside tables and another grant of $1,300 for research materials. Since the culture medium he was using cost nearly $100 for only a small amount, the additional $1,300 was gratefully received. But no research microscope. Becker never really expected it anyway.

Not long afterward a British hunter, roaming through the Ituri forest, was stricken with appendicitis. Rushed to Oicha with a ruptured appendix, the hunter was operated on by Dr. Becker and his life was saved. As he recuperated, he asked to see the doctor. "Dr. Becker, what do you want most of all? You name it and I will give it to you."

Becker smiled. "I really don't need anything personally. My salary allowance comes from a church in the United States, and I have no special needs."

"Well then," the Britisher said more gruffly, "what do you want for your hospital?"

"That isn't the way we do business here."

The Britisher seemed to be getting more and more perturbed. "Certainly you don't have all the equipment you need."

When Becker saw that his patient would not give up, he decided to ask for something exorbitant, something that no one in his right mind would think of buying for a jungle hospital even if he could afford it—a research microscope. So he said it.

The incident was all but forgotten when a few months later "the gift nobody could afford to buy" was delivered to Oicha.

As the excitement heightened over his research project, his workload increased in proportion. Each time a research team visited Oicha it meant more work. There were further experiments to be carried on after they left, new ideas to be explored.

Finally he came across a new method. He found that when a leprous nodule was placed on a special gauze platform and soaked in a chicken serum and then properly covered, protected, and incubated, the organisms apparently multiplied until the tissue on which they were growing was exhausted. After that, the number of bacilli gradually diminished.

While his chicken serum failed as a medium for growing the leprosy bacillus indefinitely, Dr. Becker saw another use for it. It could become the basis for a lepromin test, a test to determine the type of leprosy a patient had. When administered like a tuberculin test, it caused those who had lepromatous leprosy to respond negatively and those who had tuberculoid leprosy to respond positively.

Other more scientifically prepared lepromin tests had been developed previously, but Becker's chicken-serum lepromin test was relatively inexpensive, and besides, he told Cochrane, "We could supply you with barrels of it."

When Dr. Cochrane returned to Oicha early in 1958 he seemed elated. "Dr. Becker now has quite large quantities of lepromin and would be able to supply us with all the lepromin we need. As this lepromin has not been made by standard methods, Dr. Becker has called it 'nimorpel' (lepromin spelled backwards)."

Cochrane took 50 cc of the lepromin back to Great Britain to check it out. Enthusiastically he wrote back to Becker that there was no doubt about it: the reading of the results tallied over and over again with the clinical condition of the patients tested.

Cochrane wrote again in his diary in 1958: "I cannot say yet if Dr. Becker's work will lead to the cultivation of the organism, but already one useful result of this investigation is that there has now been devised a method by which lepromin can be made."

Besides the development of Nimorpel, Becker's investigations were triggering scientific researchers like Brieger, Nailer, and others with the British Colonial office. A new excitement was brought to the area of leprosy research in British East Africa.

As the research excitement mounted, Carl Becker told Marie one evening, "Cochrane is right; we'll have to decide to do one or the other—either leprosy research or continue in the total hospital ministry."

And then came word from America that a young doctor would be joining him soon at Oicha, the first doctor to be assigned to assist him in nearly thirty years of his missionary service. This seemed God's answer.

Maybe this was the Lord leading him out of general hospital work at Oicha to specialize in leprosy and leprosy research.

15

One Day's Dusk
Is Another Day's Dawn

In the back of his mind, Dr. Becker carried for years the idea that Carl Jr. would step into his shoes as a medical missionary. He seldom said anything about it, but Dr. Becker didn't need to speak in order to express himself.

Though young Carl had been a star pupil at Rethy Academy during the late '30s and early '40s, an avid reader and a handy young mechanic, he was devoid of any inclination toward medicine. As a teen-ager he had managed the hospital's carpenter shop and later had assisted his mother in the pharmacy. This was as close to medicine as he got, except for the day when his father suggested he come and watch an operation. Carl Jr. scrubbed up, donned a little white jacket, and followed his father into the operating theater much as Isaac must have followed Abraham up Mount Moriah. To Dr. Becker the operation progressed smoothly. Periodically, he stole glances in his son's direction. But halfway through the operation he looked for his son and couldn't find him, for Carl Jr. had keeled over in a dead faint. And on that spot the brief medical career of young Carl ended abruptly.

Finishing at Rethy Academy, he continued his education at Houghton College in New York State and Eastern Baptist Seminary in Philadelphia, earning degrees from each. Receiving a scholarship from the University of Pennsylvania, he earned a master's degree in English and applied to the Africa Inland Mission for service in Congo as an educational missionary. His wife, Gladys MacDonald, joined him in the application. After a year of language study in Belgium, they arrived in Congo in 1955 and were promptly assigned by the Congo Council to Oicha, where qualified teachers were needed.

At Oicha he not only superintended the large school attended by 700 children, but also guided the branch schools of the area. The Africa Inland Mission, which had long debated the offer of government subsidy for education, finally accepted it experimentally at a few stations, one of which was Oicha. At these stations the educational ministries of the A.I.M. expanded rapidly.

It was obvious that the Congolese generally had become hungry for education. This mixture of passions brought a spirit of unrest to Congo. The demand was for more and better schools, for higher wages, and for more self-rule in the churches as well as in the nation itself. No more was the white man revered as he had been a generation before. Now, no matter who he was—missionary, Belgian plantation owner or soldier—he symbolized an obstacle to the aspirations of the Congolese.

To Dr. Becker, who welcomed the growing maturity of the African church, this drive for freedom and equality had much justification. But he did not fail to recognize the huge problems that the unrest swept along ahead of it. The lack of love, the increasing materialism, the irrationality of the rising breed of Africans, he knew, would be hard to reckon with.

Not all missionaries viewed the social changes as favorably as Dr. Becker, and the A.I.M. field council meetings often exchanged forceful differences of opinion. At one point Dr. Becker suggested, "I think it might be a good idea to set a time limit on the number of years we should give ourselves to get out of Congo and leave a strong established national church to carry on." Few agreed with such a radical suggestion.

Each meeting seemed crucial; missionaries held deep convictions and sometimes were reluctant to surrender their viewpoints. Godly men were on both sides, and Dr. Becker's progressive stand was sometimes misunderstood.

But finally, an African church was established independent of but cooperating with the Africa Inland Mission. The Congolese Church was allowed to stand on its own feet; Dr. Becker felt it was a wise move.

Tall, blond Dr. Harry Wilcke joined Dr. Becker at Oicha late in 1957, the first doctor permanently assigned to work with Dr. Becker in all his years in the Ituri forest. Though not impressed with the externals of Oicha, Wilcke was impressed with Dr. Becker's sixth sense in diagnosing African ills and also his ability to organize the great work load. He was also amazed with Becker's infinite compassion for the Africans and his willingness to stop and listen to someone's problems. "The most important people in the world are his patients," Wilcke stated.

To Becker, Wilcke's arrival was an answer to prayer—but he wasn't quite sure which prayer. He remembered Cochrane's urging that he devote his time to research and let someone else take the burden of Oicha's medical work. He had prayed often about that, but he realized that he couldn't do anything about it as long as no other doctors were available. But now Dr. Wilcke had come to Oicha to assist him. Then he recalled Marie's suggestion that he slow down a bit. At his age, he should be careful not to overtax his heart.

But only two months after Wilcke arrived, Dr. Becker was stricken with a kidney-stone attack in the middle of the night. When Carolyn Saltenberger arrived to give him a shot of morphine, he was writhing in pain on his bed.

After giving the injection she started to leave, but he called to her: "Would you help me get over to my desk, Carolyn?" He was struggling to sit up at the side of his bed.

"Dr. Becker, you belong in bed," she scolded.

"Oh, I won't be able to sleep with this pain, so I thought that while the needle was working, I'd see if I could get some work done."

Everyone dreaded the days when Dr. Becker was sick. Though his health was normally excellent, occasionally he was flattened by a malarial attack. "And you know how impossible doctors can be when they get sick," said one nurse.

On his sick bed Becker would continue to work. He might try to fix a complex hospital machine that was not meant to be touched by anyone but a highly specialized mechanic or he would take apart a tape recorder or a radio. Marie dreaded those days too, because when he was sick he was restless. "It's not when he is real sick, but only when he's half-and-half that things never come fast enough to suit him."

But what his hospital staff dreaded most were the days after his illness. He had too much time to think when he was bedridden, and brand new ideas would be germinated, new procedures hatched, and old routines which had been followed for years would be scrapped.

Like a recharged battery, he bounded from his bed with indefatigable energy.

However, his kidney-stone problems in early 1958 didn't go away so easily. For three months he was hoping the stone would be passed naturally. There was too much work to be done; Congo was in too great a crisis; the A.I.M. needed every man it could muster; the Congolese Church needed stabilizing; Wilcke needed to be trained for the job; more leprosy research needed to be pursued. This was hardly the time for him to be laid up with an operation.

On the other hand, he was reminded by the home office that he was long overdue for a furlough. Certainly Marie, whose arthritis seemed to be worsening, would enjoy one. It had been seven years since they had seen their daughter Mary, who had married and settled in New Jersey. For two years they had talked about taking a quick three-month furlough, one month at Atlantic City resting; one month at Mayo Clinic in Minnesota; and the third speaking in churches and presenting the need for medical missionaries.

So as his condition became more severe and he resigned himself to the fact that the kidney stone was not going to disappear by itself, he asked Marie, "Do you suppose it's about time for our furlough?"

Upon reaching New York City, he phoned his old friend Dr. Bob Hunter, now trustee chairman of Hahnemann Medical College. "Bob, can you get me a bed at Hahnemann?"

Within a short time Becker went under the knife of Ed Campbell, noted urologist and long-time friend, and the following ten days he spent recuperating in the hospital. But Bob Hunter did more than just arrange a room and contact a urologist. He also came to the hospital one afternoon and announced to the missionary doctor, "Listen, Carl, you're going to be given an honorary degree from Hahnemann in June."

Hunter knew how to handle Becker's protests and insisted that everything was all set and that it was impossible for him to say "No." So in mid-June after reluctantly addressing an alumni banquet, Dr. Carl K. Becker received the Degree of Doctor of Humane Letters, along with a U.S. senator, Hahnemann's president, and a distinguished scientist from Australia.

Embarrassed by the praise of men, he felt uneasy in America. A friend remarked, "He ducks away from praise the way other men dodge blame." So a few days after receiving the degree, he and Marie returned to Congo.

In Congo there were greater problems than publicity. Two years earlier he had written candidly, "Bitter opposition on the part of the predominant religion here and the hindrance of nationalism are not new to us any more. But anti-Americanism on the part of the Europeans and anti-white feelings among the Africans seem definitely on the increase. And the fact that both are so unreasonable and based on such a minimum of fact only makes them the more dangerous and definitely handicaps in our work."

Increasingly, missionaries felt themselves squeezed between the Belgian colonial government and the Congolese. While Africans sometimes felt that the missionaries were dragging their heels in granting ecclesiastical independence, the colonial government sometimes felt they were moving too rapidly. For years, Protestant missions had been criticized for "preaching to the poor natives the doctrines of independence and rebellion." And the establishment of independent indigenous churches, apart from white domination, seemed to substantiate the criticism.

To add to the crisis, George Van Dusen, a former Los Angeles businessman who had served as A.I.M.'s Congo field director since 1928, was talking about retirement. He was a seemingly irreplaceable man who had guided field policies and handled financial matters of the mission for a generation. It was a crucial time in the mission's history—no time to lose such a key leader. But the rumor was that Dr. Becker was being thought of to be his replacement. Becker parried the suggestions aside. How could he possibly manage to run one of the largest hospitals in central Africa and serve as field director for the 150 Congo missionaries in the Africa Inland Mission? It was ridiculous even to think of it.

Yet when George Van Dusen became seriously ill in 1958, the name of Dr. Carl Becker was the replacement most often suggested. Becker knew he would be "on the spot" at the next meeting. Other veterans in Congo had excellent missionary records, but none of them commanded the respect that Becker did. Some of them, remembering the old days when the missionary was the *bwana*, were slow to let the Congolese take over. Becker was recognized as a rare breed, a veteran missionary with a young man's views—a combination of an older man's wisdom and a younger man's progressive spirit.

At the council meeting, when his name was mentioned, he quickly stood to decline the nomination. The work at Oicha was more demanding than ever; he felt his role was in medicine, not adminstration; and besides at the age of sixty-four he thought he was too old for the job. 'I don't see how I can possibly allow my name to be considered."

Becker sat down. The meeting continued; there were further nominations and lengthy discussions on the type of man needed for the crucial times. With independence being talked about in the future, the new field director would have to be a man universally respected by the Africans as well as the Europeans.

Once again the eyes of the council members turned toward Carl Becker. And Becker realized as the discussions extended that the meeting was not getting anywhere; it was bogged down in talk. He had never enjoyed sitting through long business meetings anyway.

Finally, he was begged to reconsider.

Rising slowly to his feet, he responded, "You can put my name down on one condition—that we have a secret ballot, and that everyone place in nomination whomever he wants."

Dr. Becker was under no delusions. He knew that his progressive views were not popular to all the old-timers. He knew that he had sometimes taken strong stands on issues where others disagreed. He knew that while there were some who supported him, there were others who didn't think his views should be dominant. And he knew also that whoever led the Congo missionaries in the next few years had to have the support of all the missionaries on the field.

A secret ballot was taken. Each council member scribbled a name on his ballot. Except for the scratching of pencils, all was silent. Then the papers were folded and the teller collected the ballots. In a few moments, the chairman of the council asked the teller if he could report on the results. The teller walked quickly to the front of the room. "Every single ballot cast had the same name on it—the name of Dr. Becker. By unanimous vote, our new field director."

The doctor shook his head. How could he possibly do the work? Yet he couldn't deny that such a unanimous call was the voice of the Lord. And if this was God's will, God would certainly provide a way or him to handle it.

It settled the matter of going into leprosy research. That would have to be done by another. Brieger was certainly well equipped to carry on what he had started. And it also settled the notion of his slowing down. Marie would just have to understand that becoming field director for Congo would mean an acceleration of work.

Robert Wilson, editor of the Evangelical Congregational magazine, wrote and asked frankly if perhaps he had made a mistake and
had bitten off too big an assignment this time.

Dr. Becker responded, "You do well to be surprised that we could
possibly accept field administrative responsibilities. It doesn't make
sense, does it? You may well know that this was not a usual election,
but presented to us as a temporal 'necessity.' If the Lord glories in
difficulties, we should certainly be a candidate for His evident
enabling."

Part of the Lord's enabling was Stanley Kline, Oicha's station
manager who assumed responsibilities as the Congo field treasurer,
and another part was certainly Dr. Harry Wilcke who served for
another year at Oicha before being transferred to Rethy station
which needed a full-time doctor.

Dark clouds ringed the sky as Carl Becker drove down the winding
road after his election. His was the responsibility not just for A.I.M.
missionaries and their families, but for an African Church struggling
like an infant to walk on its own. He had never liked to become
embroiled in fights; he had preferred to let problems resolve themselves, and they usually did. But the storm clouds on the horizon of
the Congolese Church could not be ignored.

He remembered the wise words of Emil Sywulka, A.I.M. pioneer
in Tanganyika: "I have done both pioneer work and pastoral work
and I have found that the latter is much more difficult and trying.
True, the pioneer is called upon to suffer physical hardships. But the
ready response of many, at least in Africa, makes it quite easy for the
pioneer to get to feel quite a missionary. However, it is in building up
a church that the heartbreaks come."

The church at Oicha had been like that. Outwardly, it was a
vigorous church. It had grown like an African oak and had stretched
out its branches to shelter a score of village churches in the surrounding areas. But inside, the Oicha Church had always been weak.

The dominant African tribe at Oicha had an unusually bad reputation for instability and lack of moral fiber. The Belgian mining com-
panies refused to hire these villagers; government officials spoke
disparagingly of them. Yet this was the soil from which the church at
Oicha had to grow.

While professions of faith had not been difficult to obtain, it was
quite another matter to see Christians grow into a mature, stable life.
Missionary Jim Bell had taken a boy from this tribe, Zefania Kasea,

who had been an irresponsible failure as a school teacher, and had carefully instructed him, spending much time with him until Zefania became an able pastor. But Zefania was not a forceful leader, and often he was pushed and pulled by village influences.

Carl Becker rejoiced that Zefania was still faithfully preaching the Word. He still remembered one of Zefania's sermons just after a leopard, which had been marauding the hospital area, had been tracked down and slain. The faithful pastor likened the leopard to the devil and the knives of the villagers to the Word of God, which is "quick and sharper than any two-edged sword."

And Dr. Becker remembered the Easter Sunday services, gaily decorated with foliage. The poles were camouflaged by huge palm branches and a wreath of purple bougainvillea was spotted in the center of the front wall. On each side of the platform were bouquets of African daisies and ferns in vases that had "Armour's Pork Sausage" written in big black letters on the outside. And he remembered the singing of "Christ Arose," which Zefania enjoyed so much that they sang the verses a second and even a third time.

He remembered too when the Oicha Church was the host for an African conference and 450 delegates from as far as 500 miles away came for the sessions. He had wished that the forest people be decent hosts, and he was so pleased that the Africans had whitewashed their houses inside and out and actually begged to have guests to entertain in their homes.

And he remembered when Zefania held a conference for all fifty African chiefs of the area. Missionary Claudon Stauffacher from Ruwenzori had gone hunting and had brought back nine antelope for their meat during the conference. At the closing service, after Zefania had preached a fervent message, three of the chiefs raised their hands for salvation.

And he remembered the prayers, the deeply personal practical prayers of these people. He remembered an evangelist who prayed, "Lord, I have noticed that if grease drops on to thick paper it soaks in and becomes one with the paper. So may Thy Word which we hear soak right into our lives and form a whole with them."

And he liked the prayer of the African teacher who prayed, "Lord, when our beds get bedbugs or lice in them we put them out in the sun and all the insects go away from them. So, Lord, as we come into the sunlight of Thy Presence, chase away all the bad things from our hearts."

Those were the good times. He had seen church membership at

Oicha grow from practically nothing to 1,350 baptized members, not including the thirty out-schools and churches in the district.

But he couldn't overlook the realistic side of it. He remembered that when Zefania had encouraged his church members to go out to neighboring villages on Sunday afternoons, the church members wouldn't go unless the church promised to buy new tires for their bicycles in case they wore them out.

He recalled how often church members, even church leaders, had fallen into gross immorality or had been arrested for thievery. And he remembered the first time they had a church election how they were unable to find eight church members on their entire membership roster who would be qualified to serve as elders.

He knew he had been criticized at times because he had been too patient with the forest people around Oicha. Perhaps he should have displayed an iron hand of discipline. Maybe so, but he had felt that it was necessary to enter into the cares of his fellow Christians, to sympathize with them and to pick them up when they fell—not to push them into the ditch.

This was one of the many African churches that was now self-governing. These were the people who would soon gain independence as a new nation. No wonder some of the missionaries doubted the wisdom of handing over authority to them. No wonder some of them thought that Becker's progressive spirit was dangerous. Sometimes he wondered about it himself.

Already the African church leaders were asking that certain missionaries at other stations be returned to the United States because their attitudes toward the Africans were not in keeping with the times. Already there had been work strikes on some of the mission stations, demanding higher wages.

It was a fine mess that he had gotten himself into. A person would be a fool to accept the role of the Congo field director at such a time as this. But it was a job which someone had to take, and apparently God had wanted him to be the fool who would take it.

What lay ahead? Who knew, but the Lord?

Back at Oicha there was talk of Congolese independence in the air. When Congo became independent, the new young politicians claimed, there would be banks in every town, and everyone knew that banks passed out money to anyone who needed it. If anyone was in dire need, all he would have to do was to ask an African government official, and he would dole out the money.

Dr. Becker stopped a young man passing out literature at the mission station. "Could I see one of those leaflets, young man?" he said.

"Big meeting tonight at Mbau," the lad responded, handing the doctor one of his pieces of literature.

"What's it all about?" asked the doctor.

"Freedom, Bwana, freedom."

Indeed it was. "Independence now," said the pamphlet. "Freedom from the Belgian colonialists."

That night most of the African medical staff, the school teachers and the station workers attended the big rally. The next morning at the staff prayer meeting, one of the infirmiers asked openly, "Munganga, what do you think of this talk about freedom and independence?"

The doctor didn't answer directly. Instead, he returned the question, "What do you think of it?"

Excited rumbling rose from the Africans. Big smiles beamed across dark faces; teeth glistened; happy chortles were heard.

The doctor's face was still serious. He knew it was only a surface response they had give him. "What do you really think of it?" he repeated.

"I don't know, Munganga," said one seriously.

"I'm afraid it will just mean fighting and tribal wars again," said another.

"Maybe even the missionaries will be driven out," added another.

The doctor smiled and threw out his hands as if to say, "Who knows?" Then he spoke more seriously again. "Your freedom is coming, I am sure. Only remember that the same Lord who has been with you in the past will be with us all in the future."

The following Sunday at the Oicha Church, Pastor Zefania prayed: "Lord, we are standing at the door of independence, and we don't know what is on the other side of the door. It's like standing outside of a house and wondering what the furniture is like inside, if the chairs and beds are comfortable. But we can't know until we step inside. Lord, we want You to go in with us, so whether we find it good or evil, if You are with us, it will be all right."

The white doctor in his congregation said quietly, "Amen."

16

Not Faith but Reality

"Not in the clamor of the crowded street,
Not in the shouts and plaudits of the throng,
But in ourselves are triumph and defeat." LONGFELLOW

Early in the morning, before the sun had cast its rays over the jungle, the doctor lit his kerosene lamp and opened the Word of God. Now he read in Exodus of how the Israelites were fleeing from the Egyptian hordes with all their chariots and horsemen. The word of the Lord which came to Moses that day was this: "Fear ye not, stand still, and see the salvation of the Lord, which He will show to you today . . ." (Exodus 14:33).

It was a good verse, Carl Becker thought, to remember in days of darkness and confusion. And since this was January 1, 1960, he decided to make it his "verse of the year."

It was a year of *Uhuru* (freedom), of reorganization, both for the mission and for the nation of Congo. The hospital management was handed over to a committee of Africans and the Congolese Church took on new responsibilities from the mission. It was a year also for the doctor to exercise bold leadership among Congo missionaries.

And it was the year that "Congo sort of blew up in our faces," as he put it. Scores of missionaries stopped at Oicha on their way out for a taste of Marie's cooking. In July came his hurried trip to Mount Hoyo to rescue the Scheuzgers and his bargaining with the Walesi tribesmen. September and October brought medical shortages and miraculous provisions.

Politically, Congo writhed in turbulence for the remainder of 1960. Premier Patrice Lumumba, removed from power in Leopoldville (Kinshasa), continued to maintain a strong following in northeast Congo, where A.I.M. missionaries served. In December, after Lumumba was placed under home arrest, his followers stirred themselves into rebellion against the central government and, encouraged

174

by Communist support, established a rebel capital in Stanleyville (Kisangani), only 400 miles west of Oicha.

Then in January, 1961, as the contagious rebellion of the Lumumbists swept through the jungle, Dr. Becker was quietly reading in Deuteronomy one morning: "Hear, O Israel, ye approach this day unto battle against your enemies: let not your hearts faint, fear not, and do not tremble, neither be ye terrified because of them; for the Lord your God is He that goeth with you, to fight for you against your enemies, to save you." Startling as these verses seemed in the light of Congo's current events, he felt he should adopt them as his verses for 1961.

It was not that they possessed any magic; it was simply that he believed in the God who stood behind these verses. And if it was God who had brought them to his attention at the start of the year, he could rely on them throughout the year.

Only a few days later he and Marie had evacuated in the dark of early morning at the tail end of a convoy of missionary cars, feeling their way to the plantation of the European count. And it was at this time that they had been menaced by the spear-toting Watalingi until he had bargained with them to let the others go and he would return to Oicha.

According to the U.S. Consul at Uganda, Moscow had radioed the angry Lumumbist rebels at Stanleyville to begin a systematic massacre of all whites in northeast Congo. Becker had no reason to doubt the warning; he knew the maniacal spirit of the Lumumbists.

Yet now with the Andrew Uhlingers and gallant young Herb Atkinson, he and Marie were returning to Oicha, their lives a ransom for two dozen others. On the way, he thought especially of Dr. Atkinson, only beginning his missionary experience, and he wondered if he would have had as much trust in God when he had first come to Africa.

And not until now did he recall that the Bible verse that the Lord had given him for 1961—"Do not tremble, neither be ye terrified because of them; for the Lord your God is he that goeth with you, to fight for you against your enemies, to save you."

No signs of a Lumumbist take-over back in Oicha, though. As he slowed his mud-spattered car along the Station Road, hundreds of Congolese came running out of the buildings, across the fields, from the recesses of the jungle, shouting, cheering, chanting, singing, and weeping unashamedly in an explosion of joy. For the moment, at least, it was good to be home again.

For the next few weeks Carl Becker kept in close contact with the outside world by the mission's two-way radio. To him the situation seemed as normal as could be expected.

"Is there any way you can get across the border?" radioed the anxious mission officials in Uganda.

"It would be foolish for us to try," he replied. "And much safer to stay right here at Oicha."

"Then there's no way at all we can get you out?"

"The only way I can think of is to have the United Nations helicopter fly in and pick us up. Right now that doesn't seem necessary."

In the next few days, besides celebrating his sixty-seventh birthday with Marie's home-baked doughnuts (he didn't like birthday cakes), he was greeted by a delegation of Congolese officials who again assured him of their interest in his welfare. "In fact," they told him, "we will station some soldiers here to protect you."

But it was the soldiers that he was the most afraid of; Congolese soldiers were treacherously fickle. Finally he declined the offer, "because the patients might be scared away if they saw the soldiers."

Only a few days later Patrice Lumumba escaped from prison in Katanga and was slain. His followers were incensed. According to the U.S. Consul in Uganda, the Lumumbists were now planning to retaliate by a wholesale extermination of white people starting February 15. Carl Becker didn't know how to assess the news. For one thing, the previous warning from the U.S. Consul, which had caused the evacuation of hundreds of missionaries from northeast Congo, had proved groundless. Would this warning be any more accurate? Besides, the civilian population around Oicha seemed warmly loyal to the missionaries. So when he spoke again to mission leaders by radio, he downgraded the danger he was in.

However, one mid-morning the second week in February, a U.N. helicopter dropped out of the skies, whirling into the parking area of the mission station. It stirred a crowd, as readily as it stirred up the stifling jungle air. Dr. Becker left his line of patients at the hospital and walked quickly through the milling Congolese to the plane.

The Swedish pilot stepped out of the plane and in broken English stated his mission to the doctor.

"We wish we had known you were coming," said Becker, "and we would have saved you the trip. But we see no reason to be evacuated. The situation seems quite stable at Oicha right now."

"My orders," said the pilot crisply, "are to take you back with me."

Carl Becker looked at his fellow missionaries who had now joined him.

The pilot spoke directly to them, "If you want to leave, now is the time."

No reply.

Dr. Becker looked at Herb Atkinson, separated from his wife and children. He saw Herb's jaw set, his head shaking slowly, determinedly.

He looked at Andrew Uhlinger, who had already spent a generation in Congo with his wife. Uhlinger was looking down at the brown Oicha soil, as if he had roots there. He gave no indication of wanting to be transplanted.

"We are sorry that you had to make a fruitless trip," repeated the doctor.

Dumbfounded at the reluctance of the elderly doctor to be rescued, the pilot returned to his helicopter and climbed up into the blue sky again. The five missionaries waved up at it as it whirled away. Carl Becker felt a bit lonely now. He was sure that at least Herb Atkinson did too.

Had he done the right thing in turning down his last chance of rescue? "Fear not, and do not tremble," something reminded him inside.

As Congo field director, Carl Becker felt it his responsibility to check the various mission-station properties and to encourage the believers scattered throughout the area. So one morning after a meager breakfast, he told Marie, "I think I had better go on safari today."

And off he drove, a lone missionary in a hostile nation. At one station, faithful Christians had been brutally beaten by Lumumbists because they had associated with white people. At Blukwa, he met an old Congolese pastor who told him, "I heard you on the mission radio, speaking in English to the other missionaries. I couldn't understand what you were saying, but just to know that you stayed here with us helped very much." At each station he found Christians guarding the mission properties and holding firm to their Christian convictions.

After Dr. Becker had returned to Oicha and relayed his encouraging news to the missionaries waiting in East Africa, some of them began thinking of returning. February 15 came quietly, and Doctors

Becker and Atkinson were as busy as ever with hundreds of patients; no wholesale massacre by the Lumumbists was begun.

Shortly afterwards, Herb Atkinson was sent to Kampala, Uganda, to bring the nurses back to the Congo, if they would be willing to come. Atkinson found the nurses waiting to be asked. His family also returned with him.

The rest of 1961 was one of the most difficult financially, but one of the most rewarding spiritually. Completely ignored by the Red Cross, the United Nations, and the World Health Organization, Oicha ran dangerously low in medical provisions. Ordered supplies didn't come through on time, and if they came at all, the orders were often only partially filled.

Late in 1961, the supply of penicillin was almost gone. It had been six months since it had been ordered. On Friday night, the staff gathered as usual for their weekly meeting in the Becker living room and knelt humbly in front of wooden chairs and other simple furniture.

"Tonight, I think we should ask the Lord about the penicillin," said Dr. Becker. "He knows we need it."

Dr. Becker's staff prayed earnestly, but not endlessly. Becker did not believe in long prayers and all-night prayer meetings. "Why nag God?" he had said; "He'll take care of our needs. If He doesn't, maybe we'd better take a second look at what we think are our needs. They may be just our wants."

That night it seemed to Carl Becker that penicillin was far more than a want.

The next morning a truck filled with patients pulled into the mission station. After the patients had climbed over the tail gate, two cases were dropped in the parking lot in front of the outpatient building. The penicillin had arrived.

There were tears in Dr. Becker's eyes as he opened the cases with Dr. Atkinson. "Some people might call this coincidence, Herb, but this has happened too often for that. Our staff here has prayed, and the next day it comes—sulfa, aspirin, a load of cement, penicillin. That's the way it's always been. For more than thirty years, we've been living in the midst of a continuing miracle."

When another medical supply crisis threatened, Nurse Vera Thiessen told the doctor, "In Kampala, I stumbled on a little medical supply store that some Indians run. I don't know if it's worth considering or not, but just in case we got desperate, I brought one of their catalogs with me."

She produced a poorly mimeographed collection of sheets which was purportedly a drug catalog. Dr. Becker raised his eyebrows and said nothing, but shortly sent an order to the Bombay Trading Company in Kampala, and found that Vera's random discovery was a medical gold mine. The drug problem was hereafter solved.

If anything, the food shortage was even more critical than the drug supply. Yet here too the supplies always came at just the right time. The Greek merchants at Beni had long been fond of Dr. Becker, even though they did not share all his religious convictions.

One of these Greek merchants remembered a time before independence when a little three-year-old girl was desperately ill at Butembo, a mining town seventy miles south of Oicha. The Belgian doctor of the mines, unable to help the girl, despaired of saving her life, but told the father to get Dr. Becker from Oicha.

At 9 P.M. Dr. Becker responded to the father's knock at the door. Exhausted from a full schedule of operations during the afternoon and into the evening, he had just settled down to relax at home. His muscles ached from the tension and strain of the day. "I'm so sorry," he told the Greek merchant, "but it's impossible. I simply cannot move. I'm too tired to do another thing."

As the visitor began to leave, Dr. Becker walked to the far end of his living room and back again. He had refused an urgent plea for help. He paced the floor again. No matter how tired, he had to go, and he finally blurted out. "I must go to Butembo. I must go to Butembo."

Arriving in Butembo after midnight, he examined the infant carefully, gave her the necessary injections and treatment, and by dawn the child was out of danger, enabling Dr. Becker to return to another full day's rugged routine at Oicha.

He had performed delicate operations for very moderate fees; his nurses had stayed up nights with their families. And when they asked, "Dr. Becker, what can we do special for you?" he had waved them off with his hands and said, "Nothing, nothing at all."

But the Greek colony remembered. And one day after the Oicha missionaries had knelt together for prayer and several of the nurses had reminded the Lord that their milk supply was exhausted, a pickup truck drove in from Beni, dropped six five-pound cans of powdered milk at the Becker's front door, wheeled around rapidly and sped out again. The driver was afraid that Dr. Becker would turn down his generosity if he delivered the milk personally.

A Greek baker from Beni continued to share his supplies with the

Beckers, even when there was not enough flour for his own bakery.

During this period, the Greek produce merchants were finding it difficult to get fresh fruits and vegetables, until they remembered the Oicha farming leprosy patients. The leprosy colony had diminished somewhat in the post-independence days. Hundreds of them were now being treated and released, a startling testimony to the effectiveness of the new sulphone drugs. But many of them refused to leave the leprosy colony. They found life so good to them there that they had become prosperous farmers. Their prosperity was increased further when the Greek merchants drove their trucks into the leprosy colony and purchased fruits and vegetables fresh from their *shambas* for the Beni produce markets.

Becker chuckled the first time he saw those trucks laden with produce drive out of the mission station. Who could have imagined such a thing twenty-five years ago?

While the supplies were often meager, the lines of incoming patients certainly weren't. The daily average was between 1,500 and 2,000, with some 250 bed patients, all attended to by two overworked doctors, three overworked R.N.'s and about fifty African medical assistants and nurses. Everywhere in Congo missionary doctors had a double load to carry, for Belgian doctors had evacuated at the time of independence in 1960. Patients who were once treated by government medics at Beni or by doctors at the Butembo mines now hiked or rode the back of rickety trucks to Oicha for treatment. Some even came from as far away as Leopoldville for special treatment by the famed Protestant doctor. One Congolese government cabinet member brought a personal celluloid letter signed by the President, Joseph Kasavubu, asking Dr. Becker for his own personal consideration.

Dr. Herbert Atkinson, nicknamed the "young Little Doctor" by the Africans, was like "the Big Doctor" in zeal and diligence, but he still found it difficult to keep up with the man who was pushing seventy. "There are very few missionary doctors who can deep up the pace that Dr. Becker maintains," Atkinson reported. "He was going fourteen hours a day, six days a week. When he wasn't down in the dispensary or in surgery, he was ordering drugs or dictating letters, keeping the secretaries busy just by the work he dictated in the evenings."

Atkinson's wife, Frieda, had been born and raised on the A.I.M. Congo field and had long known Becker's awesome reputation. Trained as a nurse, she assisted Marie Becker in the pharmacy when she wasn't minding her own children. And raising children in tumultuous Congo had plenty of problems of its own. Not knowing what any day would bring, the Atkinsons prepared their children for the worst and prayed for the best. Life for the children was at best unsettling. One day as their four-year-old son Daniel saw a Congolese soldier march toward the mission station with his rifle over his shoulder, he hollered to his mother, "Quick, Mommy, tell him about God before he shoots us."

Another of Oicha's acquisitions was Frieda's brother, Vic. Vic had been studying graduate engineering at a German university when he decided to visit his sister in Congo before returning home to America. He was just what Dr. Becker needed: an energetic handyman who could manage all the odd jobs that no one else could do. Without attaining missionary status with the Africa Inland Mission and without tangible financial support, Engineer Vic Paul fit in beautifully. Since he had lived most of his life in Congo, he spoke the language like an African and was accepted immediately by Africans and missionaries alike. A carefree bachelor, he joshed with the Africans, argued with government officials and soldiers, and kept the mission station operating. His vacation to Oicha had turned into a vocation.

As 1962 began, Carl Becker once again sought a Bible verse to strengthen him through the year. In January, his morning devotions led him to a verse in Joshua: "Every place that the sole of your foot shall tread upon, that have I given unto you. . . . Only be thou strong and very courageous, that thou mayest observe to do according to all the law, which Moses my servant commanded thee: turn not from it to the right hand or to the left, that thou mayest prosper withersoever thou goest."

And the doctor humbly bowed before his Lord and asked, "Will it be that kind of a year, Lord?"

It was.

Becker's fame spread in all directions. A group of South African university students touring the continent stopped at Oicha after having visited Schweitzer's Lambarene and a dozen other significant centers in the rapidly developing continent. When they returned to school and were asked to write on the highlight of their long summer's journey, all but one wrote an essay on the medical work at Oicha.

In the provincial capital of Bunia, 120 miles north, a taxi driver told a visiting journalist, "Dr. Becker just looks at you and you feel better." And when pupils in the Bunia schools were asked the name of the greatest man in Congo, the teacher expected to hear the names of Kasavubu, Tshombe, or Lumumba. Instead, the pupils chanted, "Dr. Becker."

Dr. Becker was not interested in building a monument for himself in the Congo; he was interested in building a church. He called his hospital evangelist one day and asked, "Melona, when you first came to Oicha, how many of the patients were Christians?"

"Oh, not very many, *Munganga*. A few were Muslims, but most believed in the witch doctors." Melona's brow creased deeply as he thought back through the years.

"And now, Melona?"

"Now, *Munganga*, most of them say they are Christians already."

"But, Melona, you don't seem to be very sure that they really are Christians."

"No, *Munganga*, I'm not. Sometimes on Sundays when I go into the villages I see these people and I am not so sure."

It was the answer that Dr. Becker thought he would receive, and it confirmed a new plan he had. Previously, his medical staff had gone out on Sundays to evangelize, trying to reach as many different villages as possible. From now on, he would assign each of them a village; every Sunday for a year the staff member would teach and preach in that village and seek to establish those who claimed to be Christians by concentrated Bible teaching.

Little chapels—small, crude, home-made buildings that hardly resembled churches—sprang up in many of these towns as the hospital staff took their regular parishes conscientiously. While not as many professions of faith were made during the year as had been made previously, there was qualitatively little doubt about the effectiveness of the work. Immature Christians in outlying villages now had a chance to grow into full Christian maturity.

For Yonama, the colorful, effervescent chief of the African staff at Oicha, the biggest thrill of his life came when a man he had taught week after week in a little primitive village took over the group the following year.

Coupled with the effectiveness of the new strategy of the hospital staff was the "Evangelism-for-All" program that swept through northeast Congo during these crucial years. Attempting to involve every member of the Congolese Church, which in the A.I.M. field alone now numbered 35,000, not including the catechumens, Evangelism-for-All started with house prayer meetings. After intensive prayer the Africans signed up for a training course in evangelism, a series comprised of eight separate classes designed to instruct the African believer in leading someone else to make a profession of faith in Jesus Christ. Prayer lists of non-Christians were drawn up and thousands of people were specifically mentioned in prayer to God day-by-day. In the next step of the program, church members went out two-by-two throughout the villages in their areas, spending days and sometimes weeks in evangelistic hut-to-hut calling. In the Oicha area, some of these villages were so remote as to entail a week-long safari to reach them.

The climax of the effort came as an African evangelistic team, composed of a fluent evangelist and a trumpet quartet, held a week of revival meetings in the central church of each area. Sparkplugged by A.I.M. veteran, Austin Paul, father of Frieda Atkinson and Vic, the Evangelism-for-All program proved effective wherever it went. Paul, whose teams of trumpeters had long been extremely successful in Congolese evangelism, capped his missionary career by serving as chauffeur to Congolese revivalists. Though he stayed in the background, the meetings were propelled by his driving energy.

By the time the gospel teams had blanketed Congo in 1962 and 1963, 11,000 first-time decisions for Jesus Christ had been made. All told, nearly 20,000 Africans were added to the Congolese Church as a result.

Looking into the future, Dr. Becker turned more and more of the hospital management over to his African staff. Yonama Angondia, who had been groomed for greater things since he had come to Oicha in 1944, was chosen to be the hospital's African medical director. And greater things were still ahead for the irrepressible Yonama. Yonama was surrounded by a competent African medical committee composed of the senior staff and the local pastor.

Dr. Becker had always operated the hospital on a shoestring and a mustard seed. But sometimes Africans would see money come in, and they would ask how it was spent. There was no reason why Africans shouldn't be responsible for their own hospital, so gradually more and more responsibility was heaped upon Yonama's willing shoulders. Besides financial matters, Yonama and his committee handled personnel matters and intricate problems with African patients. After independence Congolese officials who came to Oicha demanded special consideration and housing, not only for themselves but also for their entire families. If a white missionary tried to handle this he would have been charged with racial discrimination, but Yonama, who had been nicknamed the *avocat* (French for lawyer) because of his skill at settling problems in human relations, ironed out such difficulties with finesse.

In the fall of 1963, Carl and Marie Becker took a flying trip to the United States. Allergic to furloughs, they actually stayed less than two months before heading back. Dr. Becker had other than vacation purposes in mind in making the trip; foremost was his aim of recruiting young doctors for missionary service. Each of his brief furloughs had been geared to this end, and his heart was always heavy as he returned without success.

Becker also had a reunion with some of his Hahnemann classmates, who had gained wealth and prestige from their practices and had now retired in comfort. Marie, hampered by arthritis, walked with difficulty; Carl, too, was showing signs of the feverish pace he had long maintained.

His friends told him he was foolish to return to the Congo. "Face it, Carl," one said, "you are not getting any younger, you know—and Marie isn't either. You've been over there—what is it—thirty, thirty-five years now? Don't you think you deserve a rest? Stay home in America and let somebody else take over your missionary work."

The doctor found it hard to suppress a smile. "One of you fellows interested in going?"

"Come on, Carl. You're acting like a fool, going back there when Congo is in such a mess. What are you getting out of it for yourself anyway?"

For a second Carl Becker looked off into the distance—in the direction of faraway Congo—a light of impatience in his eyes. "All right, you've had a good practice here for nearly forty years, and you've made yourself a good comfortable living. But are you really satisfied with what you've gotten out of it for yourself?"

17

The Lions Stalk Their Prey

"There is no situation in human life, however
apparently adverse, that cannot be made, if God is in the heart,
a thing of perfect joy." GEORGE SEAVER

When the Simbas threatened the area in 1964, Dr. Becker was no longer Congo field director; almost seventy, he had asked to be relieved after his five-year term ended in 1963.

It had been a half-decade packed with excitement, two missionary evacuations, indigenization of the church and a successful Evangelism-for-All program. Becker had steered the craft through treacherous waters indeed, and had done it while carrying his normal load at Oicha.

Now Pete Brashler, a native of New Mexico who had served in Congo since 1940, had taken the helm, relying heavily on Carl Becker, who had been named director emeritus. Missionaries of many Protestant mission agencies had second thoughts about evacuating in 1964. After all, they had evacuated twice before, in 1960 and 1961, and most of them had returned to their stations to find everything going on as usual and some African Christians asking, "Why did you leave us? Nothing happened here." In only isolated instances was property damaged or stolen, or were there incidents of violence.

With this in mind, Brashler now wondered whether this was going to be another false alarm.

Becker didn't think so. "Look at what happened in Kwilu province." He was referring to the Baptist Mid-Missions worker, Irene Ferrel, who had been martyred by members of Lumumba's old youth group, the *Jeunesse*, early in 1964.

"But what about the Congo Church? Do you think it can stand on its own feet now?"

"We don't know, Pete. But for the past four years we've been living on borrowed time here. If the church isn't ready now, it never will be."

The Simbas (Swahili for lions) advanced with giant steps and vicious growls across the nation, capturing more by fear and superstition than by force. At first, the rebels were only roving bands of disillusioned youth, disenchanted with the Congolese government, and striking blindly back in savage terrorism. Then welded into a fighting force by skillful leaders and abetted by Communist nations, the Simbas planned a systematic take-over of the entire Congolese nation.

The Simbas claimed to be invulnerable to bullets. They were told they could retain their *dawa* (magic) if they did not wash, if they did not touch anyone who did not possess *dawa*, or if they did not touch a woman. The last was the hardest rule for them to keep.

Rebellion broke out first in southern Congo, but soon flared in isolated outbreaks throughout the eastern half of Congo. The Simbas seemed invincible. Several days before invading Stanleyville in early August, 1964, they announced their projected arrival in the city. Frightened by the Simba reputation, government soldiers offered only token resistance and soon fled in all directions.

On his radio, Dr. Becker followed the news of the advancing Simbas. From Stanleyville the rebels trumpeted their victory, proclaiming a new people's government and appealing to Leopoldville's central government to surrender. Though Stanleyville was 400 miles of dirt highway away from the Africa Inland Mission territory, there were no major towns in between—mostly dense jungle. If the rebels decided to turn eastward, they could reach Oicha in two days.

Radio Stanleyville was full of long, political speeches denouncing Prime Minister Tshombe, interlaced with cha-cha music, tirades against Americans in Congo ("Americans are killing our people"), and occasional news.

The emotional outbursts deeply disturbed the missionaries. No American soldiers were stationed in Congo; why this sudden blast of anti-American propaganda? Dr. Becker felt he knew the answer; Communists were strongly supporting the Simbas, and the Communist nations wanted to make America the scapegoat for all of Congo's troubles.

Dr. Becker listened, too, to the mission inter-communication networks, both that of the A.I.M. and that of the Unevangelized Fields Mission, which worked the area between A.I.M. and Stanleyville.

(The Unevangelized Fields Mission is not to be confused with the Unevangelized Africa Mission with which Dr. Becker began.) Caught by the lightning thrust of the rebel conquest, one of the U.F.M. stations fell to the Simbas.

Reports from missionaries in rebel-held Stanleyville were garbled. According to one report, rebels had assured them that they could continue their work without difficulty. But other indications were not so favorable. U.F.M. missionaries were first deprived of their transport vehicles; then their radio communications were cut off. One by one the U.F.M. transmitters fell silent.

Listening one night, Dr. Becker heard the last message from a U.F.M. station: "Get out while you can; you don't know how bad it is." There was little question about it now. All hopes that the Simbas would allow missionaries to carry on their work without interruption had been dashed.

On August 14, Carl Becker, Jr., who had been stationed at Aungba near the Rethy A.I.M. headquarters, left his station. He recalled, "The rebels had been reported at the town of Bafwasende, only 200 miles away. A day's trip by truck, if there were no fighting, would bring the rebels to our nearby town of Bunia, cutting off our way to escape. Bunia itself was in panic.

"The government officials who remained were trying to sort out fifth columnists by making a security check of the entire population of the town, and crowds were lined up outside their offices.

"Most of our missionaries had traveled northward on a road that led across the border away from the rebel advance. But my wife and I wanted to join my parents at Oicha. Possibly there, we thought, we could wait a bit to see if the rebels might be halted and it would be safe to return. To do this, we had to travel about fifty miles down a road that the rebels would be using. We wondered as we rounded each corner whether we might meet their advancing troops."

At Oicha, Marie became concerned when her son and daughter-in-law did not arrive on schedule. "Don't you think you had better see if they're in trouble?" she asked her husband after supper.

In ten minutes Dr. Becker was heading up the road to Bunia to find his son. He remembered the time four years before when he went on another rescue operation to find Hans Schuezger; he wondered if this one would be as adventuresome. Fortunately, it wasn't. Only a pothole and not the Simbas had delayed Carl Jr. By ten o'clock the family was re-united at Oicha.

The middle week of August was quiet, too quiet to be normal. Except for the radio, which was on almost constantly, and the efficient handling of more than 1,500 patients a day, Oicha was serene. The Swahili sign on one of the dispensaries read, "Come unto me all of you who worry and have heavy loads, and I will give you rest." Oicha seemed an oasis of rest in a jungle of tumult.

Instead of marching straight east to Bunia, however, the Simbas raced southeast of Stanleyville to Bukavu. Bukavu was Conservative Baptist territory, and Dr. Becker thought of Deighton and Alice Wentworth Douglin, stationed at Goma, only 100 miles north of Bukavu. (After graduating from college in the United States, Alice had married and returned to her native Africa as a missionary.) Another Simba group moved northeast to Bafwasende, Paulis and Dungu, into territory where the Assemblies of God, Unevangelized Fields and Worldwide Evangelization Crusade missionaries served.

Only a pocket was left outside of Simba control, a pocket on the Uganda border due east of Stanleyville. It would only be a matter of time before this prize was snatched away from the National Army as well.

Dr. Becker asked Vic Paul to check with the administrator at Beni for evacuation papers. Two hours later Vic reported, "He said we won't need to evacuate. The National Army is stopping the Simbas."

The doctor turned on his radio that night only to hear that another town in north Congo had fallen. "Vic, you'd better go back and tell that administrator that he doesn't have all the facts. The Simbas are not being stopped, and we will need his signature to get out of Congo."

The following afternoon the administrator came to Oicha and talked to Dr. Becker. He told about the thousands of excellent soldiers in the Nationalist Army and the wonderful generals they had. The Simbas may have taken a few cities but they have just been defeated in a major battle at Bukavu, he reported.

"But that is not what my radio says," replied the doctor patiently.

"Then your radio must be telling you lies,'" snapped the administrator, and stomped out of the doctor's office.

On August 22 Dr. Becker heard that the American embassy in Kampala, Uganda, would have a special message for them at 11 A.M. The staff gathered in silence around the Becker radio to hear the message: "We strongly advise all Americans to leave Congo immediately. Pack lightly, as you may have to leave your cars at the border and walk through the bush to Uganda."

Field Director Pete Brashler repeated the embassy advice on the mission network. Then he read Jeremiah 39:17,18: "But I will deliver thee in that day, saith the Lord: and thou shalt not be given into the hand of the men of whom thou art afraid. For I will surely deliver thee, and thou shalt not fall by the sword, but thy life shall be for a prey unto thee: because thou hast put thy trust in me, saith the Lord."

On the mission network, missionaries reported conditions on the various stations. Some felt rather strongly that it was premature to leave. Some who had left in 1960 and 1961 thought they had made mistakes about evacuating in the past and they should not be too hasty now.

"That isn't the point," others said. "If we stay in Congo and the rebels take over, the national Christians will be endangered by our presence. And we would be shot not because we stand for the gospel of Jesus Christ, but because we have white faces."

"As far as I can see," said Pete Brashler, "there's nothing to be gained by staying. We won't be helping the advance of the gospel, we won't be helping our families, and we won't even be helping our own country."

This time Carl Becker agreed.

"Let's wait until tomorrow," Dr. Becker told the missionaries who had gathered at Oicha. "Then we can get an early start. Vic, tell the administrator in Beni that we need our evacuation permits now."

That evening several officials from Beni came, interrupting a prayer meeting at the Becker house. "We have heard that you are planning to leave us. Why do you want to do that?"

The doctor replied that they had been ordered to leave by the American government.

The African officials looked at one another. Then one spoke, "Dr. Becker, we can let all the other missionaries go, but we cannot let you go. If you go, what would happen to the hospital?"

The doctor smiled. "You know Yonama and Benjamina. They will take care of your injuries and diseases."

But the officials were uncertain. "No, you must stay here. All the other missionaries have our permission to go."

Afterward, during a lengthy session, the missionaries decided that all would leave the following morning—except, of course, Dr. and

Mrs. Becker and Vic Paul. Most of them had young children who would be endangered by staying. Vic Paul would continue to try to get permission for the Beckers to leave, and as soon as that permission was granted, the Beckers would evacuate also.

However, Dr. Becker's three nurses, Olive Rawn, Jewell Olson, and Mary Heyward, were not happy with the decision (Vera Thiessen was on furlough and Carolyn Saltenberger was at Rethy.) "If you are staying, we are staying," they told Dr. Becker adamantly.

"Don't be foolish," the doctor replied. "This is no place for single women!"

"But if you are detained, you will need nurses to assist you at the hospital."

The doctor finally gave in. "Well, all right. Sleep on it and decide individually what you will do. Personally, I think it's foolish for you to stay."

The next morning the three nurses all arrived at the six o'clock prayer meeting in uniform, ready for work. Independently they had each made their choice to stay at Oicha with Dr. Becker. Later in the morning they, along with the Beckers and Vic, waved good-bye to a caravan of fourteen missionaries and eleven children who were leaving for the Uganda border.

During the next few days the officials visited Oicha often, but still they would not permit Dr. Becker to leave. Each day Dr. Becker heard of the advancing Simbas; one by one the northern mission stations of the Africa Inland Mission went under Simba control—Dungu, Aba, Adi, Rethy, and finally Bunia.

The administrators sent soldiers to guard Oicha as the advancing hordes moved closer. The Nationalist soldiers consoled Dr. Becker, "Do not worry, *Munganga*; we will die with you." More optimistically, the administrator kept insisting that the Nationalist troops were turning the tide and that Dr. Becker's radio was telling lies.

"Do you want us to stay here and be killed by the Simbas?" Dr. Becker asked the administrator one day.

"Oh, no," came the reply. "We will let you go if the Simbas arrive."

But that might be too late, as Dr. Becker realized very well.

The following day Yonama and Vic Paul went again to Beni to convince the administrator. The Simbas were now advancing south of Bunia on their way to Oicha. There were no more towns standing in their way.

Yonama pleaded, "If you do not let him go, he will not be able to come back to us after the Simbas leave."

The administrator stared back at him, "If I do let him go, do you think he will want to come back?"

Yonama smiled broadly, his white teeth gleaming. "The *mun-ganga* has the face of a white man, but Congo has his heart. He will come back; yes, I am sure that he will come back."

Slowly the administrator reached for his pen and scribbled his signature on the piece of paper, authorizing Dr. Becker's evacuation.

Two hours later a seventy-year-old missionary and his wife were chauffeured out of Congo by Vic Paul in a bouncy pickup truck. They were closely trailed by three sedate missionary nurses in a jeep. Vic's driving left much to be desired that day as they raced along rutted roads to the border. The pickup swerved from side to side, and going around corners Dr. Becker thought that Vic would end up in one of the many ravines. Concerned about Marie's proneness to carsickness, Dr. Becker asked, "Vic, everything all right?"

"Fine, Doctor, fine." His eyes were riveted on the road.

"You're sure?"

"Yes, yes, I'm fine."

They drove further, but Vic's driving didn't improve. Finally he slowed down and managed an apologetic smile toward the doctor. "I didn't want to say anything until we crossed the border, but this steering wheel doesn't work right. I have to turn it a full revolution before it moves the wheels at all."

They stopped in a vain attempt to fix the malfunctioning, but being unsuccessful, they journeyed on in the same uncertain way to the border.

That night, safe in the Uganda town of Kasese, Dr. Becker asked Vic to ask the blessing. "Dear Lord," the engineer prayed, "we thank Thee for this food, and we thank Thee for a safe and comfortable trip." He paused and then added, "Relatively speaking, that is. Amen."

18

The Escape of
the Two Hundred

Yonama Angondia was packed with energy. Stocky, handsome, and animated, he always made himself known in a crowd. Quick-tongued, he was sometimes too glib. And he spoke more expressively with his eyes and more dramatically with his hands and arms. Sometimes his flamboyancy dunked him headfirst into trouble, but he always bobbed up again.

His magnetism was captivating. In the States, he would have been a hard-sell salesman who would repeatedly win trips to Bermuda. But Yonama was born in Aru, Belgian Congo, 200 miles north of Oicha. And while attending a Bible study class in a secondary school, he heard the dramatic story of Noah. Young Yonama felt the waters overflowing him and realized that he too was outside the ark. That day he became a Christian.

Recruited by Dr. Becker in 1944 for medical training, Yonama had a rocky road to dependability and stability. It was Yonama who was the choir director at the main Oicha Church, and decided to start a choir for the leprosy camp too. At the first rehearsal 650 leprosy patients showed up.

It was also the irrepressible Yonama who, having heard that a choir would be chosen to sing at the Belgian World's Fair, announced that he would be going, and even took a special trip to Uganda to purchase a small bag for the trip. For weeks he told everyone of all the grand European sights he was going to see. Then came the audition: unhappily Yonama didn't pass the test.

Yonama came from a tribe in the far North, which pulled the four lower front teeth of all adolescent boys. When he arrived at Oicha, he was surprised to find that toothlessness wasn't in style. So after learning about the possibilities of modern dentistry, he went to a Brethren missionary dentist who periodically visited Oicha and asked if he could have a dental bridge made. For two weeks after he received the bridge his hospital efficiency was sub-par: he was spending too much time in front of a mirror practicing his smile so that all four of his new teeth would show.

A natural show-off, Yonama loved loud and garish colors for his clothing and bedecked himself with dazzling pins. For a long time he wore a brilliant woman's brooch on his tie. But Yonama wasn't all strut and show, and Dr. Becker realized it. Dr. Becker's patience and long-suffering along with Yonama's unflappable spirit combined to make of him a leader of his countrymen. In addition to being a top-notch medical assistant, Yonama constantly used his bright sense of humor to take the edge off the hospital's grim routine. And as Yonama the *avocat*, he was always sought out by the Congolese whenever there was a problem between patients, between staff members, or within a family unit.

So when Dr. Becker and his fellow missionaries were forced to flee from the Simbas in August, 1964, it was Yonama Angondia, Oicha's African medical director, who was left responsible for both Oicha and the dispensary at Ruwenzori.

But Yonama, though he had lived in Oicha for twenty years now, was still considered a foreigner in the area. As the Simbas came closer and closer to Oicha, Yonama and other senior medical staff members, all imports from A.I.M. stations farther north, felt the increasing hostility of the local residents. When the Simbas came, would these forest people turn against them? Yonama and his medical staff were afraid that they would. So just as Dr. Becker had turned the work over to him, Yonama felt it best to turn the work over to male nurses, who came from the forest tribes around Oicha. Ofeni of the Mbuba tribe, Paul Kamba of the Nandi tribe, and Fanweli of the Suti tribe were chosen, since these tribes were more acceptable to the Simbas.

And the Simbas were coming closer. Not far from Oicha, a major battle was fought in which 400 Simbas and an untotaled number of the National Army were slain. The bodies were carried through Oicha and thrown into the Semliki River. Every two or three days, Yonama heard of a different battle on a different site. According to reports the Simbas always suffered the greater casualties, but there were too many Simbas. When the National Army would go to fight the Simbas in one place, the rebels would attack in another.

In the village of Oicha the forest people carried arrows, spears, and machetes, but the rebels, now well armed from Communist

sources, were attacking with heavy machinery and tanks. The villagers felled huge trees across the roads to stop the Simba advance,
but the rebels cut through the timber and moved them out of the way
as though they were toothpicks.

Finally, on September 23, 1964, guards at the edge of the village
came running. "The Simbas are coming, the Simbas are coming."
There was no time to lose.

Yonama alerted the nurses—both men and women—and the
pastors and many of the stronger patients. He told them to evacuate
quickly. He suggested that they follow a small stream that ran east of
the hospital and go to a hill five miles away. He would meet them
there later. Nearly 200—including many of the medical staff and
their families—fled from Oicha that day. The following morning he
made the rounds as usual, checking all the hospital houses and starting the electricity generator. He didn't want those patients who could
not evacuate to become frightened. He explained the situation to
Ofeni, Paul Kamba, and Fanweli. He would return to Oicha if he
could, but it might be better for the rest of them if he were not
around.

At 8:00 A.M., September 24, soldiers of the National Army came
to Yonama for medicine and he gave them what they needed. As
they left Oicha they ran into a pocket of Simbas. Shortly after 9:00
Yonama began hearing staccato gunfire and explosions of shells. He
stayed at Oicha as long as he could to see how the battle was going,
but an hour later news came that the strength of the National Army
had given out.

As the National Army retreated, soldiers yelled to the people
standing along the roads, "Get away as fast as you can; the Simbas
are coming." The villagers fled into the bush, leaving the roads deserted.

The gunfire continued. Around noon shots were coming closer.
About an hour later the Simbas had reached the outskirts of the
mission. Yonama could see it all—heavy weapons, twenty armored
cars, machine guns, and artillery. The Simbas circled the mission as
Yonama watched. It looked as if he were trapped in a den of lions.
The hospital patients were wailing and groaning in terror. Yonama
tried to remain calm. He knew that if he panicked, all the patients
and the remaining nurses would do so too.

Yonama ventured out in front of the hospital to get a better view.
Up the road, shells were being fired at the church. Then he heard

shells from every direction—from the Beni road, from the Kano road, and even from across the valley. There was no doubt about it now; he was completely surrounded. And the trap was closing slowly upon him; the lions were moving in for the kill.

He retreated into the hospital; the shells were falling in the hospital yard. He prayed for strength. "When you are surrounded on all four sides by the enemy, what else can you do but look up?" Yonama thought.

Inside the hospital, patients were shouting at him, "Yonama, what can we do? We'll all be killed. Yonama, help us!"

Yonama thought fast. He gathered all the patients in front of him and said, "Listen carefully." The shells were shrieking outside. Yonama's voice was clear and direct, but occasionally it was drowned out. He tried to appear calm, though inside his heart was beating madly.

"Those of you who can't leave the hospital, crawl under your beds. You'll be safer there. The Simbas probably will not hurt you if you are very sick, and they will probably leave tomorrow. Ofeni will be in charge here and he will take good care of you." Yonama paused. "It is necessary for me to leave Oicha for a while. If any of you wish to come with me, you may, but I think you may be safer here. Good-bye and may God take care of you." Yonama went out the back door into the operating area; a score of more patients followed him.

The Simbas, now advancing onto the hospital grounds, spotted Yonama and the fleeing patients. Yonama jumped down into the stream-bed, with the Simbas still in sight. He passed behind the leprosy camp, and the leprosy patients waved at him, revealing his location. They shouted at him to come up to their houses to hide. Bullets screamed over his head.

"If I do, they will search and find me there," he shouted back. Shots came now from both sides of the stream. The hospital patients trailed Yonama in terror. The tall elephant grass along the banks of the stream provided a minimum of cover.

An hour later Yonama came to the Oicha River (at places hardly more than a trickling stream), and checked again on the patients. Not one of them had been wounded yet. "We are going to have to cross this river. Do it as quickly as you can and then dive into the bushes on the other side." The forest foliage would afford more protection on the other side.

As they scurried across, shots whistled by their heads; still no one was hit.

In the bush on the other side of the Oicha River, Yonama yelled, "They know exactly where we are now, so we'd better crawl; put leaves and shrubbery on your head. Keep as close to the ground as possible." Like snakes the fleeing Africans wiggled through the brush. Finally, after two hours the shooting ceased, and at dusk Yonama and his followers reached a hunter's camp where they stayed overnight.

The next morning Yonama sent a male nurse back to see what had happened at Oicha. In an hour he returned with this report: Seven had been killed, including a teacher named Gidiona.

The two names at the top of the Simba list for execution had been Dr. Becker and Yonama. The Simbas made it a practice to kill the leaders of the village first. Once the heroes everyone admired were slain, the Simbas felt they could take over. At Oicha they were disappointed to find neither of their prime targets—the American Dr. Becker and the African Yonama Angondia.

The Simba rebels had been aiming at Oicha for some time. Even though Oicha was just a small village in the middle of the forest, they had heard of the fame of the hospital and its miraculous medicines. When they had difficulty in capturing Oicha, they assumed that it was because of the *dawa* (magic) of Dr. Becker. Then they decided they would capture Oicha at any cost, execute Dr. Becker, and make Yonama show them how the *dawa* worked before they executed him.

In the hospital itself, the Simbas had crudely operated on some patients, cutting open the skulls to remove the brains. On others they cut out pieces of flesh and then sewed them back up again.

The report convinced Yonama that he could not return to Oicha. Shortly after he had received this report, late in the morning on September 25, 1964, Yonama heard airplanes coming. He watched silently as they flew over the forest, and then released sixteen bombs on top of little Oicha. Yonama felt sick. He rounded up his coterie of followers. "You had better stay here. You will be safe enough at this cabin for a few days, and then you may go directly to your homes. It would be best not to return to Oicha for awhile. They do not want to kill you; but they want to kill me, so I must leave you."

They asked him where he was going and he refused to tell them. "If I did, they would torture you to find out." As he left the group, he

asked solemnly, "Pray for me, my friends; I will be praying for you."
Then he disappeared into the jungle thickness.

All day long he trudged through mud and swamps until he finally
found a road; all night long he followed the road. It was pouring rain
now. The rainy season had begun with a fury, but Yonama couldn't
afford to stop. Finally at seven the next morning, he climbed to the
hill selected as the rendezvous with the 200 others who had escaped
a day ahead of him.

They were surprised to see him, for according to one report, he
had been cut up with a knife by the Simbas. Yonama urged them to
move on immediately. "The Simbas will surely find us here. We must
move on, get across the Semliki, close up the Ruwenzori dispensary,
and then get into Uganda where the Simbas can't get us."

So they continued their escape. Near the Semliki they found the
little village of Poto, where they were halted and asked where they
were going. When Yonama explained their situation, the local chief
called his people together, all of whom were armed with arrows,
spears, or machetes. After the village meeting, the chief told the
refugees that they would not be allowed to pass through his village.
He explained that he would not allow Oicha's doctors and nurses to
leave the area, though he assured them of safety if they stayed with
him.

Yonama didn't trust the chief, but there was nothing he could do.
That night, however, as he and the others were preparing a place to
stay on the outskirts of Poto, a Christian who lived in the village
sneaked over to him and whispered, "My people want you to stay
here so they can give you over to the Simbas. Get away from here if
you can."

Yonama decided to act quickly. He went immediately to the chief
and said, "Let us take our wives and children to our dispensary at
Ruwenzori. Then when all the shooting is over, we will come back to
Oicha."

The chief was adamant, though once again he assured them of
their safety.

"We appreciate your kindness," Yonama argued, "but for our
children it will not do to stay here. We have no food for them, and
you do not have enough food either. Let me lead the others to
Ruwenzori, and then I will come back to stay with you."

The chief nodded slowly. "Yes, we will let your people go if you
give us 15,000 francs" (about $50 at the time).

Yonama replied that he didn't have that much money, but he would gladly give everything he had.

"No, 15,000 francs or else you cannot leave."

The refugees' escape hopes seemed dashed. Had the Lord brought them so far only to turn them over to the Simbas? No, the God that Yonama knew was not like that. He prayed silently. Then looking intently at the chief, he said boldly, "I know what you want to do. You want to hand me over to the rebels. But what you do not know is this: the rebels have already shot at me for over two hours and could not hit me. My God has been taking care of me." In back of the chief, many of the villagers with their spears and machetes had now gathered, but Yonama wasn't going to stop now. "I want to tell you something. For twenty years I have lived here in the forest at Oicha near your village. For twenty years I have helped Dr. Becker heal your children, your wives, and many of your men too. Over and over again you have come to me, and I have given you medicine that made you well. Yes, and just this week one of your men came with a strangulated hernia and I operated on him, and he is still alive today. This is all true and you know it. But if you are not thankful for all I've done for you, you can go ahead and give me over to the enemy. If you are not thankful, you can do with me as you wish. All I ask of you is that you lead these wives, these nurses, these pastors, and these children to safety. That is all I ask."

The villagers were silent. Then came a few murmurs from the men. Slowly the chief turned and muttered a few words to them. Then he turned again to face Yonama, "You have spoken well. We have decided that because of all you have done for us all these many years, we will charge you only 3,000 francs (about $10) to pass through our village."

Together the Oicha refugees pooled their money and handed it to the chief. But as they were beginning to move on, the chief returned to talk again to Yonama. "We have changed our minds."

Yonama didn't understand why.

"We have noticed that you have a different-colored man with you. We will let you go, if you wish, but you must leave this different-colored man with us. We can return him to the rebels so that they can kill him."

The man the chief referred to was a light-colored African, and the African chief saw no reason to let him live.

"But you don't understand," Yonama insisted. "This man came to the hospital because he was sick, and we gave him a bed. When someone is sick, I do not ask about his color. And since he was nearly well when the Simbas came, he fled with us. God has entrusted his life into my hands, and I will not betray him."

The chief could not follow Yonama's logic. "You should leave him to die. I do not understand why you show him kindness."

Yonama continued. "But I do not see his color. All I know is that he has been sick."

The chief relented. "I suppose that if you are foolish enough to take a man of a different color along, that is your business."

Hastily, the refugees left Poto and marched along the road north of the Semliki toward Uganda. That afternoon a friend from Oicha caught up to Yonama on a bicycle and urged him to hurry. "They are searching for you everywhere and they know that you are trying to get to Uganda. Take my bicycle; you must get away quickly."

Yonama conferred with the others and then rode on ahead. When he reached the Semliki River, he found fishermen, some of whom were friends of his. He told them about the 200 others who were coming and asked them to guard them for the night. They agreed to do so.

But when he told them where he was heading, they replied, "But you can't! The chief on the other side of the river has put up a big barrier and is guarding it closely. His men have arrows, spears, and machetes. If you try to cross, they will kill you."

"Is there another way to Ruwenzori?" Yonama asked.

"There is no other way."

"Then do not worry about me; God will open the way for me."

Yonama continued on. He knew very well the reputation of the village across the river. He knew that this was one village where the gospel had never really penetrated. Evangelists seemed fearful of the area. Of all villages in that section, this one was most certainly rebel in its allegiance.

Yet if this was the only way, God would open it for him. Yonama's faith was just that simple.

As he neared the other side, he heard the gruff voice of a guard: "Who is it?"

"Yonama Angondia from Oicha," he replied.

"Yonama Agondia?"

"Yes, I am Yonama."

"Greetings. Open the barrier quickly. Let Yonama in."

Yonama was stunned by the friendly reception. But when he entered the guard's hut, he found that among the guards selected by the chief for the day were several who had been to Oicha for treatment. One had even worked in Yonama's garden. Quickly they gathered around Yonama and let him recount the battles around Oicha and how the Lord had delivered him from the Simbas and from the Poto villagers. Then Yonama told how the Simbas had butchered people at Oicha and how entire villages had been massacred.

"You should tell this to our chief," they said.

In a short time the chief came to the hut where Yonama was. Yonama explained how the rebels came and killed all those in authority, the chiefs, the police, and the soldiers. Anyone holding bows and arrows would also be killed. Yonama glanced around and saw all the men nervously fingering their machetes and spears.

Immediately, the chief ordered the weapons to be thrown away and the barrier to be torn down.

"Incidentally, I have 200 friends who will be coming this way tomorrow. Will you tell your guards to let them pass through your territory?"

The chief agreed. Then he took Yonama to his home village, Kamango, only eight miles from the Uganda border. There Yonama slept with the African pastor of the city, a man who had been converted in Oicha.

The next morning Yonama continued to Ruwenzori where he talked to the church leaders and packed up the medicines. When word came that the rebels were only seven miles away, Yonama got on his bicycle again, intending to pedal his way around the gigantic Ruwenzori mountain into Uganda. But he had no strength remaining. The Christians of Ruwenzori heard of his fatigue and they took turns pushing him on his bicycle up the steep trail until they brought him safely to the Uganda border.

A few days later he found the other Oicha refugees, who had bypassed Ruwenzori, awaiting him at a rest camp at Bundibugyo, just inside Uganda. They were all exhausted. Many had sores on their feet; others had contracted various illnesses during their forced march. They were desperately hungry, some suffering from malnutrition. But not one of them died.

At Bundibugyo Yonama continued to receive news from Oicha. He heard that the rebels thought they had him trapped when he first fled from Oicha, but after firing at him for two hours, their ammunition gave out and they had to go back for more. Other Simbas were sent out to kill the escapees and had trailed them to Poto. There they took the chief, along with the headman of the village and six others, back to Oicha with their hands tied behind their backs. Because they had permitted Yonama and the Oicha refugees to pass through their village, all eight village leaders of Poto were shot.

This news affected Yonama deeply. He could nevertheless rejoice that they had escaped to Uganda. They were alive. But their journey and trials were not yet over. Instead of Simbas, they were confronted by poverty, helplessness, insecurity, and hunger. Was starving in Uganda any better than being butchered in Congo?

Somehow, somewhere they would have to find Dr. Becker. If only they could get word to him, he would know what to do; he would find a way to help them.

19

Terror at Night, Healing by Day

"When I saw that unwearied patience,
that unflagging zeal, those enlightened sons of Africa,
I became a Christian at his side, though he never spoke to me about it."
HENRY M. STANLEY IN REGARD TO DAVID LIVINGSTONE

Dr. Becker folded and refolded his hands as he sat in the home of Harold Amstutz, general field director of A.I.M., in Kampala, Uganda. It had hardly been a month since he and Marie had left Oicha, but it had seemed much longer. Why did God want him to sit around in Kampala? His mind was at peace about it, but his body and instincts were restless.

"Of course, you could take a furlough if you wished," Amstutz suggested. "At seventy, you're entitled to a little rest."

There were too many loose ends for him even to consider it right now. What about Yonama and the medical staff? What about the desperate medical needs in Congo? What about an inter-mission medical-training center?

All the American missions in northern Congo were having trouble finding missionary doctors to fill the gaps, and this dire need coupled with Congo's uncertain future seemed to draw all the mission boards together. Now seemed to be the ideal time to plan an inter-mission medical-training school. Through the years, Dr. Becker had never given up on the idea. Recently he had been writing to medical missionaries all over northern Congo. Not too long ago he had received a reply from Dr. Paul Carlson of the Evangelical Covenant Church, indicating his interest in the inter-mission project.

Suddenly, Dr. Becker looked up at Amstutz. "Any news about Paul Carlson?"

"Nothing." Amstutz shook his head. Only a few days earlier, reports had come that Dr. Carlson had been captured by the rebels.

"He was interested in this inter-mission medical school, you know."

Amstutz nodded. "Prospects for it don't look too good right now. In fact, nothing looks too encouraging right now, when you look at Congo."

The two missionaries speculated about the future for several minutes before Becker indicated his impatience at sitting around in Kampala. Amstutz mentioned a need at a mission station in northern Uganda. "One of the British doctors of the Church Missionary Society is ill—had to take a rest for a few weeks. They need a temporary replacement badly."

There was a gleam in the elderly doctor's eye.

"It's not exactly a vacation resort!" Amstutz added.

For the next six weeks the Beckers served at Amudat Hospital on the Sudan border on the backside of the desert. An arid area, it was as different from Oicha as it could be. Oicha was a mass of trees and foliage which blotted out the sky and camouflaged the ground; Amudat was sky and sandy, barren soil—hardly anything but thorn bushes speckled the vicinity.

The area was inhabited by Suk tribespeople, who wore earrings and metal and bead necklaces that weighed up to ten pounds. For a scant living, they raised skinny cattle.

While at Amudat, the Beckers received fragmentary reports from Congo. According to these reports, Oicha had been sacked, hospital patients had been chased from their beds, medical men had fled to refugee camps, a Catholic mission at Beni had been burned with six priests and nuns killed. It was just enough information to whet his appetite for more. He wrote to Brethren missionary Bill Deans, now in Kampala, to be on the lookout for Yonama if he should show up there.

Then in mid-October, Yonama Angondia wrangled permission to leave the refugee camp at Bundibugyo and travel the 225 miles to Kampala. He knew that Field Director Amstutz was there, and he knew that Amstutz could locate the *munganga* for him. Without delay Amstutz drove Yonama the long journey to the edge of Uganda and Dr. Becker's temporary post. Yonama related his harrowing escape from Oicha and embellished it with graphic details for full effect. He told also of how the work at Oicha was being carried on by Ofeni, Paul Kamba, and Fanweli, and how Zefania would continue to preach the gospel as faithfully as ever.

But Yonama and the others were becoming restless in the refugee camp, and Dr. Becker understood exactly how they felt. "Surely, Uganda can use men of their caliber," he told Amstutz later.

"Don't forget, Doctor," Amstutz replied, "these men are Congolese, and Uganda doesn't want to get mixed up in the mess over there. Around Bundibugyo, you know, they already have a civil war going on, and the Uganda government has its hands full trying to control that."

Becker prayed more fervently than ever for his African aides; he wished that he could help them in some other way, but he too was a refugee in a strange land. Before the Beckers finished their stint at Amudat, they received feelers from other Church Missionary Society doctors about the possibility of coming to their relief. His own Africa Inland Mission leaders were interested in transferring him to Kola Ndoto, Tanzania, south of Lake Victoria. There was a new doctor there and a heavy medical load. Someone with Dr. Becker's wealth of experience would be of tremendous aid. So he flew 500 miles south into Tanzania and surveyed the work. He wasn't keen about going so far away from Congo, nor of leaving his African medical staff to flounder at Bundibugyo, but he realized the Lord often worked in stange ways, and if God wanted him in Tanzania, He could take care of the 200 Oicha refugees at Bundibugyo.

While waiting for approval from the Tanzanian government, Becker and Amstutz tried to assist the Oicha refugees. After penetrating Ugandan red tape and securing official permits, they collected a supply of blankets, food, clothing, and medicines, and set out for Bundibugyo.

Dr. Becker was saddened by what he found at the refugee camp. His friends, along with other refugees from Congo, were jammed into two large government buildings. Daily they received a pitifully small refugee's allowance of corn flour and beans. In addition, some of the Oicha medical staff were working in local gardens and earning an East African shilling (14 cents) a day.

Back in Kampala Dr. Becker couldn't remove the sight of those refugees from his mind, yet he realized there was little he could do. A few pieces of clothing now and then, a little extra food, a few shillings—but what was that among so many?

When Christmas 1964 came he was still waiting in Kampala for Tanzania's approval to move. Phone calls had been made to its capital city of Dar-es-Salaam to speed the action, but no word came. And ever since the American-backed paratroop landing at Stanleyville to try to rescue the ill-fated Dr. Carlson and other U.S. citizens trapped there, any Yankee was under suspicion in Tanzania, which had shown considerable interest in the Simba cause. It was quite questionable whether Tanzania would approve Dr. Becker's request in the near future.

But 200 miles south of Oicha, Conservative Baptists were criss-crossing the Congo-Uganda border to maintain their hospital in Ruanguba. Because this hospital had been without a doctor for some time, the Baptists urged Dr. Becker to come and help them. Even as he received the urgent request, Uganda authorities began raising objections to the frequent border crossings by the missionaries in that area, thereby clouding the future of Ruanguba.

Dr. Becker wrote at that time: "None of these doors are either completely closed or open for us. And so we are dependent on the Lord's further guidance from day to day. Although we can help refugees if we stay in Uganda—and someone needs to be on hand here pending clarification of the Congo situation—it is evident that we cannot stay here indefinitely."

Yes, that was quite evident. Just before Christmas many whites were forcibly expelled from Uganda, and according to reports others might be forced to leave shortly. One missionary had just been given twelve hours' notice to get out of Uganda. And the visitor's visa that the Beckers possessed was due to expire December 31. The present mood of the Uganda government was against renewing such visas.

Late in December, however, as Becker and Amstutz were visiting Bundibugyo again, a well-dressed African introduced himself to them as E. B. Bwambole, the parliamentary secretary of the Ministry of Commerce and Industry in Kampala and a member of the parliament from Toro South, the province in which Bundibugyo was located. "Gentlemen, if you have a little time, I would like to show you something," he said matter-of-factly.

The two missionaries listened politely.

He described a place not many miles south of the refugee camp. "It isn't much," he admitted. "A few buildings in poor condition, but it once was a government dispensary and leprosarium. Unfortunately, we have been forced to close the dispensary there because of extreme violence in the area. Frankly, gentlemen, it isn't an ideal place for a hospital—too much bloodshed, you know. But the buildings are all there, and if you want them the government will consider a request to permit you to use them."

Although neither Becker nor Amstutz was enthusiastic, they consented to visit the place with him. They drove down the east side of the Ruwenzori mountain range and across a strip of the Queen Elizabeth National Park. Elephants and buffaloes grazed along the road; farther up the foothills were numerous deer.

"Only fifteen miles from the border," Bwambole said.

Dr. Becker recognized the area because he had come frequently to the border to pick up drugs and other supplies. "This dispensary must be only seventy-five miles from Oicha and yet I never knew it existed."

Bwambole laughed. "It is pretty well disguised. It is about ten miles off on a side road in a hidden valley. A very beautiful setting." Soon he was zigzagging along the side road up into the Ruwenzori foothills, passing roadblocks manned by Uganda soldiers, who waved at the official car as it passed.

"Why the roadblocks?" asked Amstutz.

"Surely you know that this area has been designated a 'danger area,' because of the fighting. The tribe throughout this area—the Nandi tribe, you know—resents the Toro government ruling over them. About three years ago, they set up their own government and have refused to have anything to do with the national government. Periodically, fighting breaks out between the Wanandi and our government troops." The official added that some of the Wanandi, especially those who lived in the valley, had been cooperating with the government, and so the hill people considered them traitors to their tribe. "So quite frequently the Wanandi of the mountain battle their own tribesmen in the valley. In fact, that's the major trouble right now. Many homes have been destroyed; many good people have been killed; most of the valley people are living in terror."

Dr. Becker could hardly contain himself. To him it was sardonically amusing that when the government could not keep enough order to maintain a hospital, it called on missionaries to do it.

"Here it is, right up here," Bwambole advised.

"Where?" asked Amstutz. The trail was so overgrown with weeds that it was difficult to follow. Finally they approached some buildings. Weeds hid the few rundown shacks. Doors had been torn off and windows broken.

"This was the leprosy camp," explained Bwambole. "About two

miles down the road is the dispensary at Nyabirongo." He turned to look at the missionaries who seemed unimpressed. "It must be hard to visualize a medical program here, but this area does need medical attention. There are no doctors or nurses, but thousands of needy people."

Carl Becker began thinking of Yonama and Melona and the others. When he began listening to the Uganda official again, the latter was saying, "I really do not know if I could get permission for you to take over the work. For one thing, this is a government dispensary, and we do not give away our property to religious organizations. For another thing, you are an American who has served in Congo for many years. That is not a good thing these days either."

Yet Bwambole showed far more enthusiasm for the project than either Harold Amstutz or Carl Becker, who agreed only to think about the matter. They had informed Bwambole that they would consider taking it over only if they had complete freedom to preach and teach the Bible without restriction. This presented another problem to Bwambole.

Becker realized all the problems involved. But it was all in God's hands. He was not eager to take on the problems of Nyabirongo dispensary if God was not in it. Tanzania would be better than that; even returning to the United States—perish the thought—would be better.

Becker did not know what the next day would hold. It could be Tanzania with the A.I.M., Congo with the Conservative Baptists, the deserts of Uganda with the Anglicans, or trying to resuscitate an abandoned government dispensary in the foothills of the Mountains of the Moon.

Finally, the months of waiting were ended. The Uganda government gave its approval to a land-lease agreement with the A.I.M, if Dr. Becker were in charge of reviving the Nyabirongo dispensary. Although it meant starting a new hospital, Dr. Becker felt that it answered so many questions that it must be God's will.

Nurses Jewell Olson and Mary Heyward, along with engineer Vic Paul, were waiting for the word to rejoin him; the Uganda government even permitted the Oicha refugees to be released for service at Nyabirongo.

Five months after they had evacuated from Congo, Carl and Marie Becker moved into a small, two-room pillbox at Nyabirongo. The doctor surveyed the physical property carefully. At the leprosy settlement was a school building with most of the windows broken and a main building in only slightly better condition, plus eight smaller shacks in back. Two miles around the other side of the horseshoe road at Nyabirongo were four two-room homes and four dispensary buildings.

Marie Becker said, "What this needs is a good Pennsylvania Dutch housecleaning." With soap and water, paint, and whitewash, the missionaries renovated their quarters. Then they fixed doors and windows and rebuilt walls torn down by mountain rebels. Finally they were ready for business.

The African staff moved into houses in the village which had been deserted because of the civil war. Accustomed to living in a danger zone, they refused to let such disturbances bother them.

Not long after Nyabirongo reopened, the African staff gathered with the missionaries one Sunday afternoon under a small grove of trees near the Anglican pastor's house in the village. There were only a few chairs there. Most sat on large grass mats or on the ground. Behind them the foothills of the massive Ruwenzori range rose sharply. Little groups of huts with terraced gardens and clumps of trees stretched far up the mountainside.

This was a testimony meeting: the Africans had gathered to praise the Lord for His faithfulness during troubled times. Carl and Marie sat quietly, listening, rejoicing. One after another rose to tell of how the Lord had helped them in their weakness. Many quoted verses from the Psalms or from the account of the Israelites' journey from Egypt to Canaan. Several babies had been born during these months and the mothers testified how the Lord had given them a strength they did not think possible. Other mothers had carried small children on their backs. They had slogged through the forest on foot, sometimes in pouring rain, sometimes cutting away the growth with machetes before they could continue.

One nurse had been unable to leave Oicha with the rest of the group because of illness. Seized by rebel soldiers, she was threatened with death the next day, but she had escaped into the forest. Seriously ill, she was found by friends and nursed back to health in their small mud hut. What comfort she had found in singing hymns and recalling verses from the Psalms!

Recalling that testimony meeting, Dr. Becker commented, "As I listened, my own heart was thrilled to feel, in the presence of that group of Christians, renewed hope and assurance for the church in

Congo. And I thought then that there was no place on earth that I would rather be than right there with them."

The Congolese assistants may have felt like the Israelites who had come out of the wilderness, and Yonama no doubt felt a bit like Moses, but Nyabirongo was certainly not a Promised Land flowing with milk and honey. Battles were being fought around them every week. One of the first surgical patients handled by Dr. Becker was a man with a bad spear wound, the result of tribal war. The doctor removed a three-inch spearhead from the man's back.

At least one night a week the mountain rebels would sound a warning before they swooped down on the villagers and kidnapped, killed, or wounded some innocent villagers. Out they came on the hills, played their wooden flutes, and shouted their cry, "Mai, mai." The villagers below cowered in terror. Sometimes the mountain Wanandi sent a written message, and sometimes the warning of an impending attack filtered down the hillside by messengers. But whenever it came, the villagers panicked. Patients at the hospital were terrorized as well and, despite their infirmities, often fled the hospital to hide in the hills.

A sixteen-year-old expectant mother, hearing of a coming attack, ran out of the hospital. Mary Heyward, in charge of the maternity ward, knew that the girl would die if she was not returned to the hospital. Her baby would have to be delivered by Caesarean section in the next few days. Up somewhere in the hills, wherever she had fled, she would die for certain. So Mary Heyward and two Congolese chased after her.

They climbed up through gardens which seemed almost vertical, pushed through tall grass and over rutted trails. Finally they arrived at the mountain village where the girl lived. The Wanandi men of the village warned Mary Heyward that it was not safe for her there and that she should return to Nyabirongo before she was mistreated.

But Mary, lean and gray from her seventeen years of missionary service, replied obstinately, "I will not go back unless that girl goes back with me. If you don't let her return, she will die on your hands within the next week."

The veteran nurse won the argument. The girl returned to the hospital and that night the baby was born by Caesarean section, delivered by Dr. Becker.

Not long after Nyabirongo's newly whitewashed buildings began shimmering in the Uganda sun, the leader of the mountain Wanandi and several of his lieutenants approached the doctor. The leader told the doctor that, since he ruled the area, the hospital was under his control. It was not to be questioned.

Not wishing to antagonize the rebels, Dr. Becker replied calmly, "Did you ask me to come here?"

"No," the leader admitted.

"Did you tell me I could use these buildings?"

The leader shook his head.

"It was the government of Uganda that invited me, and so I must consider what they say. However, I am here to serve you, to heal your bodies and to tell you about the God in Heaven. The members of the central government will not be coming here for medicine, but you and your people will. They have invited me, so I am under their jurisdiction; but the people I will serve are your people and so I am your servant."

The delegation went away satisfied with the decision.

Nyabirongo faced other problems too. About a month after it was reopened, two large trucks arrived and several men jumped off and removed everything from the hospital buildings, under order from the Uganda government. Patients were laid on the floor while beds, mattresses, sheets, and blankets were removed. All tables, cupboards, chairs, medical instruments, basins, and buckets were hauled into the waiting trucks. And the trucks pulled out down the narrow road, leaving Nyabirongo stripped and naked.

"I don't understand this. The Minister of Health told me that all equipment would be left for our use," Dr. Becker told his staff. "But the Lord knows all about it." He paused a moment and then a half-smile appeared on his face. "The Lord is good to us, isn't he?" The staff was quiet, not understanding how he could rejoice in the midst of calamity. "Don't you remember that hotel man who came here two days ago? He dumped a truckload of old cots in the back of the leprosy camp. No, I don't think the Lord has forgotten us yet."

In the meantime Vic Paul and Mary Heyward rushed off to the nearest city of Kasese to buy as many blankets, basins, mattresses, and pieces of enamelware as their meager missionary allowances would permit.

A week later, when a government official came by, Mary Heyward talked bluntly: "It hasn't been easy trying to care for our patients with practically nothing."

The official seemed flabbergasted. "Didn't Dr. Becker have all his own hospital equipment?"

Mary's hands were on her hips. "When we came out of Congo, Dr. Becker carried just one suitcase with him, and you can't outfit a hospital from one suitcase."

Within another week the trucks returned with all the equipment. It was just a mistake, the men explained.

Despite the continuing difficulties and the civil war surrounding Nyabirongo, the work grew. Early in the morning long lines waited outside the dispensary. When rumors of raids filtered down from the hills, only 300 Ugandans stood in front of the dispensary, but when the weather was good and the situation settled, the number doubled.

In three months, Nyabirongo was a different place. The buildings were spotlessly sanitary on the inside and neatly whitewashed on the outside. Nyabirongo had been developed into a hospital of nearly 100 beds. There were Quonset hut wards for leprosy patients, TB patients, diphtheria patients, and those with other contagious diseases. Day by day, Dr. Becker sat in his office behind a crude wooden table, talking to patient after patient. And in the pharmacy Marie Becker, her arthritic leg now heavily braced, perched on the stool in a small pantry jammed with drugs of all kinds, stirring up a brew of liniment, a favorite African remedy. Jewell Olson jauntily strode along the road, singing "Hujambo" and "Habari" at the hospital guests, on her way from ward to ward. Hospital evangelist Melona, thin and angular, fixed his deep-set eyes on the waiting patients and explained to them how God loved them and sent His only Son, Jesus Christ, to die for them.

Assisting Dr. Becker on the Nyabirongo medical staff, while Dr. Atkinson was on furlough, was young Keith Waddell, a British-trained medic. Two miles down the road at Nyabirongo, Mary Heyward oversaw the maternity wing and the surgical wards with characteristic crisp efficiency. It was also her job to manage the Oicha-trained girl nurses. Vic Paul was every place, running a mechanics' school, fixing a worn-out generator, driving to Kasese for supplies, and doing things no one else could do.

After nine months at Nyabirongo, Melona approached Dr. Becker, "Would you like to see something?" He pulled a well-worn notebook from his pocket and opened it in front of the doctor. Page after page was full of names and addresses.

"These are people who have become Christians through the hospital ministry," he explained. "I think there are probably others too, some who didn't respond openly, some who simply asked for prayer but didn't say what for, or some who were led privately to Jesus Christ by someone else and I didn't know about it. But these are the ones who have responded to my ministry."

Dr. Becker took the notebook in his hands and flicked through the pages. "How many names are here, Melona?"

"I counted them before I came. There are 551 names here."

Each weekend the African staff as well as the American missionaries went out into the villages, following up on the decisions made for Christ during the week.

Day after day the Christian gospel of peace was heard in the valley, and night after night the war cry of the rebels was heard in the hills. One night the rebels descended from the mountains in an especially savage attack. The Uganda Army was called, but came too late. The Wanandi rioters had escaped into the hills again. But just to let them know that the Army had come, a few of the soldiers fired their rifles up the mountainside in the direction of the rebels.

In the middle of the following night, when all was quiet at Nyabirongo, there was a knock at Dr. Becker's door. The doctor pulled on his khaki trousers over his pajamas and opened the door. There lay the leader of the rebels who had been critically wounded by a stray shot the night before. His friends had brought him to the hospital to die.

In the dead of night Dr. Becker ordered him brought to the operating room and summoned his nurses Mary Heyward and Jewell Olson. After successfully removing the bullet, he ordered the rebel placed in a private room so that angry villagers would not come and kill him.

Day by day he grew stronger and day by day the hospital staff witnessed to him, telling the story of Jesus' love. After three days Carl Becker noticed that the man's personality had changed markedly. He was no longer the hostile, bitter, angry rebel leader. He seemed to possess a new spirit.

But somehow the word got out to the Uganda Army and they came to arrest the insurrectionist. Dr. Becker stood in the doorway. "I'm sorry, but he is still my patient and I cannot leave him. He is a very sick man and he needs hospital care. When he is better, you may come and get him." The doctor's word was sufficient.

Two weeks later the Army came a second time to take him away.

Still on a stretcher, he was placed in the back of an Army truck. Mary Heyward asked him if he would like to take a Swahili New Testament. His eyes brightened. "Oh yes," he responded. "Yes, I would."

And as Dr. Becker watched the truck move slowly down the knoll on which Nyabirongo stands, he could also see the hardened rebel clasping the New Testament tightly to his chest.

20

Home Is Where the Heart Is

The weather was good for flying on July 28, 1965. A few puffs of clouds scattered themselves across the Congolese sky, and a few cumuli lay in waiting to the east, perching behind the Mountains of the Moon, like a leopard crouching in the jungle.

Les Brown, Missionary Aviation Fellowship pilot from England, was checking his gas supply at the Bunia airport, just 100 miles from Oicha. The missionaries' gear was all stowed in the back of the single-engine Cessna 185, and the passengers hoisted themselves aboard.

There were four passengers that day:

Tall, trim, graying Sidney Langford, Brooklyn-based general secretary of the Africa Inland Mission, was an ex-Congo missionary himself. He had come to East Africa a month earlier for a field conference and had stayed around to investigate the possibilities of re-entering turbulent Congo. From Nairobi in Kenya he had flown to Congo's capital of Leopoldville to make sure that an MAF plane would be permitted to enter northeast Congo from Kenya.

Veteran Plymouth Brethren missionary Bill Deans, short and dapper for his thirty-six years of Congo missionary service, was the second passenger. Deans had spent most of his life at nearby Nyankunde and had made it into an arsenal of Christian literature for all of central Africa. One of the last to leave the previous fall, Deans had been one of the first to return.

No less a veteran was young, energetic Bill Stough, a second-generation Congo missionary. Still in his early thirties, Stough had lived most of his years in Congo. Since his return to the field in 1957, he had served at A.I.M.'s Aba station.

The last passenger was Dr. Carl K. Becker.

Waiting for Les Brown to take off from Bunia on the last lap, Dr. Becker felt good to be home again in Congo. It had been a long wait for a man who never enjoyed waiting. He had nothing against Nyabirongo; in fact he praised God for the opportunity. But it wasn't

Congo, even though it was so nearby. And he was always reminded that Nyabirongo was only a transition in his life, a hallway between two rooms. Nyabirongo could never be a permanent settlement for him.

But was anything permanent? The events of the past five years had proved indisputably that Congo wasn't permanent either. However, if any place was "home," it was Congo; Manheim, Philadelphia, Boyertown were only tenting places in the wilderness. Congo was his Promised Land—strange land of Canaan.

It was only eleven months that he had been out of the country. But only once before in thirty-six years of missionary service had he been outside of Congo longer than that. In fact, he had been in the States for a total of only thirty months since 1929 and for only eleven months since 1945.

As the crow flies, Nyabirongo was but fifty miles from Oicha, over a closed border. News was scarce, too scarce for Dr. Becker, who was still concerned for Oicha. And the news sources weren't too reliable, so habitually he tried to filter out as much of the obviously exaggerated bad news as possible.

There had been rumors of massacres of whole civilian populations, especially in the Oicha area. And there had been rumors that the entire church at Oicha had apostatized to the Simbas; that the hospital and all the homes had been utterly destroyed; that famine was sweeping the land; that those who had been left by the Simbas were starving to death; that little girls eight to ten years old were kidnapped by the Simbas and forced to cook for them; that little boys the same age were pressed into military service. Some of these rumors were undoubtedly true, but Dr. Becker hoped and prayed that not all of them were.

To find out the truth was one reason he had to come on this trip. But he was also wondering how long it would be until he could resume work in Congo, until a medical training school for Africans could be set up, and until he could return permanently.

The worst part about traveling those fifty straight-line miles from Nyabirongo to Oicha was that he had to make a 1,200-mile detour to get around that closed Congo-Uganda border. All these miles were necessary because western Uganda was off limits for all aircraft. This was Uganda's method of maintaining neutrality in the face of Congo's troubles.

A few days earlier he had gone to the nearest telephone—at

Kasese's Hotel Marguerite, thirty miles away—contacted Harold Amstutz in Kampala, and received the word he had been waiting for.

"Everything's clear for the trip; M.A.F. has the government OK and wants to leave the day after tomorrow if you can make it to Nairobi by then."

"Don't worry, Harold; we'll be there!"

The next morning, Marie packed a bag lunch for Vic Paul and her husband to share, and at dawn the 275-mile trip toward Kampala began. They bounced along a rutted lane across Queen Elizabeth National Park, whizzed through the busy little village of Mbarara, and finally met a paved road which they followed the rest of the way, arriving in ample time to catch the East African Airline flight to Nairobi, where M.A.F. was headquartered.

Early the following morning, Les Brown, Bill Stough, and Dr. Becker were in the air, heading for Congo. Langford, coming from the opposite direction, would join them at Bunia, as would Bill Deans, already in Congo. The first leg of the trip was southwest across Tanzania, just south of Lake Victoria, over Mwanza where David Livingstone's heart was interred, and then into the tiny Connecticut-sized nation of Rwanda, where they set down at Kigali, smallest capital in the world. After refueling they lifted off northwesterly, crossing the Congo border. Then hugging the western side of the Congo-Uganda border, with the volcanic peaks of Nyamulagira and Nyiragongo rising 14,000 feet high to their left, they soared over huge fields of lava flow at the edges of Albert National Park. As the plane skirted the west side of Lake Edward in the Albertine Rift, a massive ridge shot high into the air. For pilot Les Brown, it was just another geologic phenomenon, similar to the Great Rift of Kenya. But to the silent passenger in back it was more than that. Just on the other side of that ridge lay Kitsombiro, where he had started his career thirty-six years before. And on the landfloor there were numerous speckles marking villages where he had healed men's bodies and preached to men's hearts.

Fifteen minutes later, flying almost due north, they had left the shores of Lake Edward behind and entered the wiggly Semliki River valley. Dr. Becker could not see it, but he knew that Katwa lay over that ridge, Katwa where his leprosy experience had really begun. Off to the right, a scant thirty miles away, lay Nyabirongo, which he had left two days ago. From this high up Nyabirongo seemed only minutes away from Congo; but on the ground it had seemed months.

Not far below them was the escape route where Vic Paul had tried to steer his car with an almost non-functioning steering wheel only eleven months earlier. It was amazing how an airplane could span not only the miles but also the years.

Following the Semliki northward, they passed within the shadow of giant Ruwenzori. And there off to the right nestled against that enormous mountain was the Ruwenzori dispensary, the place where he had almost settled; but God—life seemed to overflow with that phrase—had steered him to Oicha.

Even now Oicha was off to the left. Les Brown had just pointed out toward the western horizon what was probably the town of Beni, and Oicha lay only twenty miles north.

Should he ask the pilot to fly over Oicha now? He would love to see it from the air. After all, it was home. No, there would be time for that later. It was late in the afternoon now, and it got dark an hour earlier Congo time than it did in East Africa. There was no need to waste precious fuel just to satisfy a doctor's fancy.

Up ahead the Semliki emptied itself into Lake Albert.

Les Brown turned to Dr. Becker: "Bunia should be just off to the left up there, shouldn't it?"

"Yes, I think so; that's probably Bogoro over there, and then over that ridge should be Bunia. You won't miss it; it's quite a city—at least for Congo."

And indeed it was. Now he could see Bunia, the new provincial capital, a substantial town of upwards of some 10,000 people.

Dr. Becker smiled. No reason for Marie to be concerned about my flying in a single-engine plane. Safer than driving a car!

Brown landed smoothly on a modern airstrip and taxied to a stop by a fairly large but quite deserted airport.

From the air Bunia looked calm and peaceful indeed. At the airport was Sid Langford, who had landed a few days before from Leopoldville, and intrepid Bill Deans who had driven his car into Congo from Kampala a month earlier.

As they drove from the airport to customs and immigration offices on Bunia's main street, Deans chatted casually about the atrocities that had plagued Bunia under Simba occupation. He pointed out the open area in the middle of the street where a statue of Lumumba had stood only a few weeks before. The pavement around it was still stained with blood; it had been the execution spot for hundreds of

Bunia citizens. All told, some 2,000 or more had lost their lives at Bunia. Many of the soldiers were buried along the airstrip. Along the broad paved main street were public buildings, stores, and residences, almost all of which had gaping bullet and shell holes in the walls. Windows of most of the main buidings were smashed.

And they heard the story of Zebediah, one of the pastors of the church at Bunia. Arrested on false charges that he owned a radio transmitter, he was savagely beaten and abused. He cried to God for help, and the Simba soldiers mocked him. Finally he and nineteen others were marched toward the Lumumba statue for execution. Suddenly the colonel ordered the nineteen prisoners to count off by twos. The one's were executed; the two's were returned to prison. Zebediah was a two.

Back in the prison he was tortured again, but because of his testimony he led eight other prisoners to Jesus Christ.

Later Zebediah was released and he walked back to the church where Bunia Christians were kneeling in prayer for him.

Bill Deans pointed out a new government hospital sitting decorously on a hill outside the city. "Beautiful building, maybe, but no doctors. Not a doctor in 40,000 square miles."

The next morning, as soon as it was light, Langford, Stough, and pilot Brown left for a day's survey of the A.I.M. stations that lay farther north. Bill Deans asked Becker to go with him to Nyankunde where several emergency operations were awaiting his surgical consideration. At the same time he could look the station over to see if it might serve as the future medical training center.

A few hours and several operations later, Bill Deans and Dr. Carl Becker were strolling across the Nyankunde compound, pacing off distances for new buildings, pointing off to the left where an airstrip could be built, making plans for an inter-mission medical training school—a prayer finally turning into a reality.

The following morning Dr. Becker and Bill Deans returned to Bunia, rejoining the trio who had finished their inspection trip of the northern stations. So now there were five men in the Cessna 185 heading toward Oicha.

What would Oicha be like? That was the question in everyone's mind, especially in the mind of Dr. Becker. Much of the fiercest fighting had centered around Oicha. How much physical damage had been done? How had the young national church stood up?

Waiting had never come easy for Dr. Becker, but these last few days of waiting were among the most difficult of his life.

Now he had forty minutes to go to cover the 100 miles from Bunia to Oicha. He wondered why they had never thought of using airplanes earlier. How many cars had he worn out; how many hours had he spent in traveling this 100-mile stretch?

The plane lifted off easily from the airstrip and crossed the rolling plains with their varying hues of green. Down below Dr. Becker could see little villages of thatch-roofed huts, splotches of bushes, and the dark shadow of the plane on the ground. They were following the rutted, winding road which led across the Shari River and over a field that Bill Deans said was the site of a vicious battle. Dr. Becker could identify banana and paipai trees; huts, square and circular; shambas, small and large, and lone scrubby trees.

After they had passed Nyankunde, he could see the rolling plains merging slowly into the forest to the right and the mountains of Isamba and Ami to the left, tinted by wispy clouds.

Babiru huts graced the ground like the shells of acorns; long-horned cattle grazed aimlessly. And then the Ituri forest began. At first the hills seemed to fight against it and occasionally broke out above in rebellion over it; but soon the forest conquered all, and all became a sea of broccoli, broken up only by meandering streams like the Shari, the Luna, and the Ituri. In the massive forest occasional 200-foot high trees seemed to lord it over the masses of lower foliage, with brilliant flame trees occasionally breaking up the monotony of green.

And then they spotted a trail in the forest, a long thin thread of brown, which suddenly, unexpectedly, blossomed into an African village.

"Our African evangelists have preached there," Dr. Becker thought. He knew the place well, but couldn't quite recall the name. Thirty years ago he had no trouble remembering names.

Underneath were more wisps of clouds, giving a fantasy atmosphere to the jungle scene. Then over to the left loomed huge old Ruwenzori, far higher than you would think—stately, unperturbed by cloudy intrusions. And on the right, spreading like a fungus as far as Stanleyville, was that jungle of broccoli. And then they spotted the main road, the much-traveled dirt road that linked Oicha with Nyankunde, Bunia, and points north. And now all along that road little villages popped up, dotting the road with horizontal patches of brown. And then there was a little brick church in a village.

It gave Dr. Becker a good feeling.

He knew exactly where he was now. All the torturous twists and turns of that road could not confuse him now. In less than a minute he would see beloved Oicha again.

Then there it was, breaking up the forest into bright green shambas and three long brown fingers cut into the seemingly impenetrable forest. The forest seemed impenetrable, but at Oicha the forest was not the worst enemy.

Dr. Becker spotted the church and the hospital buildings and even his old house as Les Brown dipped his wings so that he could have a good look.

He could see children waving to the plane and then running into houses to tell others to come out and see.

The nearest airstrip was ten miles farther down the road, almost to the little town of Beni. From Bunia the missionaries had sent word to Greek merchants at Beni, asking them to furnish Dr. Becker with transportation from the airstrip to Oicha when they arrived on Saturday.

Les Brown flew first to Beni, circling twice low over the business section of town to attract the attention of the merchants, and then he headed back up over the road to the airstrip.

At the airstrip they were surrounded by Congolese soldiers stationed there to guard it. They chatted in Swahili, explaining their business and showing their official papers to the captain of the troops.

Soon people began swarming onto the airstrip. Boys and girls, young mothers with babies on their backs, old men on crutches—all streamed out of the jungle to see whom the plane had brought to them.

Three Greek merchants pulled their cars off the road onto the lane that led to the airstrip. The five missionaries piled into one car with the driver, while the other two cars returned to Beni.

The ride was only ten miles by the jungle road. Huge trees lined the sides, and interspersed with the trees were little thatch-roofed huts. Then almost immediately the forest became alive with people. Children ran up to the edge of the road to get a good look at the car, and then turned and shouted, "Doctor!" Others shouted, "Beck-air, Beck-air!" Excitedly, they ran back into the forest to spread the news. And soon the roads were lined with people. The shouting passed the news faster than the car could go on the forest trail. As the car came closer to Oicha, the crowd became enormous, hardly permitting the car to move.

Finally, the car pulled off the main road, onto the palm-lined station road that led to Dr. Becker's house. At last the car could go no farther and pulled to a stop.

Dr. Becker was almost knocked down as he stepped from the car; everyone was trying to shake hands with him at once. The people wanted to carry Dr. Becker on their shoulders, but he denied them their request.

The happy doctor spotted Lazaro, several of his Pygmy friends, and dozens more that he knew by name. And then pushing his way through the crowd came Benjamina, his operating-room assistant. Benjamina threw his arms around the doctor and wept. Then, wiping away his tears, he said, "Dr. Becker, we have a serious operation in there, and we need your help."

As quickly as he could, Dr. Becker moved toward the hospital. When he entered it seemed like a different world. The outside noise was muted; the hospital itself seemed almost barren, for the patients all had gone outside to see what the commotion was about. Then into the operating room. Dr. Becker was pleased to note that cleanliness had been scrupulously maintained.

Benjamina had been doing minor operations with the doctor for years and during his absence had performed considerable major surgery as well. But the case before them was different. This woman had been suffering from a strangulated hernia for four days; she would soon die if they did not operate.

Benjamina explained that they had prayed earnestly about the operation and had felt it was the Lord's will for them to attempt it. And so they had strapped the woman on the table and had scrubbed up and had readied all the instruments for the delicate operation.

Then there was the excitement outside. To Benjamina it seemed a miracle—could that be Dr. Becker, or was it a vision, just his imagination? He had come just when he was needed most.

Dr. Becker turned around to Sid Langford. "I think I had better help them, if you don't mind. It shouldn't take too long."

The doctor was glad to get away from the milling crowd outside and into the tranquility of an operating room. And besides, it was good to feel needed. He walked into the scrub room and prepared himself for the operation.

An hour later Dr. Becker emerged from the operating room. The operation had been difficult but successful; he was glad he had been there to handle it.

But the crowds were thicker than ever. The news had spread throughout the forest, and hundreds of Africans swarmed all over the Oicha mission station. As the door opened in front of the hospital and Dr. Becker stepped out, great shouts rent the air. "Beck-air, *Munganga*, Doc-tor!"—it was deafening.

Dr. Becker noticed that many were dressed only in rags, though many of the women still wore their colorful wrap-arounds. Two Pygmies had pushed their way up to the front and stood in their unashamed nakedness with broadly beaming faces. There were patients from the leprosy camp and young nurses and medical assistants.

"Thank you, Lord, for letting me see Oicha again," he prayed quietly.

Later in the afternoon he met with church leaders and hospital infirmiers.

Paul Kamba apologized: "It's nothing like it was before. We don't have the supplies, and we don't have anyone who can do those impossible operations that you always did so easily. And medicine is so hard to get."

Dr. Becker understood. These men were working under severe handicaps—a meager education, minimal equipment and medical shortages. He was sufficiently pleased to find they were still carrying on the medical program in his absence, but he wanted to know also how many patients they were treating daily.

Benjamina seemed to avoid the question and tried to change the subject. "Remember when we used to have twenty-five or thirty big operations a week? We can't do that now."

"I know, Benjamina; but how many come now?"

Benjamina looked down at the clean floor, and toed it with his sandals. "Only about 500 to 600 a day now."

Dr. Becker was pleased. "Why, that's wonderful." That was as many as were coming to Nyabirongo each day. Yes, Dr. Becker was pleased, pleased that the work hadn't been totally demolished by the Simbas, pleased that the hospital was still maintaining its medical standards, pleased that these infirmiers were still efficiently treating 500 to 600 patients daily.

But another matter concerned him even more—the spiritual side of Oicha—the church which had such a shaky existence even when bolstered by missionaries. Now wrenched by the tortures of the Simbas and without the steadying of the missionaries, what would be left?

He turned to the elderly pastor, Zefania Kasali, and directed his question to him.

Zefania beamed. "Do you know what, *Munganga?* Two weeks ago, we had a baptismal service and 108 were baptized. Besides that, many of our church members were once lukewarm, but the Simbas growled so loud that these people became afraid and have gotten on fire for God again. And besides that, *Munganga,* the church now has an evangelist who is preaching all the time out in the villages."

The doctor was pleased, very pleased.

"But there is bad news." Zefania paused before he continued, "Have you seen your house yet? That is sad, very sad. I don't know why they did it, *Munganga.*"

With Bill Stough and Les Brown leading the way, the quintet of missionaries pushed their way through the crowd across the station road to the Becker home.

Zefania had warned him, but he still wasn't quite prepared for what he saw. Simba slogans were scribbled on the walls, windows were broken, and the rooms were depleted of furniture. The only thing that remained was his personal library, and these hundreds of books were strewn over the floors. Simbas had built fires in the bathroom and in the hall in vain attempts to burn it all down, and the walls and ceilings were singed brown from the attempt.

Dr. Becker had never put much stock in material possessions, and he and Marie had shunned the expensive and exclusive. But this was home; it was more home than any place that he and Marie had ever lived in.

He didn't understand his own reaction, but suddenly he felt very weak and old and tired inside. It was something that he could not tell to anyone, not even to Marie.

After a few minutes, recuperating from his exhaustion, he walked slowly to the other homes; each betrayed the same Simba savagery. It was surprising that the hospital itself was not more badly damaged. But the Simbas were always unpredictable.

The African leaders at Oicha then invited the missionaries to a special banquet hurriedly prepared for the occasion, a sumptuous meal of chicken, sweet potatoes, boiled plaintains, and African spinach.

Afterwards the fivesome drove back to Beni, where they had permission to stay overnight under the protection of the military post there. But the following day they returned to Oicha in time for the Sunday church service.

It was a tearful reunion as Dr. Becker stood before the Oicha congregation. The benches were filled and many Africans were standing in the back; he could even see some peeking in from outside through the open windows. The church comfortably seated 800; there must have been more than 1,000 there, Dr. Becker thought. Even two government officials had come to welcome the *Munganga Mukubwa.*

Dr. Becker had been asked over and over again if he were going to stay, and there were many who begged on their knees in front of him not to return to Uganda, but to stay with them at Oicha.

Quietly and calmly he stood in front of the congregation and explained the situation. Because his government feared that Simbas were still lurking in the forest that surrounded Oicha, it would not give him permission to return. But as soon as possible he wanted to come back to Congo. After all, this was his home and there was work yet to be done.

When he had finished speaking, there were tears in his eyes.

Perhaps the story of Dr. Becker's return to Oicha, however, was best told by a Congolese Christian who described the visit this way:

"Today was a big day at Oicha. This is the day Dr. Becker came here together with the director of the A.I.M. At seven this morning we saw something like a big bird circling over our heads and over the forest near Oicha. It went toward Beni. We wondered what this meant.

"After a while a car appeared carrying five white people. Among them was a person who looked like Dr. Becker. He waved his hand at the people. After a little while we saw that the road was filling with people as many as the sands on the seashore. They were wearing clothes of all colors—some had shorts and shirts, some long robes, others wore wrap-arounds or skirts. Truly the road was filled with people as it must have been on that day Jesus entered Jerusalem. On the mission station there was no place to stand. Even Dr. Becker did not have a place where he could walk. In his usual humble spirit, he refused to allow the people to carry him. He almost fell because of the people who wanted to talk to him. But he talked only to the church elders and the medical committee.

"Then we looked in the direction of the leprosy camp at Mbimbi. All the sick who were well enough came out of the hospital to go to see him. We saw cripples of all kinds coming—those who walked with crutches, some with fingers missing, some with toes gone, and some who crawled on hands and knees like goats, all coming to see their father. There was much noise. Some shouted, others rang bells in praise. Every eye watched while others spoke. The father and friend of everyone had come, the friend of lepers. Dr. Becker went into the hospital and inspected it as well as all of the homes of the missionaries. He even operated on one woman. After he had finished talking, they went back to Beni to sleep.

"The next day he returned and greeted the congregation at church. People hid their faces and wept. They wanted to detain him. They said that he should not leave, this wonderful *bwana* who loves the Congolese. Lazaro and his crippled wife said, 'If our father leaves, he leaves us to die now, but God bless him.' A little later he returned to Beni. In a few minutes we saw the bird going back from whence it came. The cripples with fingers missing raised their mutilated hands and waved them piteously. If you had been here you would have cried.

"After a little while the bird was lost to our sight.

"Don't forget me in your prayers."

Epilogue

On December 6, 1965, the Beckers in their Chevvy, along with Nurse Jewell Olson in her Jeep, Vic Paul in his Volkswagen, African assistant Yonama Angondia, and three other African assistants—a party of eight in all—bumped their way down Nyabirongo hill in Uganda, crossed the borderline Ishasha River, and re-entered Congo again.

It had now been fifteen months since the evacuation of Oicha, and for all except Dr. Carl Becker who had briefly visited his old haunts on flying trips, it was their first look at the damage the rebels had inflicted.

After spending their first night at the Conservative Baptist station of Ruanguba, and the second at the home of Greek merchant and friend Davidopoulos in Butembo, they finally drove into the Oicha hospital grounds late the third night, cheered by villagers who recognized them in the full moon.

The next day the Africans told how they survived the rebel occupation. Some had hid like animals for three months in the forest, under banana leaves, sleeping in hollow tree trunks and moving whenever they heard rumors of rebel approach or of gunfire.

A woman with leprosy hobbled over to say, "The Lord was good to me too. I couldn't run." She had no hands or feet. "I just locked my door, sat down and prayed, while the gunshots kept going ka-ka-ka right over my head."

Pastor Zefania commented that never before had they known more complete harmony between Christians of different tribes in the Oicha church.

Then the eight travelers continued on their way to Nyankunde, where missionary Earl Dix was preparing buildings for Dr. Becker's long-dreamed-of medical training school.

Throughout the vast area of northeast Congo, Carl Becker was the first doctor to return. The medical needs were enormous. Aided by sky-hopping Missionary Aviation Fellowship service, Becker at seventy-two continued his whirlwind schedule visiting stations from Oicha to Aba periodically, rebuilding a hospital at Nyankunde and planning the future of the medical training school.

Cautioned by mission officials and urged by his nurses as well as fellow missionaries to slow his pace, Becker saw only the mountain of work that surrounded him.

Then in mid-1966, Carl Becker fell by a Congo roadside, after suffering three heart seizures in one day. Marie was at his side as he lay quietly for two hours, completely helpless. Believing that he had only hours left to live, he asked that Carl Jr. be called from his missionary teaching chores at Bogoro station.

But gradually he felt steadier, stronger, and after returning to Nyankunde and having a good night's sleep, he appeared at hospital devotions early the next morning and insisted on resuming his hospital routines.

A nurse reprimanded him, "Why, Dr. Becker, you should be ashamed of yourself. You shouldn't be working like this after suffering three heart attacks yesterday. You should be resting in bed!"

And the doctor responded softly, "If this is to be my last day on earth, I certainly don't want to spend it in bed."

With such an indefatigable spirit, he finally saw the establishment of the Inter-Mission Evangelical Medical Training Center at Nyankunde; four mission boards—Christian Missions in Many Lands, Worldwide Evangelization Crusade, Unevangelized Fields Mission, as well as the A.I.M.—were cooperating in the project.

Despite immense problems in the re-occupation of northeastern Congo that seriously affected finances and personnel, plans surged forward. By the end of 1966, four doctors were at the Center and two more were on their way.

As many as 1,500 people were coming daily to Nyankunde for treatment, and Dr. Becker was looking forward to the completion of a 200-bed hospital. Airplane connections and radio kept the Nyankunde Center in close touch with hospitals at Oicha, Rethy and Aba as well as with the many smaller dispensaries. Doctors were dispatched by airplane to handle emergencies at distant dispensaries manned by African infirmiers, and made monthly safaris by air, performing twenty to twenty-five operations each visit. Dr. Becker, besides supervising the Nyankunde Center, continued to keep Oicha as his responsibility and also managed to handle three other outlying dispensaries on monthly visits.

And on October 1, 1966, the Center for Advanced Medical Training was opened at Nyankunde with thirty African students fully qualified for the course.

His dreams were coming to pass; his prayers were being answered.

But for Dr. Becker, there was still more work to be done. The French-language *Service d'Information Protestant* commented: "Dr. Becker, without any doubt the most renowned doctor in Northeast Congo, has not slowed his pace; if there is a difference in his pace, it has increased once again."

And Dr. Becker was ready for more work.